APPROACHES
TO THE STUDY OF
SOCIAL STRUCTURE

Approaches to the Study of Social Structure

edited by

Peter M. Blau

A Publication of
The American
Sociological Association

THE FREE PRESS
A Division of Macmillan Publishing Co., Inc.
NEW YORK

Collier Macmillan Publishers
LONDON

The Free Press
A Division of Macmillan Publishing Co., Inc.
866 Third Avenue, New York, N.Y. 10022

Collier Macmillan Canada, Ltd.

Library of Congress Catalog Card Number: 75–2809

Printed in the United States of America

printing number

  2 3 4 5 6 7 8 9 10

Library of Congress Cataloging in Publication Data
Main entry under title:
Approaches to the study of social structure.

   Bibliography: p.
   Includes index.
   1. Social structure--Addresses, essays, lectures.
2. Sociology--Methodology--Addresses, essays, lectures.
I. Blau, Peter Michael.
HM131.A63   301.18   75-2809
ISBN 0-02-903651-8

Poetic lines from "Under Which Lyre: A Reactionary Tract for the
Times" (1966) Copyright 1946 by W. H. Auden. Reprinted from COL-
LECTED SHORTER POEMS 1927–1957, by W. H. Auden, by permis-
sion of Random House, Inc. (*See p. 21.*)

Contents

About the Contributors

WALTER L. WALLACE was born in Washington, D.C. He received a B.A. from Columbia, an M.A. from Atlanta, and a Ph.D. from Chicago. He was Professor of Sociology at Northwestern before assuming his present positions at the Russell Sage Foundation and as Professor of Sociology at Princeton. His main books are *Sociological Theory* and *The Logic of Science in Sociology*.

TALCOTT PARSONS was born in Colorado Springs, Colorado. He obtained an A.B. at Amherst, studied at the London School of Economics, and earned a Dr.Phil. at the University of Heidelberg. He has retired from his post as Professor of Sociology at Harvard University and is a member of the American Academy of Arts and Sciences. Among his numerous books are *The Structure of Social Action* and *The Social System*.

ROBERT K. MERTON was born in Philadelphia and received an A.B. at Temple. His M.A. and Ph.D. are both from Harvard. He held the post of Professor and Chairman of Sociology at Tulane before relocating to Columbia, where he was the Giddings Professor of Sociology before becoming University Professor. Merton is a member of the National Academy of Sciences. He has written *Social Theory and Social Structure* and *The Sociology of Science*.

SEYMOUR MARTIN LIPSET, born in New York City, obtained a B.Sc. at City College and a Ph.D. at Columbia. He was Professor of Sociology at Berkeley before becoming Professor of Sociology at Harvard, which is his present position. Lipset is a member of the National Academy of Sciences. He is the author of *Political Man* and the senior author of *Union Democracy*.

GERHARD E. LENSKI was born in Washington, D.C. and earned both an A.B. and a Ph.D. at Yale. He was chairman of the Department and is Professor of Sociology at the University of North Carolina at Chapel Hill. He is the author of *Power and Privilege* and the co-author of *Human Societies*.

GEORGE C. HOMANS was born in Boston and received a B.A. from Harvard, where he later was a Junior Fellow. He is Professor and Chairman of Sociology at Harvard, and a member of the National Academy of Sciences. His best-known books are *The Human Group* and *Social Behavior: Its Elementary Forms*.

WILLIAM J. GOODE was born in Houston, Texas, and obtained a B.A. and an M.A. at the University of Texas. His Ph.D. is from Pennsylvania State University. He is Professor of Sociology at Columbia University. His published works include *World Revolution and Family Patterns* and *Explorations in Social Theory*.

LEWIS A. COSER was born in Berlin and studied at the Sorbonne. He has a Ph.D. from Columbia. He held the post of Professor of Sociology at Brandeis and currently is Professor of Sociology at the State University of New York at Stony Brook. Coser is the current President of the American Sociological Association. His publications include *The Functions of Social Conflict* and *Masters of Sociological Thought*.

JAMES S. COLEMAN was born in Bedford, Indiana, and earned a B.S. at Purdue. His Ph.D. is from Columbia. He has been Professor of Sociology at Johns Hopkins and currently is Professor of Sociology at the University of Chicago. He is a member of the National Academy of Sciences. Coleman is the author of *The Adolescent Society* and principal author of *Equality of Educational Opportunity*, the so-called Coleman report.

TOM BOTTOMORE was granted both a B.Sc. and an M.Sc. in economics at London. He has held the post of Professor and Department Head of the Political Science Department of Simon Fraser University (Vancouver), and presently is Professor of Sociology at the University of Sussex. He is the current President of the International Sociological Association. His published works include *Elites and Society* and *Classes in Modern Society*.

PETER M. BLAU, born in Vienna, obtained his A.B. at Elmhurst College and his Ph.D. from Columbia. He was Professor of Sociology at the University of Chicago before moving to his present position as Professor of Sociology at Columbia University. His publications include *The Dynamics of Bureaucracy* and *Exchange and Power in Social Life*.

ROBERT S. BIERSTEDT was born in Burlington, Iowa and earned a B.A. at the State University of Iowa. He has an M.A. and a Ph.D. from Columbia University. He has been Professor and Chairman at the City College of New York and at New York University, and is now Professor of Sociology at the University of Virginia. Among his publications are *The Social Order* and *Emile Durkheim*.

Introduction: Parallels and Contrasts in Structural Inquiries

Peter M. Blau

This book presents different theoretical approaches to the sociological study of social structure. The diverse conceptual schemes and theoretical viewpoints of the various authors reflect the existing state of the field. As Merton notes in the next chapter, sociology is characterized not by a single comprehensive theory of social structure but by a plurality of theoretical orientations and paradigms, because structural analysis "is both polyphyletic and polymorphous,"* deriving from different theoretical traditions, the most important of which are rooted in Durkheim's work and Marx's, and hence assuming a variety of forms. Far from considering the coexistence of these diverse and often conflicting theoretical perspectives a sign of the pathology of sociological inquiry, Merton looks upon them as a sign of the discipline's vigor and emphasizes that complementary views are essential for a thorough understanding of social structure and that competing theories make vital contributions to the advancement of knowledge in a field. Lipset also discusses the complementary understanding of social life provided by contrasting theoretical approaches, specifically functionalism and Marxism, and he examines the substantial areas of agreement that closer inspection reveals between these presumably quite contradictory theoretical schemes.

☐ I am grateful to Theodore A. Sledzinski for assistance in editing this book and preparing this chapter.
* Citations without references are taken from chapters in this volume.

The *raison d'être* of this collection is to juxtapose various theoretical conceptions of structural analysis and thereby make apparent their parallel as well as their contrasting features.

"Focus on Social Structure" was the theme of the 69th meeting of the American Sociological Association, held in Montreal in August, 1974. The papers in this volume are revised versions of the thematic presentations made at the plenary sessions by nine social theorists, with comments on some of them by three others. Explicating the theme, the meeting's program stated:

> Many different approaches have developed to improve our understanding of social structures and their dynamics. They center attention on a great variety of subjects, including the class structure and its significance for historical developments; the evolutionary process of increasing differentiation in social structures; the dialectical processes of structural change; the division of labor with its consequences for interdependence and conflict; the forms of associations that structure social relations; the structural-functional analysis of institutional subsystems; the status-sets and role-sets that help clarify the dynamics of social structures; the structural roots of deviance and rebellion; the interrelations between environment, population, and social structure; the microstructures emerging in face-to-face interaction; the construction of social reality; the structural analysis of kinship and myths.
>
> Everything in social life can be viewed with a focus on social structure as well as from a socio-psychological perspective. Whatever the specific orientation, the structural approach is designed to explain, not the behavior of individuals, but the structure of relations among groups and individuals that finds expression in this behavior. The ultimate objective is to advance by means of such sociological explanations our knowledge about society, how it changes, and how it can be changed.

Most of the topics mentioned in this statement as examples of structural analysis are dealt with in some of the following chapters. This is not to say that the papers here represent all approaches to the study of social structure, let alone all subjects of structural inquiry. There are so many fine distinctions in structural conception that it is impossible to include all viewpoints in a single volume. However, some major structural approaches that are not represented or are underrepresented should be mentioned. The most conspicuous absence is Lévi-Strauss's structuralism. Although this approach seems to have gained wide acceptance among social scientists in Europe and in some intellectual circles in the United States, most

American sociologists have rejected it, as have most American anthropologists, and none of the social theorists asked was interested in presenting Lévi-Strauss's views. An indication of the critical attitude of many sociologists toward Lévi-Strauss is that three authors in this volume criticize his structuralism (Homans, Goode, and Bottomore). Another set of theoretical orientations not represented are ethnomethodology, phenomenology, and symbolic interactionism. As a matter of fact, in one of the plenary sessions Harold Garfinkel gave a paper representing ethnomethodological structural analysis, "Naturally Organized Ordinary Activities," but unfortunately he decided to withdraw his paper because he could not revise it to his satisfaction in time for publication. Finally, whereas Marx's theory influences the conceptions of many authors, the only one of them who presents an explicitly Marxist view, Bottomore, is interestingly enough the only author who is not an American but a European, a fact indicative of the wider acceptance Marxism has among European than among American sociologists.

Although no claims can be made that all views of structural analysis are equally represented in this volume, a wide spectrum of sociological conceptions of social structure is presented by the papers in it. The objective of this introduction is to point out some of the underlying differences and similarities.

The Range of Vision

Social structure refers to the patterns discernible in social life, the regularities observed, the configurations detected. But the nature of the patterns and shapes one can recognize in the welter of human experience depends on one's perspective. One important difference in perspective, though not the only one, is the range of our vision, whether we view things from a distance to encompass the larger picture or whether we stand close up not to lose sight of details. "The Water Lilies" by Monet must be looked at from a considerable distance to appreciate the beauty and composition of the painting, which becomes a jumble of colored dots when one stands too close. Van Eyck's "Arnolfini and His Bride," on the other hand, must be viewed close up to notice such details as the intriguing reflection of the couple in the mirror, which become blurred when one stands too far. Analogous differences in range of vision determine which aspects of social life are examined to disclose a pattern and thus the kind of social structure perceived. A sociological perspective designed to reveal the broad panorama of historical developments and institutional systems conceals the minutiae of the social life of individuals, and a perspective suited for penetrating deeply into human relations and face-to-face interaction loses sight of the larger historical and institutional context.

This contrast in range of vision is dramatically illustrated by the difference between Lenski's and Homans' analysis. Lenski adopts a long-range and macrosociological perspective, as he is interested in the pattern that underlies the entire sweep of history. His evolutionary thesis is that long-run directional trends characterize history and govern the structures of societies. Even so pronounced a difference in social structure as that between the Soviet Union and the United States appears to be merely a minor departure from the dominant trend toward increasing structural complexity in this long-range holistic view, which centers attention on patterns of historical developments that extend over many centuries. The perspective Homans adopts is the polar opposite of Lenski's. It focuses on the elementary social behavior exhibited by individuals in their daily social relations, the psychological processes governing it, and the group structures to which it gives rise. In his own words, Homans' major aim is "to explain the properties of certain simple structures using as general propositions the propositions of behavioral psychology." The intensive study of sociopsychological processes and the psychological principles governing them is for Homans the necessary foundation for any theory that seeks to explain the structure of human relations and social behavior in groups. In most of his work, he deals with face-to-face groups. While Homans restricts the scope of his vision to reach greater psychological depth in his explanations, Lenski is willing to sacrifice such depth—and, indeed, criticizes reductionist tendencies—for the sake of a more comprehensive view of social life.

The difference between Parsons and Coleman exhibits the same contrast in theoretical perspective in somewhat less extreme form. Parsons' macrosociological focus is not primarily on the evolutionary pattern of history, though he accepts evolutionary principles, but on the interrelations of different institutional subsystems in a larger institutional system. He emphasizes that these interdependent institutions, the analysis of which is his version of structural analysis, must be clearly distinguished from the people in the various collectivities of society. A theoretical scheme on such a high level of abstraction—

not quite so macrohistorical as Lenski's, yet more abstract—makes people disappear from view, and with them not only the motives and behavior of individuals but also the structures of social relations and the differentiated collectivities in society. The starting point of Coleman's analysis is the opposite of that of Parsons': individual behavior, not social institutions. Although Coleman is more interested than Homans in the complex structural configurations in large collectivities, his basic assumption, like Homans', is that a systematic theory of social structures must start by explaining individual behavior and build up to higher levels. Accordingly, the first premise of his theory is that individuals rationally strive to maximize expected utilities. Then he distinguishes interest from sentiment relations and draws three further lines of distinction among forms of interest relations. The analysis of the structure of interest and control relations among persons in a group has the purpose of deriving the collective interest of that group. The interests of various groups so derived become the basis for analyzing on the next level the structure of relations among groups. Thus, whereas Parsons abstracts the institutional systems on which he focuses from persons, the rational actions and social relations of persons are the foundation on which Coleman builds his inquiry even when he is concerned with complex structures on higher levels.

The sociological perspective of some authors directs attention to an intermediate range of social structure that takes into account both microsocial and macrosocial phenomena, but without either grounding structural analysis in rational individual behavior or seeking to encompass the entire course of history or entire institutional systems. Merton makes this explicit: "structural analysis in sociology must deal successively with micro- and macro-level phenomena . . . [and] therefore confronts the formidable problem . . . of developing concepts, methods, and data for linking micro- and macro-analysis." As a single theory can hardly hope to encompass adequately the diverse issues posed by the structure of societies and the structure of small groups, Merton advocates that we should concentrate on developing multiple theoretical paradigms in sociology instead of attempting to build one overarching theory. Lipset's and Blau's papers also exemplify intermediate perspectives in their attempts to connect microlevel and macrolevel analysis (and so does, in some respects, Coleman's paper, since he too endeavors to connect these levels). On the microlevel, Lipset analyzes two forms of rationality, in an elaboration of Weber's conceptual distinction, and he then relates these on the macrolevel to structural changes in society. Blau discusses the relationship between structural differentiation, conceived in macrosociological terms, and processes of social integration, conceived in microsociological terms.

Another perspective that may be juxtaposed to a holistic concern with the underlying structure of all societies and all human history is a focus on the distinctive constellation of historical conditions in a society. Here the range of vision is narrowed in time rather than social space, and attention centers on the significance of historical circumstances rather than individual behavior for an understanding of social structure. As Bierstedt notes in his criticism of Lenski's evolutionary thesis: "One can appreciate the virtues of holism without subscribing to an evolutionary theory." This viewpoint also finds expression in Bottomore's criticism of Lévi-Strauss's concern with universal structural properties: "a Marxist thinker cannot be a 'pure' structuralist in the manner of Lévi-Strauss, for the Marxist theory has at its starting point the idea of historically distinct social structures; and . . . it aims to locate all social phenomena in a specific historical context." Coser criticizes structural evolutionism, especially the assumption that modernization makes the structure of all societies inevitably more and more alike, from the same standpoint. He emphasizes that an "exclusive focus on structural factors ignores the processes that modernization sets into motion in specific and concrete societies." The analysis of structural conditions, which only determine the potentials for change, must be supplemented by the analysis of historical processes, which determine which of these potentials become realized.

In sum, three different sociological perspectives can be contrasted with that of Parsons and Lenski, who both adopt the widest range of vision, different though they are in other respects, and who assume that universal principles govern the social structure of all societies and structural change throughout history. Their approach is most holistic, ahistorical (in the sense of ignoring particular historical conditions, not in the sense of ignoring change over time), and most general in the all-inclusive claim of its theoretical assumptions; and each of the three alternative perspectives to it departs from it in one of these three respects but not in the others. The alternative perspective of Homans and Coleman focuses on human behavior and relations as the fundamental elements without which social structure would not exist and which consequently must be analyzed to derive systematic explanations of social structures. The objection here is to holism, but these theories are also ahistorical and most general, that is, claim to be universally applicable. Bottomore and Coser, on the other hand, accept a holistic approach but object to one that is ahistorical and stress the importance of taking distinctive historical conditions and processes into account in order to understand the structures of societies and changes in them. Finally, the alternative approach best represented by Merton demands that we develop multiple theoretical paradigms in sociology rather than endeavor to construct a single all-inclusive theory, lest we cannot satisfactorily deal with diverse macrosociological and microsociological problems and their connections. In this case, neither the holistic nor the ahistorical character of social theories is denied, but the monistic claim of theories to be completely general and universally relevant is rejected.

The Antithesis of Social Structure

Since the concept of social structure is often defined implicitly by the way it is used in the analysis, not explicitly, one way to infer its meaning for various authors is to examine its antithesis, the counterpoint that serves as background for bringing out the features of social structure. An elementary contradistinction to structure in social life is chaos, formlessness, idiosyncratic human behavior that exhibits no regularities and hence is unstructured. Only if social behavior reveals some consistent, more or less persisting regularities can we begin to speak of it as being structured. Appropriately enough, Homans, whose prime concern is the study of elementary forms of social behavior (1974), uses this most elemental contradistinction in his explicit definition of social structure as "those aspects of social behavior that the investigator considers relatively enduring or persistent."

The sheer fact that comparatively enduring patterns of behavior can be discerned, which is the criterion of structure for Homans, is the very antithesis of social structure for Merton. In Merton's view, social structures develop as the result of the external constraints social conditions impose upon the choices and behavior of human beings, social constraints that alter the patterns of behavior from those that would otherwise be manifest, for example, as the result of psychological conditioning. Homans' reference to "social behavior" might be interpreted to indicate that he too restricts attention to behavior that is socially constrained, but this is not so. He seems to mean by social behavior all behavior that finds expression in social situations, and his analysis discloses that he is primarily interested in the influences on this behavior of psychological factors, such as reinforcement, valued rewards (utilities), and satiation (1974:15–50), and only secondarily in the influences of social factors. Merton, on the other hand, contrasts the structural conception of behavior in terms of social constraints with the interpretation of behavior in terms of inherent utilities, reinforcement, and other psychological factors (see his quotation from Stinchcombe).

The absence of external social constraints on conduct is also the antithesis of social structure for Parsons, Lipset, and Blau. In Parsons' and Lipset's theoretical scheme, the nature of these social restraints on human conduct is specified. Institutionalized norms and values are what regulate the behavior of the members of a society and maintain order among them. According to this conception, the study of social structure involves the analysis of social norms and values, their legitimation and institutionalization, and their functional interrelation. This concern with the regulatory force of established institutions creates the danger that order and stability are overemphasized and conflict and change are neglected. Aware of the danger of such a bias, for which their functional scheme has frequently been criticized, both Parsons and Lipset respond to this criticism in their papers. Parsons deals with media of interchange and notes: "The introduction of a theory of media into the kind of structural perspective I have in mind goes far, it seems to me, to refute the frequent allegations that this type of structural analysis is inherently plagued with a static bias, which makes it impossible to do justice to dynamic problems." And Lipset devotes much of his paper to the thesis "that all social systems inherently contain contradictions, the resolutions of which press for social change." One might say that Lipset's antithesis to social structure, conceived as normative order, is social change but that he seeks to arrive at a synthesis of the two by connecting them in his analysis of structural contradictions.

The antithesis of structural inquiry for several authors is the investigation of historical processes. Thus, Coleman contrasts his earlier conceptualization of social conflict "as an autonomous process, self-sustaining and with an internal logic and dynamic" with his present one in terms of the structural configurations that determine the outcome of conflicts. Bottomore also juxtaposes "structural and historical modes of studying social life—namely, the contrast between society conceived as a fixed, stable, and persisting structure and society conceived as a process in which there is continual breakdown and renewal. . . ." For Coser, similarly, the antithesis of structural analysis is the analysis of social processes, notably the social processes in which conflicts between groups are acted out and social change is thereby effected. But both Coser and Bottomore use the antithesis of the study of process versus the study of structure simply to emphasize the importance of a synthesis between the two. The analysis of structural conditions must be complemented by an analysis of the historical processes through which social structures undergo continual change; otherwise we cannot understand, and may even overlook, the dynamics of structural developments.

Whereas historical developments are also the antithesis of social structure for Lenski, he goes beyond Coser and Bottomore in synthesizing the two. For what he juxtaposes to the study of social structure is not so much the study of historical processes as historical particularism, that is, the study of the distinctive historical constellations in various societies and periods. Historical developments are incorporated into the concept of social structure in Lenski's evolutionary scheme, which is concerned with the directional trends that shape and structure the course of history and thereby determine the structure of societies. Such a conception of social structure that encompasses patterns in historical time as well as social space differs sharply from the concepts of Bottomore and Coser, who stress the distinction between general structural conditions and particular historical processes and circumstances, as previously noted, and who, precisely because they insist on that distinction, consider the study of structural conditions and historical processes to be both essential and complementary. They want to synthesize the *analysis* of historical and structural factors, while Lenski seeks to synthesize historical developments and structural conditions *themselves* in his evolutionary scheme.

The Mental Image

I shall attempt now to infer the mental image that various authors have of social structure, the main idea in their conceptualization of social structure. It must be inferred, because some do not explicitly define the concept and some that do then reveal in their discussion that the terse definition fails to capture the distinctive meaning social structure seems to have for them. Most sociologists' concept of social structure is rich with connotations and implications, to which a single definition cannot easily, if at all, do justice. This is undoubtedly the reason that many choose to abstain from supplying a definition of the concept. The variety of aspects of social life typically embraced by the concept of social structure makes it hazardous to attribute one core image to an author, and not all readers will agree with my classification, nor will probably all authors. In my judgment, the three core images of social structure are those of configuration, of substratum, and of differentiation.

Goode refers to "genuine structures in the strict sense that the *arrangement of the parts* controls much of the variance in the phenomena. Wittgenstein said in this connection that we should pay attention to the network, the geometry of its arrangement, and not to the characteristics of the things that net describes. . . ." This image of a configuration among elements that has distinctive significance can be exemplified by the arrangement of dots in a cross or in a square, since the cross or the square we see is not an inherent property of the dots but results from the relationships among them in the way they are arranged, which is probably the most specific meaning of the statement that the whole is greater than the sum of its parts. The configuration of social relations among people appears to be the basic image of social structure for Coleman, Homans, and Merton.

Coleman is explicit in considering social structures to be configurations of social relations—in his words, "structural configurations." Specifically, by social structure he refers to people's "objective control relations," as Wallace notes, that is, "the objective things people do and can do to each other." Wallace points out that this conception of structure in terms of objective relations contrasts fundamentally with Parsons' emphasis on "the indispensability of subjective orientation to [the] definition of social phenomena." Although Coleman calls attention to the fact that both he and Parsons are concerned with purposive action, people's purposes are not constituent elements of social structure in his scheme, as the value orientations determining purposes are in Parsons', but influence the structure only indirectly. Coleman distinguishes forms of social relations depending partly on the character of people's purposes (interests versus sentiments) and mostly on objective conditions (notably who has control over actions and whom the consequences affect). The specific form of social relations, in turn, governs the structural configuration that develops among persons in groups or, on higher levels, among groups and organizations in society.

Whereas Homans initially defines social structure broadly as enduring social behavior, it becomes apparent in his examples and his analysis, in the paper here and in his other work, that he primarily means enduring behavior that finds expression in configurations of relations among persons and their positions. Note the illustrations he gives of social structure immediately after defining it as enduring behavior: "formal organizations"; "a complex of positions and roles"; "a certain distribution of occupations and income—a stratification system"; "a certain pattern of interaction and activity among the members of a small group." Implicit in these examples is the image of a configuration of social relations or relative positions. Indeed, in the only chapter of his last book with the word "Structure" in the title, Homans (1974:167–92) analyzes the configurations of interpersonal networks in groups manifest in matrices of sociometric choices and social interaction.

Merton's discussion of social structure also conveys the mental image of configurations of social relations among statuses and roles. He speaks of "the social distributions (i.e. the concentration and dispersion) of authority, power, influence, and prestige [that] comprise the structures of social control" and of "people occupying various positions and strata in that structure. . . ." The task of structural analysis on the microlevel is, for him, to investigate how these social configurations, not the parts composing them, influence human choices and conduct, in accordance with Goode's strict definition of structure as the control over phenomena exerted by the *arrangement* of parts. Merton's recent theoretical work on status-sets and role-sets (1968:422–38) directly centers on the complex social configurations resulting from intersecting statuses and role relations.

A different image of social structure is that of a fundamental substratum that molds social life and history—a deep structure, in Lévi-Strauss's terms, that determines the superstructure, in Marx's. Three authors—Parsons, Lipset, and Bottomore—may be considered to conceive of social structure as a substratum abstracted from people's conduct and relations, though the attributes of the substratum posited by Parsons and Bottomore are diametrically opposed. For Parsons, social structures consist of institutional systems of legitimate norms and values that govern people's orientations. Accordingly, Wallace calls attention to the crucial role subjective orientations play in Parsons' theoretical scheme. It is important not to mistake the meaning of the word "subjective" here. Parsons' orientations are not the subjective, variable sentiments and attitudes of individuals but the social values and norms that are firmly grounded in the institutions of society (as Wallace indicates). Indeed, Parsons strongly emphasizes, here and elsewhere (for example, Parsons and Smelser, 1965:14–16 and *passim*), that institutions must be clearly distinguished from and never be confused with collectivities of people and the manifest organization of their social relations. Thus, he abstracts institutional systems from people's observable social conduct and relations and treats these systems of institutionalized norms and values as the substructure that shapes social life.

Lipset essentially accepts Parsons' conception of social structure as being constituted of social norms and values, though he conceives of norms and values in less abstract terms, as indicated by his specification that norms are "expected patterns of behavior held in the minds of individuals." Nevertheless, these standardized expectations are anchored in society. However, Lipset concentrates in his paper on the discussion of the contradictions and conflicts to which a complex system of values and norms gives rise, because not all the elements in such a system are consistent and because even consistent ideals and standards can give rise to strife and conflict. Incompatibilities of various social values and norms engender strain and instability. "The assumptions about value consensus with respect to stratification imply that hierarchical systems are inherently contradictory," for general agreement on the scarce goods that are most valuable inevitably leads to conflict over the distribution of these goods. Of course, value consensus does not exist in all respects, and Lipset examines how the difference in value orientation between adherents to an "ethic of responsibility" and believers in an "ethic of absolute ends" is reflected in conflicts between generations and social strata. These contradictions and conflicts create pressures for social change. Thus, Lipset's image of social structure as a substratum of social values and norms is akin to Parsons', but his focus on the change-generating contradictions in the structure links his analysis to Bottomore's. He bridges these contrasting theoretical approaches in a deliberate attempt to reveal the overlap between the functional scheme of Parsons and the Marxist scheme, which Bottomore adopts.

Bottomore initially refers to the structure of a society as "a certain order, a specific interconnectedness of the diverse elements, or spheres, of social life"; but he quickly modifies this conception in order to take changes in social structure into account. He consequently suggests "the idea of social structure as a changing reality produced by processes of destructuration and restructuration," a conception he derives from Gurvitch. However, Bottomore considers this notion of structure as a continuous process also unsatisfactory, as it fails to explain the discontinuities manifest in revolutionary changes in social structure. Major transitions from one type of social structure to another are the result of increasing contradictions that develop in social structures, and Marx deals with two kinds of contradictions—class conflict and the growing disjunction between productive forces and relations of production (that is, between technological developments and economic organization, in the broadest sense of the terms). "The first of these should not perhaps be regarded as a structural contradiction at all since it involves rather the opposition and conflict between actual individuals and social groups. . . . On the other hand, the second contradiction *is structural* and might be conceived as producing, through its own development, a major change in the form of society." In this formulation, Bottomore clearly considers social structure to be a substratum of objective conditions and contradictions that governs the actual relations of people and groups and thus class conflict. To be sure, he goes on to criticize extreme versions of Marxist determinism, like Godelier's, which assume that structural contradictions directly determine the transformation of one type of society into another. And he stresses that historical developments influencing class struggles must be taken into account to ascertain whether and when the mere potentialities for social change created by structural conditions are in fact realized. Yet Bottomore's image of social structure refers not to the conflictual relations of social classes but to an underlying substructure abstracted from observable social life, as is the case for Lipset and Parsons. This formal parallel must not, of course, obscure the profound difference between his conception of the substructure and the contradictions in it in terms of objective "materialistic" conditions and their conception in terms of subjective normative orientations.

A third mental image of social structure visualizes it as a multidimensional space of the differentiated social positions of the people in a society or other collectivity. The focus here is on the forms and degrees of social differentiation among people that are reflected in their social relations, not primarily on the configurations of social relations among persons or positions, nor on a substratum abstracted from people and their social life. Coser, Blau, and Lenski represent this viewpoint. For Coser, structural analysis entails the study of the consequences for social life—especially for conflict and change—of differences in objective social positions and of changes in the distribution of these positions. His emphasis on objective conditions becomes apparent at the very beginning of his paper in his criticism of "subjectivism." By objective positions he means largely socio-economic and political positions which have implications for differences in power, as indicated by his illustrations of structural analysis. He refers to such factors as differences in socio-economic status, rural-urban differences, changes in the occupational distribution resulting from migration and increased industrial employment, and "the resistance of back-country farmers to the pressures of encroaching commercial capitalism" in Colonial New England. The impact of different social positions and of different distributions of these positions must be investigated to discover "the structurally rooted interests and values that lead men to engage in conflicts with each other" and to join social movements. Such structural analysis is for Coser necessary for understanding social change, though not sufficient without being complemented by an analysis of the social processes that actually precipitate change.

Whereas Coser examines the significance of differences in social positions among individuals and groups, Blau and Lenski examine the significance of differentiation itself, of the variations among societies in the forms differentiation among people assumes and in the degree of differentiation in various respects. This is evident in Blau's statement that "concern is not with the occupations of individuals but with the extent of variation in their occupational positions, which is indicative of the division of labor; not with the income of individuals but with the distribution of incomes in a society, which reflects income inequality." Structural analysis in this view involves comparative studies of societies (or other collectivities) to ascertain the conditions that influence various forms of differentiation, the interrelations of these forms, and their consequences for social change and social life generally. Lenski's conception of social structure is essentially the same. He distinguishes societies on the basis of their "structural complexity," which refers to the degree of differentiation among people in various respects, such as the amount of division of labor, the extent of inequality, and the multiple lines of status differences observable in complex societies.

The Roots of Social Structure

Finally, let us examine what the matrix of phenomena is in which the social structure is assumed to be rooted. What kinds of phenomena basically determine the characteristic features of social structures and therefore must be analyzed to explain these features? The answers various authors give to this question were mostly implicit in the foregoing analysis and can be summarized briefly. The roots of social structure may be located in the psychological make-up of the individuals whose social conduct and relations compose the structures, or in the interdependence of social conditions themselves, or in external conditions beyond social life. For ecologists, the natural environment is such a realm beyond the social structure in which it is rooted; and although none of the authors here adopt an ecological approach, some do conceive of the social structure as being ultimately governed by a realm beyond it.

For Homans and Coleman, social structures are rooted in psychological processes of individual behavior, notably the rational choices of individuals in seeking to maximize expected rewards or utilities through their behavior, which is the basic psychological assumption of economic theory. The starting point for explaining social structures must therefore be psychological explanations of the behavior of individuals who are engaged in social relations with other individuals. Once simple structures of interpersonal relations have been explained in this manner, this knowledge can be used to derive from it explanations of more complex social structures. In this scheme, the analysis of psychological processes of human choice is the necessary foundation for a theory of social structure and, indeed, seemingly for all theories in the social sciences.

Most authors confine their attention to social factors and seek to account for certain structural features by analyzing the influences on them of other social conditions, including other structural features, without searching for any nonsocial phenomena in which social life is ultimately rooted. They thereby follow a well-known maxim of Durkheim (1938:110; italics omitted): "The determining cause of a social fact should be sought among the social facts preceding it and not among the states of the individual consciousness." This restriction of the conceptual framework to social factors, which implicitly denies the relevance of any nonsocial origins, characterizes the approach of Merton, Blau, Lipset, and Coser. Even when Merton examines human choices on the microsociological level, he is concerned with the structural constraints that affect these choices and thus with social conduct, not with the psychological processes underlying them. On the macrosociological level, he similarly focuses on the effects of some social factors on others, as illustrated by his statements here, which refer to his analyses elsewhere, that "social structures generate social conflict," that "social structures generate differing rates of deviant behavior," and that "social structures generate both change within the structure and change of the structure" (italics omitted). Such a framework confined to social facts is also manifest in Blau's attempts to trace the interrelations of various forms of differentiation and their significance for social change, for example, the analysis of how the division of labor is related to status inequalities and of the impact of consolidated inequalities on social change.

The sources of social conflict and change are the central concerns of the papers by Coser and Lipset, and both locate these sources in the social structure. To be sure, there is an important difference, owing to the different theoretical conceptions of social structure of the two authors. Whereas Coser considers group conflict and social change to originate in differences in objective social positions, Lipset considers them to originate in contradictions in social values and norms, which for him are the constituent elements of the social structure, but which for Coser are rooted in the differentiated objective positions that compose the social structure in his view. Nevertheless, both limit their analysis to social phenomena and treat social change as being rooted in the social structure, though their conceptions of social structure are not the same. Both also stress that the investigation of conditions in the social structure can only discover the potentials for social change and cannot alone explain which changes actually come to pass, a point made by Bottomore as well. Coser notes that one must analyze the implications of structural positions for social relations and for concerted social action of people similarly placed in the social structure in order to explain which groups become mobilized to initiate change and what changes occur. He cites Marx's discussion of French peasants as an illustration of this need to take into account the social relations and processes that mediate and effectuate the influences of structural conditions on social change.

Three authors conceive the social structure to be rooted in and ultimately governed by a matrix of phenomena that are analytically distinct from social life and lie in a realm beyond it. For Parsons, who is an outstanding representative of this viewpoint, this realm beyond the social system is the cultural system, which he defines in one place (1961:34) as consisting of " 'patterns' of meaning, e.g., of values, of norms, of organized knowledge and beliefs, of expressive 'form.' " To be sure, values and norms are also the fundamental elements of the social system. However, Parsons always insists, as in this volume once again, on the importance of the analytical distinction "between the social system and the cultural system, in our technical sense of the terms." *Institutionalized* values and norms compose the social system, as reflected in such institutional subsystems of the social system as the economy and the polity, whereas the abstract system of meanings and beliefs underlying values and norms comprises the culture. For instance, Parsons considers knowledge to be an element of the cultural system and rationality to be the corresponding element of the social system. Knowledge is the basis for rationality. In parallel fashion, the cultural system generally is the basis for the social system. Thus the characteristics of the culture, an analytically distinct infrastructure, determine the characteristics of the social structure. Wallace calls attention to this exogenous causal domination of the social structure in his comments: "Parsons speaks of a 'cybernetic control hierarchy' and by this he means that . . . the cultural subsystem controls the social subsystem." The social system, in turn, controls the personality structure of individuals and thereby human behavior. In sharp contrast to Homans and Coleman, Parsons views the social structure as being governed by a system of cultural meanings beyond both society and individuals. As he (1966:113) himself notes, referring to this cybernetic control, "I am a cultural determinist, rather than a social determinist."

External conditions also ultimately determine the features of social structure for Lenski and Bottomore, but their conception of these conditions provides another contrast with Parsons' scheme. The progressing technology, not the culture that gives meaning to values, is what shapes the major features of social structure. Lenski finds much "evidence of the strong link between advances in technology and change in social structure" and considers the complex structures of today's industrial societies to be essentially the result of their advanced technology. He specifically criticizes cultural explanations of social structure: "not much of the basic variance in social systems seems to require the invocation of cultural values." Bottomore's position is not so unequivocal. On the one hand, he places much importance on the study of historical processes for understanding how social structures change and the characteristics of the social structures that have emerged. On the other hand, he concludes that the most fundamental structural contradiction in which these changes are rooted is that between productive forces and relations of productions. Since Marx's thesis is that established productive relations and class structures cannot forever stem technological progress but inevitably are transformed by its productive forces in the long run, Bottomore's Marxist scheme may be classified, like Lenski's, as one that treats the progressing technology as the ultimate source of social structure and changes in it.

Concluding Remarks

Four ways to distinguish the approaches to the study of social structure presented in this book have been suggested: the antithesis juxtaposed to structure, the mental image of that structure, the matrix in which social life is rooted, and the range of social phenomena encompassed by the theoretical perspective. These are, of course, not the only criteria on the basis of which differences and similarities in sociological approaches can be categorized, and a few others have been mentioned in passing. Nor do these classifications necessarily refer to the topics the authors themselves stress most in their papers.

The four kinds of distinctions made are relatively, though not entirely, independent dimensions of structural conceptions, as becomes apparent when any two are cross-tabulated, inasmuch as there is little relationship between them. Thus, the antithesis of social structure inferable from the analysis is not predictive of the basic image of social structure an author seems to have. The three authors whose structural image was classified as entailing configurations of social relations imply in their discussions three different counterimages or antitheses: that of Homans is idiosyncratic behavior lacking persistent regularities; that of Merton is behavior that, though exhibiting such regularities, is not socially constrained; and that of Coleman is an autonomous social process unfolding through time. Similarly, authors whose image of social structure is a substratum that molds social life may consider the antithesis of structure the absence of social restraints, as Parsons does, or the process of history, as Bottomore does; and the same difference in antithesis can be detected among authors whose structural image is the differentiation of social positions, such as Blau and Coser.

Neither the antithesis nor the image of social structure in a theoretical scheme makes it possible to derive the matrix of phenomena outside the social, if any, in which the social structure is rooted and which shapes its features. Coleman and Homans consider psychological choice processes to be at the roots of social structure, but their antithesis is not the same. Four authors share the notion that sociological inquiry does not involve a search for the ultimate roots of social life in conditions outside it and governing it. Yet two of them differ with respect to both antithesis and image of social structure (Coser and Lipset), and the two others differ with respect to image (Merton and Blau). The three authors who do examine exogenous phenomena beyond the social structure that determine its character differ in the antithesis juxtaposed to it (Parsons and Bottomore) or the theoretical image of it (Bottomore and Lenski) or both (Parsons and Lenski).

Finally, none of these three dimensions—antithesis, image, and roots—coincides with the range of social life encompassed by the theoretical perspective. Lenski and Parsons have the most macrosociological perspective, but their schemes differ in two other dimensions, as just noted. One contrast with this macrostructural view is the microsocial focus of Homans and Coleman, whose antithesis to social structure is not the same. Another contrast with a macrosociological interest in broad structural uniformities independent of particular circumstances is a perspective concerned with distinctive historical conditions and processes. Coser and Bottomore have this perspective in common, yet their theoretical images of social structure are unlike, and so are their conceptions of the basic roots of social life. Still another perspective seeks to combine macrosociological and microsociological analysis while avoiding extreme versions of either. Merton, Lipset, and Blau (and Coleman, too) represent this view, though they have three different theoretical images of social structure.

I must reiterate in closing that these categorizations are mine and may not accurately reflect the intentions of the authors, despite my endeavor not to impose my own theoretical viewpoint on this introductory discussion. The time has come to let the authors speak for themselves.

2

Structural Analysis in Sociology

Robert K. Merton

> . . . *Solipsists declare*
> *That no one else is there,*
> *Yet go on writing—for others.*
>
> . . . *Behaviorists affirm*
> *That thinkers do not learn,*
> *Yet go on thinking—undismayed.*
>
> . . . *Subjectivists find*
> *That it's all in the mind,*
> *Yet go on sitting—on real chairs.*
>
> . . . *Popperians deny*
> *That we can verify,*
> *Yet go on searching—for the truth.*[1]

When Alvin W. Gouldner, my friend, colleague-at-a-distance, and onetime student, entitled his recent book *The Coming Crisis of Western Sociology* (1970a), he rather understated the case. For it can be argued, without paradox and with as much persuasiveness, that sociology has been in a condition of crisis throughout its history.

□ Written while I was a Fellow at the Center for Advanced Study in the Behavioral Sciences, this paper was supported by a grant from the National Science Foundation to the Program in the Sociology of Science, Columbia University. Helpful criticism was provided by fellow Fellows: Joshua Lederberg, Yehuda Elkana, Arnold Thackray, and Harriet Zuckerman.

[1] An imperfect extension of three lines from Auden's lyrical repudiation of social science, "Under Which Lyre: A Reactionary Tract for the Times" (1966) :
  . . . *existentialists declare*
  That they are in complete despair,
  Yet go on writing.

The Chronic Crisis of Sociology

Sociology has typically been in an unstable state, alternating between phases of extravagant optimism and extravagant pessimism amongst its cultivators about their capacity, then and there or at least very soon, to find abiding solutions to the problems of human society and the problems of human sociology, that is, solutions to the major social problems and the major cognitive ones.

As the population of sociologists attained a critical mass, the rate of such diagnoses quickened. Just about every generation of sociologists has managed to identify *its* time as a decisive moment for better or for worse in the development of the discipline. Those of us who have lived long enough to have observed this behavior over a span of decades can easily bring to mind some of the more striking diagnoses of crisis. For myself, it is enough to select the year 1956, when Georges Gurvitch (1956) announced "the crisis of sociological explanation" and Pitirim Sorokin (1956) itemized another version of the crisis in his *Fads and Foibles in Modern Sociology*.

Quite understandably, every doctor making the diagnosis prescribes a formally identical but substantively different therapy: See things and do things my way. The grave crisis will take a turn for the better if the collective patients will only adopt the diagnostician's own sociological perspective—be it Gurvitch's dialectical sociology or Sorokin's integralist sociology or, more recently, Gouldner's reflexive sociology. Nor, as we shall see, need this prescription of one's own theoretical commitment be an occasion for cynical amusement. After all, what cognitive basis—not, mind you, social or psychological or political basis—what cognitive basis should there be for subscribing to a theoretical perspective other than believing it to be at once more fruitful, more comprehensive, and more cogent than its rivals?

The aspects of sociology that have been taken to provide the signs and symptoms of crisis are of a familiar kind: a change and clash of doctrine accompanied by deepened tension, and sometimes abrasive conflict, among practitioners of the craft. The clash involves the strong claim that existing paradigms are incapable of handling problems they should, in principle, be capable of handling. It is in this sense that we can describe sociology as having experienced chronic crisis,[2] intermittently broken only by short surprising periods of relative calm. As distinct from the actual ongoing condition of the discipline, the periodic *sense* of crisis erupts at moments when sociologists become particularly aware of conspicuous inadequacies of cognitive or practical performance, typically as gauged by heightened aspirations for larger accomplishment.

On the social plane, this intensified awareness of inadequacy among sociologists (and their far-from-silent observers in the larger society) is occasioned by dynamic social systems generating new major troubles or aggravating old ones, such events undercutting what purported to be acceptable solutions to major social problems. I refer here in particular to those often pesky and, in a world of very imperfect knowledge, inevitably unanticipated consequences [3]

---

[2] "Chronic crisis" is not the paradoxical phrase it may seem to be. Beginning at least by the early 1930s, Horkheimer (1932) intermittently examined the "contemporary crisis in science." And although Boudon (1971b) remarks that many sociologists have "rightly" spoken of the current "crisis of sociology," he promptly goes on to observe that "sociology is more or less permanently characterized by a situation of latent crises." Apart from its special aptness for describing the condition of sociology through the years, the term "chronic crisis" acquires more general relevance now that, in Musgrave's account (1971), T. S. Kuhn (1962, 1970a, 1970b) has amended his thinking so that periods of "normal science," rather than being "dogmatic periods *between* crises," are now seen to be "full of crises of their own."

Thanks to my colleague, Robert Nisbet, I am put back in mind of what I should never have forgotten: historian Elizabeth L. Eisenstein's heavily documented observation that for our present-day, crisis-minded scholars, "every era once regarded as 'transitional' is now presented as an age of 'crisis.' . . . One may read, in chronological sequence, about the political crisis of the early Italian Renaissance and the aesthetic crisis of the late Italian Renaissance; about innumerable crises—including an 'identity crisis'—precipitated by the Reformation; about a general European crisis in the early seventeenth century (1560–1660) ; about a crisis of the European conscience in the late seventeenth century (1680–1715) ; and about the 'age of crisis' immediately following, during the eighteenth-century Enlightenment (1715–1789). Four centuries of crisis thus have to be traversed even before arriving at those classic late-eighteenth-century points of departure for our present twentieth-century crisis: political revolution in France and Industrial Revolution or the so-called Great Transformation in England." Eisenstein, "Clio and Chronos: An Essay on the Making and Breaking of History-Book Time," *History and Theory* 6 (1966) : 36–65, at 38. When a composite of historians declares the last four hundred years or so a time of continuing European crisis, perhaps we sociologists looking at our short collective past may be indulged in finding it to be one long crisis.

[3] The problem of those residual unanticipated consequences is not really solved by a thoroughgoing rationalism, not even through use of the recipe thoughtfully devised by Bertie Wooster as he sternly advised his man: "Always anticipate everything, Jeeves. It is the only way." But as the immortal Wodehouse makes clear, the trouble is that most of us are less sanguine than Bertie and all of us far less knowing than Jeeves.

of our purposed social action, individual and collective (Merton, 1936). As social dysfunctions accumulate in society or concentrate in one or another of its sectors, there develops an increasingly acute sense among practitioners of the social sciences that the state of their knowledge does not begin to measure up to the requirements of the situation.

On the cognitive plane, the intensified awareness of inadequacy is generated by the dynamics of sociological thinking and inquiry, variously distributed among the aggregates making up the community of sociologists, which open up new problems, also not foreseen, that put back in question some of what had been taken as reasonably settled knowledge. A major crisis in a science develops when inconsistencies of theoretical expectation and actual observation accumulate to the point of becoming notorious among those at work in the field, no longer to be accommodated by a lengthening chain of *ad hoc* hypotheses designed to "save the phenomena" (Duhem [1908] 1969). This in turn brings with it *specified ignorance:* the express recognition of what is not yet known but needs to be known in order to lay the foundation for still more knowledge. Paradoxically, then, a sense of crisis can be occasioned by new knowledge resulting in more exacting demands being made on old knowledge.

The social and cognitive processes within the collectivity of sociologists thus interact with developments in the environing society to produce variability in appraisals of the state of the art. When historical demands coalesce in both cognitive and social domains, as they appear to have done in the late 1960s, they generate an acute sense, in place of the acceptably or even agreeably chronic sense, of less than adequate performance in developing cognitively powerful and socially applicable paradigms. Such historical times of trouble transform chronic sociological aches into acute sociological pains. It is then that observant doctors are apt to advance their diagnosis that sociology is in deep crisis.

The sociologists engaged in making that diagnosis are only doing in their own domain what they are called upon to do in other domains of society and culture. After all, a principal task assigned the sociologist and the other breeds of social scientists is to identify the character and sources of social discontent. Aggregated discontent signals underlying inadequacies in the structure of the social system or in the values and expectations developing in that system, or both.

Not by analogy with medicine, but in their own right, social scientists observe that the processes giving rise to aggregated social complaints are not necessarily known to those expressing them. The same considerations invite analytical sociologists to adopt the role of metasociologist by diagnosing their own collective condition and by prescribing appropriate therapy for the ailments they find.

Were I called in as a consulting physician to diagnose the condition of sociology today, my opinion would be this: that superimposed on the chronic crisis of sociology to which I have referred is an acute crisis of a particular kind. This is the "crisis of prosperity," a general type identified by Tocqueville in his time and by Durkheim, a learned and independent "student" of Tocqueville in his.[4] Sociology faces a crisis of abundance today partly as the result of an abundance of social crises. The great transformations taking place in much of the world confront sociologists with the immense task of investigating them effectively and of arriving at science-based recommendations for coping.

It is the newly-won standing of sociology resulting from *some* advancement of knowledge that leads sociologists to stumble as they think themselves ready to select or to accept the assignment of helping to solve these large practical problems. The effective demand for solution of social problems far exceeds the current capacity of sociological knowledge and the current resources of sociological manpower and womanpower. As an unnecessary but understandable result, that demand far too often meets with nominal approximations to the genuine article. Sociologists who want to believe or who claim that enough is known or is immediately knowable to provide guidelines for coping with this or that massive social problem manage to put the entire discipline on premature trial. Their make-do investigations or off-the-cuff pronouncements of instantly achieved truths gain temporary credibility from the actual but severely limited achievements of scrupulous social science. But this oracular sociology filled with swift answers to tough questions can only lead to disillusionment, not least among students and new recruits to the field. The demands made of a sociology precisely

---

[4] The quotation marks indicate that Durkheim was of course only a close student, not a pupil of Tocqueville. Nor is there any direct evidence that Durkheim's notion of a crisis of prosperity (Durkheim [1897] 1951: Book II, Chapter V) is based upon Tocqueville's chapter entitled "Why the Americans are so Restless in the Midst of Their Prosperity" (Tocqueville [1835] 1954: II, Chapter XIII).

because it has been slowly advancing accelerate at a rate that only widens the gap between expectation and accomplishment, a situation well calculated to produce a deepened sense of cognitive crisis.[5]

Reinforcing the malaise among sociologists deriving from excessive practical demands prematurely accepted and inadequately met is the malaise deriving from developments in neighboring cognitive domains. Chief among these, in my opinion, is the impact of ideas being variously advanced by Popper, Kuhn, Lakatos, Feyerabend, Toulmin, and many another in the philosophy of science. Often poorly understood by sociologists on the periphery of that currently tempestuous discipline, some of these ideas are sometimes taken to indicate that subjectivity reigns supreme in the physical and life sciences and so, it is inferred, it must surely reign in the social and behavioral sciences. Sociologists drawing this gratuitous inference take it as license legitimatizing a total subjectivity in which anything goes since, as they believe they have learned from the philosophers, objectivity in science is only a figment. I say no more about this subject now, as I shall be returning to it later. Here, it is enough to note that current anxieties and acute doubts expressed by those experiencing a "crisis of sociology" are often explicitly connected with ideas much debated in today's philosophy of science.

This tentative diagnosis of the current sense of crisis in sociology as deriving from developments in both the social and the cognitive domains is not incompatible with the tentative diagnosis advanced by Ben-David (1973). He sees the recent expressions of dissatisfaction with sociological theory by Gouldner (1970a), Friedrichs (1970) and Runciman (1970; see also 1963) as resulting from a particular change of academic generations since the end of the Second World War. Not that sociological criticism and dissent are new; not that assumed consensus on the substance of sociological theory has been replaced

---

[5] By this point, it must be evident that I consider that the form of malaise expressed by some sociologists about the condition of theoretical sociology today does not constitute a deep crisis in the strong sense of involving basically new controversy over fundamentals. The main lines of argument have a long and easily accessible history. Were that history carefully reviewed, the most recent announcements of crisis in sociology would be recognized as a continuation of theoretical issues long under debate.

Perhaps it is in this sense that the new book by the Polish sociologist Sztompka (1974: 182) concludes with the judgment: "Finally, I believe that the so-called crisis of contemporary sociology is nothing but a new myth of the discipline, and that in fact there exists a solid foundation on which to base further, much needed theoretical efforts."

by marked dissensus. Rather, as Ben-David summarizes it (and I quote him at length since many sociologists do not see the journal in which his article appeared):

> This unity of the profession [in the immediate post-war period] was not based on the existence of anything resembling a "paradigm" for theory and research, such as postulated by Thomas Kuhn as the characteristic of a "normal science." There was no paradigm in sociology, and sociologists were often very critical of each other's approach. Consensus existed only in one respect, namely that all sociologists accepted the scientific method as relevant to sociology, and the scientific morality as binding for sociologists. They clearly demarcated science from ideology, and if, on occasion, they accused each other as crypto-ideologists, this was done in the name of value-free science, not as a denial of the possibility of an objective value-free sociology.
>
> My hypothesis is that the passing of this consensus in the late 1960s was due to a new change of generations. The generation which obtained its Ph.D. in the 1960s consisted of young people for whom the problem of sociology versus ideology did not have the same crucial importance as for their predecessors. The choice between the two did not appear to them as a choice between inevitable intellectual disappointment and moral failure on the one hand, and the reasonable likelihood of solid, though probably slow advance, on the other hand. The lesson of the previous generation was not entirely lost on them, and they were probably more sceptical of ideology than young people used to be in the 1920s and 1930s, but they were also sceptical about social science and sociology. Lacking the experience of liberation from ideology, they could find in sociology few past achievements or great intellectual opportunities to command their loyalty to the profession. Listening to the self-criticism of the sociologists of the adult generation, they found it difficult to share the loyalty to, and the unshaken belief in, sociology of the latter. Therefore, questioning the very possibility of a scientific sociology, and considering the possibility that the demarcation line between sociology and ideology drawn in the 1950s may not have been final, does not have for them the same meaning of totalitarian threat as for the older generation.
>
> This development, in conjunction with the confusions of present-day sociological theorizing, can explain the outburst and the timing of the dissatisfaction and the radical questioning of the logical basis of sociology which occurred in the late 1960s. [Ben-David, 1973:471–72]

Were I called in as a consulting physician to review not only the diagnosis but also the recommended therapy, my opinion would be this: that the chronic crisis of sociology, with its diversity, competition and clash of doctrine, seems preferable to the therapy sometimes proposed for handling the acute crisis, namely, the prescription of a single theoretical perspective that promises to provide full and exclusive access to the sociological truth. The reasons for my opinion are clear, if not compelling. No one paradigm has even begun to demonstrate its unique cogency for investigating the entire range of sociologically interesting questions. And given the variety of these questions, the past prefigures the future. Periodic claims to the contrary turn out to be only premature claims to theoretical closure. What's more, were the proposed therapy actually adopted, it would produce something far worse than crisis. It would lead to stasis: the stagnation of sociological inquiry as a result of premature agreement on a single paradigm that is claimed to be an exhaustive guide to investigating the wide range of sociological questions.

In having adopted the medical metaphor of *crisis* through the years, sociologists are of course not alone. Practitioners in other intellectual disciplines of a far more exacting kind have long used the same figure of speech to express their reasonable discontent with the condition of this or that part of the discipline. But, as we all know, metaphors are not to be taken literally. To do so is only to mislead or to be misled, since few metaphors are heuristic analogies. In picking up the metaphor of crisis, therefore, I do not intend to push it without limit in order to achieve or to impute a *reductio ad absurdum*. The term *crisis* remains a faded metaphor: neither a literal meaning nor a close analogy but only a loose figurative and not especially heuristic meaning transferred from one domain of experience to another.

In the domains of science and scholarship, a sound diagnosis of crisis, chronic or acute, means that the given discipline is found to be incapable of dealing with parts or aspects of the reality with which it does or "should" concern itself. In its strong form, the diagnosis of crisis in science involves unresolved fundamental paradoxes. To identify such paradoxes is itself no small achievement. It requires and signifies considerable scientific development, as with Planck's [6]

[6] This is the same Max Planck, it will be remembered, who in his youth abandoned the study of economics because of its difficulty and, of course, the same Planck whose observation on the rise of new truths in science is perhaps the most often quoted of its kind. Gerald Holton (1973 [1950]: 394), Bernard

deep formulation at the turn of the century which was designed to resolve the paradoxes confronting the classical theory of the emission and absorption of light. In a somewhat weaker form, the diagnosis of crisis identifies pertinent problems which, it is claimed, the concepts, ideas, and methods available to practitioners cannot adequately handle. This is the case with Morgenstern's recent (1972) account of "thirteen critical points in contemporary economic theory." But in neither the strong nor the weak form does it follow that scientists come through their crises only by collectively inventing a unified theory capable of solving the entire range of problems in their discipline.

The *ideal* of a unified comprehensive theory is not here in question. Like other ideals of the Pareto type T (Pareto, 1935: III, 1300–1322), this one may be functional, even when not attained, for advancing the state of sociological knowledge. But when the ideal is mistaken for the current thing, it becomes dysfunctional to that quest. Taken seriously as a guide to all research programs, the premature claims to theoretical closure in sociology which are the only kind of claims that can be staked out by the theoretical monists amongst us would only lead to much misguided effort, with disillusionment followed by something like stasis. For however effective some current paradigms may be in their own limited terrain (still to be adequately mapped), they have no sufficient claim to monopolize the search for sociological understanding. As we have briefly noted and shall see more fully in this discussion, it is not so much the plurality of paradigms as the collective acceptance by practicing sociologists of a single paradigm proposed as a panacea that would constitute a deep crisis with ensuing stasis.[7]

Barber (1961), Kuhn (1962: 150), Hagstrom (1965: 283), Greenberg (1967: 45), and Zuckerman and Merton (1972: 309), among sociologists of science, have variously drawn upon the remark that "a new scientific truth does not triumph by convincing its opponents and making them see the light but rather because its opponents eventually die, and a new generation grows up that is familiar with it" (Planck, 1949: 33–34). As Scheffler (1972: 370–71) has noted, it is the sort of aphorism that easily and mistakenly lends itself to an unexamined relativism and subjectivism.

[7] There is apparently a growing body of sociological opinion to this same effect. In January 1975, while this paper was in press, Shmuel Eisenstadt and I discovered during my visit to Jerusalem that for several years we had been independently developing much the same themes about the plurality of sociological theories, the nature of their interrelations, the recurrent insistence on a *recent* crisis in sociology, and the connections of all this to the structure of the community of sociologists and to critical developments in the environing society. Until now, both of us had developed these ideas in the form of oral

On the Limited Case for Structural Analysis

All this may explain why I do not consider that the paradigm of structural analysis developing through the years provides the only way out of the periodically announced crisis in sociology. In paraphrase of Winston Churchill on democracy, I regard the paradigm of this kind of structural analysis as the worst theoretical orientation in sociology—except all those other orientations that have been tried from time to time. Plainly so, or I should not continue to put my effort into it. But that is far from saying that structural analysis, this variant or any other, provides an exclusive and exhaustive theoretical base. Quite otherwise. Structural analysis has generated a problematics I find interesting and a way of thinking about problems I find more effective than any other I know. Moreover, it connects with other sociological paradigms which, the polemics notwithstanding, are anything but contradictory in much of what they suppose or assert. This is no doubt an unbecoming pacifist position to adopt at a time when the arena of sociology echoes with the claims of gladiators championing rival doctrines. Still, recent work in structural analysis leads me to spheres of agreement and of complementarity rather than to the alleged basic contradictions between various sociological paradigms. This is nothing strange. For it is not easy to

publication: Eisenstadt, in lectures at the Hebrew University; I, in lectures at Columbia University. And now we are putting these ideas into print: he, on the large scale, in his forthcoming book with M. Curelaru entitled *Sociological Theory, the Sociological Community and 'Crisis' of Sociology:* I, on the small scale, in this paper. For a preliminary paper based upon that book, see Eisenstadt (1974). Too late to have their substance drawn upon for this paper are two reflective articles by Gallino (1972), and Pizzorno (1972) in Rossi which Eisenstadt called to my attention.

In February 1975, while this paper was still in press, Stefan Nowak, of the University of Warsaw, gave me a copy of the paper he had presented to the VIIIth World Congress of Sociology at Toronto a few days before I was presenting this one to the American Sociological Association in Montreal. Again, there is a striking and, to me, comforting parallelism (a fitting response to independent multiples in science and scholarship). Nowak sees the "crisis" as long characteristic of sociology, disposes of "the old dream of systematizing all relevant theoretical knowledge about society into one 'unique' and all-inclusive theory," and notes that "we will have to live for a long time with many *partial theories*—mutually complementary, and cumulative in different senses of the term, applicable to different aspects of social reality, answering to different theoretical questions, and useful for different practical social purposes" (Nowak, 1974: 12–13).

achieve even mildly plausible sociological doctrines (paradigms, theories, conceptual schemes, models) which contradict one another in basic assumptions, concepts, and ideas. Many ideas in structural analysis and symbolic interactionism, for example, are opposed to one another in about the same sense as ham is opposed to eggs: they are perceptibly different but mutually enriching.

This, then, is the context for my enjoying the autobiographical license which Peter Blau has granted a dozen or so of us in these chapters. As chief architect of the symposium, he evidently decided that the ordinary standards of decorum calling for the disguise of personal ideas in impersonal discourse could be safely relaxed for the occasion, enough for each contributor to engage in the plenary self-indulgence of reflecting in public about some of his own favorite ideas. Or as Blau put it in his charge, each of us is to set forth "the distinctive significance of your approach to providing systematic explanations of social structure and their dynamics."

In my case, the temptation must be resisted—at least in part. For to discuss this aspect of my work would be only to repeat part of what Charles and Zona Loomis (1961: 246–326); Filippo Barbano, in a series of papers, among them one subtitled "The Emancipation of Structural Analysis in Sociology" (Barbano: 1959, 1966, 1968, 1971); Walter Wallace (1969: 24–59); M. J. Mulkay (1971: Chapter 5); and, most analytically, Arthur Stinchcombe (1975) have worked out as the essentials of this mode of structural analysis, more deeply and more critically than I am prepared to do.

In place of these complex, detailed accounts, I only sketch out basic components of this variant of structural analysis in the form of a series of stipulations. Though the term "stipulation" is taken from the adversary culture of the law, I use it only to indicate provisional agreement on the kind of structural analysis under discussion here. With such agreement, I can proceed to the rest of my subject: the place of that mode of theorizing in the cognitive and social structure of sociology and in relation to some current ideas in the sociology and philosophy of science.

Fourteen Stipulations for Structural Analysis

These, then, are fourteen stipulations of this one variant of structural analysis.

It is stipulated:

1. *That* the evolving notion of "social structure" is polyphyletic and polymorphous [8] (but not, one hopes, polymorphous perverse): that is, the notion has more than one ancestral line of sociological thought and these differ partly in substance and partly in method.

2. *That* the basic ideas of structural analysis in sociology long antedated that composite intellectual and social movement known as "structuralism."[9] Spanning a variety of core disciplines, structuralism has lately become the focus of a popular, sometimes undiscriminating social movement which has exploited through undisciplined extension the intellectual authority of such iconic figures as Ferdinand de Saussure and Roman Jakobson in linguistics, Claude Lévi-Strauss in anthropology, Jean Piaget in psychology and, most recently, François Jacob in biology. In short, although structural analysis in sociology today has been affected by certain communalities of structuralism serving as cognitive context—for example, certain parallels between Saussure and Durkheim—it does not historically derive from these intellectual traditions any more than, say, the input-output form of "structural analysis" developed by Wassily Leontief (1952) in economics.

3. *That* structural analysis in sociology involves the confluence of ideas deriving principally from Durkheim and Marx. Far from being contradictory as has sometimes been assumed, basic ideas drawn from their work have been found to be complementary in a long series of inquiries through the years, ranging from the social-structural sources of deviant behavior and the formation of bureaucratic personality to the growth and institutional structure of science (Merton, 1968, 1973). In a more compact form, a paradigm proposed for functional analysis in the 1930s and published in 1949 drew attention to the overlaps, not identity, of these theoretical orienta-

---

[8] Boudon (1971b: 9–10) adopts the image of a "polymorphism of sociology" in a related but different sense to refer to various forms of sociological work: a "brilliant essay," "an empirical descriptive study," a verifiable "analytical theory" or a "speculative theory" pointing to directions of inquiry.

[9] The burgeoning literature on structuralism is practically inexhaustible, and no good purpose would be served by supplying a long list of titles here. The works of the masters are easily accessible and require no mention, except, perhaps, for the overview of Jean Piaget (1970) and the masterly history of heredity with its successive disclosure of structures by François Jacob (1973). Boudon (1971a) is a serious effort to differentiate and formalize the major conceptions of social structure in relation to notions of structure in other disciplines. For other secondary works, see Viet (1965), Ducrot *et al.* (1968), and Robey (1973).

tions. For examples, the basic concepts of "contradictions" in the one and of "dysfunctions" in the other; the fundamental place accorded "conditions" of society in Marx and of "structural context" or "structural constraint" in structural analysis and, in the domain of the sociology of knowledge, Marx's postulate that men's changing "social existence determines their consciousness" corresponding to Durkheim's conception that collective representations reflect a social reality (Merton, 1968: 93–95, 160–61, 516 ff.).

The intertwining of these strands of thought has not gone unnoticed. Stinchcombe's analyses (1968: 80–101; 1975) of the overlapping sets of theoretical ideas generated his term "Marxian functionalism," while Gouldner takes repeated note of my "emphasizing [the] affinities" between them, concluding with the compact observation about the analysis in "Social Structure and Anomie" that "Here, in effect, Merton uses Marx to pry open Durkheim" (Gouldner, 1970: 335, 402, 426, 448, and, for the aperçu, 447). Kalàb (1969: 15–20) describes Marx's method as "dialectically conceived structural analysis" and notes the interdependence of "historical and structural analysis" as did the exemplary historian Herbert Butterfield some years ago when he described the major contribution of Marxism to historiography as one of having "taught us to make our history a structural piece of analysis" (1951a: 79–80). In one instructive volume, Giddens (1971) has recently analyzed congruities in the writings of Marx, Durkheim, and Weber, and in another, Sztompka (1974) finds close congruities between functional and Marxian analysis, just as Pierre L. van den Berghe did in short compass more than a decade ago (see also Malewski, 1959, 1967). Berghe's conclusion states the case pointedly:

> Our central contention is that the two major approaches which have dominated much of social science present partial but complementary views of reality. Each body of theory raises difficulties which can be resolved, either by rejecting certain unnecessary postulates, or by introducing concepts borrowed from the other approach. As functionalism and the dialectic show, besides important differences, some points of convergence and overlap, there is hope of transcending *ad hoc* eclecticism and of reaching a balanced theoretical synthesis. [Berghe, 1963: 705]

4. *That* since the confluence of elements of Durkheim and Marx has been evident from at least the 1930s, it cannot be taken, as Gouldner (1970: 341 ff.) proposes it should be taken, as another sign of the crisis he ascribes to both functional and Marxist sociology in

the 1960s.[10] Put more generally, it is being stipulated here that far from necessarily constituting a sign of theoretical crisis or decline, the convergence of separate lines of thought can, and in this case, does involve a process of consolidation of concepts, ideas, and propositions that results in more general paradigms.[11]

5. *That,* like theoretical orientations in the other social sciences, to say nothing of the physical and life sciences, structural analysis in sociology must deal successively with micro- and macro-level phenomena. Like them, it therefore confronts the formidable problem, lately taken up anew by Peter Blau (1964) and many another, of developing concepts, methods, and data for linking micro- and macro-analysis.[12]

6. *That,* to adopt Stinchcombe's important and compact formulation on the micro-level:

> . . . the core process conceived as central to social structure is *the choice between socially structured alternatives.* This differs from the choice process of economic theory, in which the alternatives are conceived to have inherent utilities. It differs from the choice

[10] In this connection, I must disown Gouldner's avowed conjecture that, in the 1930s and 1940s, I "sought to make peace between Marxism and Functionalism precisely by emphasizing their affinities, and thus make it easier for Marxist students to become Functionalist professors" (Gouldner, 1970, 335). Here, Gouldner surely does me too much honor. I had neither the far-seeing intent nor the wit and powers thus to transmogrify my students.

[11] This stipulation is of long standing. I have been arguing for the importance of theoretical consolidation in sociology since the 1940s (Merton, 1968: Chapter 2, esp. 49–53).

[12] It seems safe to stipulate rather than to discuss this conception at length now that it has found its way into that depository of "established knowledge," the textbook. (On the significance of the textbook in different disciplines, see Kuhn, 1962: 163–65). Thus, in discussing Blau's "exchange structuralism," Jonathan Turner writes: "Bridging the Micro-Macro Gap. One of the most important analytical problems facing sociological theorizing revolves around the question: To what extent are structures and processes at micro *and* macro levels of social organization subject to analysis by the same concepts and to description by the same sociological laws? At what levels of sociological organization do emergent properties require the use of additional concepts and description in terms of their own social laws?" (Turner, 1974: 292).

And, without indulging in easy and misplaced analogizing, sociologists must take a degree of interest in the reminder by the polymathic physicist Richard Feynman that, in connection with the laws of physics, "we have found that the behaviour of matter on a small scale obeys laws very different from things on a large scale. So the question is, how does gravity look on a small scale? That is called the Quantum Theory of Gravity. There is no Quantum Theory of Gravity today. People have not succeeded completely in making a theory which is consistent with the uncertainty principles and the quantum mechanical principles" (Feynman, 1965: 32–33).

process of learning theory, in which the alternatives are conceived to emit reinforcing or extinguishing stimuli. It differs from both of these in that . . . the utility or reinforcement of a particular alternative choice is thought of as socially established, as part of the institutional order. [Stinchcombe, 1975]

7. *That,* on the macro level, the social distributions (i.e. the concentration and dispersion) of authority, power, influence, and prestige comprise structures of social control that change historically, partly through processes of "accumulation of advantage and disadvantage" accruing to people occupying diverse stratified positions in that structure (subject to processes of feedback under conditions still poorly understood).[13]

8. *That* it is fundamental, not incidental, to the paradigm of structural analysis that *social structures generate social conflict* by being differentiated, in historically differing extent and kind, into interlocking arrays of social statuses, strata, organizations, and communities which have their own and therefore potentially conflicting as well as common interests and values (Merton, 1971: 796; 1968: 424–25). (I shall have more to say about this presently.)

9. *That* normative structures do not have unified norm-sets. Instead, that *sociological ambivalence* is built into normative structures in the form of incompatible patterned expectations and a "dynamic alternation of norms and counternorms" in social roles, as this "sociological ambivalence" has been identified, for example, in the spheres of bureaucracy, medicine, and science (Merton and Barber, 1963; Merton, 1973: Chapter 18; Mitroff, 1974).

10. *That social structures generate differing rates of deviant behavior,* variously so defined by structurally identifiable members of the society. The behavior defined as deviant results, in significant degree, from socially patterned discrepancies between culturally induced personal aspirations and patterned differentials in access to the opportunity structure for moving toward those aspirations by institutional means (Merton, 1968: 185–248; 1971: 793–846).

11. *That* in addition to exogenous events, *social structures generate both change within the structure and change of the structure*

[13] Since appearing in the sociology of science in 1942, the idea of "accumulation of advantage" in systems of social stratification (which relates to the notions of "the self-fulfilling prophecy" and "the Matthew-effect") has been developed in a series of investigations: Merton, 1973: 273, 416, 439–59; Zuckerman and Merton, 1972: 325; Zuckerman in press, Chapter 3, passim; Cole and Cole, 1973: 237–47 passim; Allison and Stewart, 1974: 596–606; Zuckerman and Cole, 1975.

and that these types of change come about through cumulatively patterned choices in behavior and the amplification of dysfunctional consequences resulting from certain kinds of strains, conflicts, and contradictions in the differentiated social structure (Merton, 1968: 176–77).[14]

12. *That,* in accord with preceding stipulations, every new cohort born into a social structure it never made proceeds differentially, along with other age cohorts, to modify that structure, both unwittingly and by design, through its responses to the objective social consequences, also both unanticipated and designed, of previous organized and collective action (Merton, 1936).

13. *That* it is analytically useful to distinguish between manifest and latent levels of social structure as of social function (with the aside that structuralism as expressed in other disciplines—for example, by Jakobson, Lévi-Strauss, and Chomsky—finds it essential to distinguish "surface" from "deep" structures) (cf. Gouldner, 1957–58: 463, passim; Barbano, 1968: 55–57).

14. And, finally, as will become evident in the rest of the paper, it is stipulated as a matter of theoretical principle (rather than as a stab at conspicuous modesty) *that,* like any other theoretical orientation in sociology, structural analysis can lay no claim to being capable of accounting exhaustively for social and cultural phenomena.

From these severely condensed stipulations, it must be plain that this variant of structural analysis in sociology is deeply indebted to the classic mode of structural-functional analysis developed by my teacher, friend, and colleague-at-a-distance, Talcott Parsons.[15] But

---

[14] This is stipulated in spite of the recent critiques by Runciman and Nisbet. Both agree that it is badly misplaced to charge functional or structural analysis with not having any "theory of social change," and they make their case in the best way: by stating that theory and criticizing it. In a series of works, Nisbet strongly criticizes the idea of structurally or immanently generated social change as being theoretically untenable. I remain unpersuaded. His analysis only shows that sources exogenous to social structure *also* operate to produce change, a position altogether congenial, as he evidently recognizes, to those of us who do not take structural analysis to exhaust all aspects of social phenomena. Nisbet (1969; 1970: 178, 194–96; 1972), Runciman (1970:43).

[15] The library of books in which Parsons has developed his conception of structural-functional analysis cannot be listed here. A small sample would include his first big book, *The Structure of Social Action* (1937) which is his Summa contra Utilitarianos; *Essays in Sociological Theory* (1949) and *The Social System* (1951), which together make up his Summa Sociologica, thereafter further developed in a variety of directions, partly represented in *Structure and Process in Modern Societies* (1960) and *Sociological Theory and Modern Society* (1967), two collections of papers that live up to the title of the books in which they are collected.

the variant differs from the standard form in, for me, two major respects, substantive and metatheoretical.

Structural Sources of Conflict and Deviant Behavior

Substantively, the variant doctrine makes a large place for the structural sources and differential consequences of conflict, dysfunctions, and contradictions in the social structure, thus representing, as I have noted, an intertwining of central strands of thought in Marx and Durkheim. I find it significant that Ralf Dahrendorf, long tagged as a "conflict theorist" in the sometimes demi-mythic classifications of theoretical sociology, noted this basic point years ago. In his chapter, signally entitled "Die Funktionen sozialer Konflikte," Dahrendorf observed that this mode of structural analysis:

> . . . enables Merton, in contrast to Mayo, to accept the idea that conflicts may be *systematically produced by social structures.* There are for him circumstances where the structures of roles, reference-groups, and institutions to some degree *necessarily generate conflict.* But where do these conflicts arise, and what is their significance? It is at this point that he introduces the concept of "dysfunction" which has been used so much since. . . . This step forward [in the development of functional analysis] lay above all in its indication of the possibility ("on the structural level") *of a systematic explanation of conflict.* [Dahrendorf, 1967: 268–69; italics inserted]

Much the same observation was made independently by Hans Goddijn (1963: Chapter 4) in noting that this mode of structural analysis finds "the origins of social conflict within the social structure itself, namely in the antithesis of social positions. For that reason, this analysis can be seen within the context of a sociology of conflict."

Gouldner has made the same kind of historical-and-analytical observation about the structural analysis of deviant behavior. Easily breaking through the make-believe barricades that would obstruct even restricted passage between theoretical orientations stemming from Marx and Durkheim, he notes the overlap between them. As I cannot improve upon Gouldner's own formulation, I borrow it. He observes that certain theorizing on deviant behavior:

> . . . should be seen *historically,* in terms of what it meant when it first appeared and made the rounds. In this context, it needs

emphasis that Merton's work on *anomie* as well as Mills's work on "social pathology" was a *liberative* work, for those who lived with it as part of a *living* culture as distinct from how it may now appear as part of the mere *record* of that once-lived culture.

There are several reasons for this. One is that both Merton and Mills kept open an avenue of access to Marxist theory. Indeed both of them had a kind of tacit *Marxism*. Mills's Marxism was always much more tacit than his own radical position made it seem, while Merton was always much more Marxist than his silences on that question may make it seem. . . . Merton always knew his Marx and knew thoroughly the nuances of controversy in living Marxist culture. Merton developed his generalized analysis of the various forms of deviant behaviour by locating them within a systematic formalization of Durkheim's theory of *anomie*, from which he gained analytic distance by tacitly grounding himself in a Marxian ontology of social contradiction. It is perhaps this Hegelian dimension of Marxism that has had the most enduring effect on Merton's *analytic* rules, and which dispose him to view *anomie* as the unanticipated outcome of social institutions that thwarted men in their effort to acquire the very goods and values that these same institutions had encouraged them to pursue. [Gouldner, 1973b: x–xi]

These observations on deviant behavior like those on social conflict are sharply at odds with the hackneyed and immutable notion, current in some sociological quarters, which holds that a theoretical orientation called "conflict sociology" is inescapably opposed to the mode of structural analysis under discussion here. In a way, Dahrendorf, Goddijn, Gouldner, and not a few others had falsified that claim before it became current. The fixed claim, made out of whole cloth, imputes to this kind of structural analysis the undisclosed assumption that societies or groups have a *total consensus* of values, norms, and interests. This imputed (rather than documented) assumption presumably contrasts with the assumption that social conflict is somehow indigenous to human society. But, of course, social conflict cannot occur without a clash of values, norms, or interests variously shared by each of the social formations that are in conflict. As we noted in the eighth stipulation, it is precisely that kind of socially patterned differentiation of interests and values which leads structural analysis to hold that social conflict is not mere happenstance but is rooted in social structure (Merton, 1971: 796–97).

All apart from the Dahrendorf-Goddijn-Gouldner observations and my own reiterations to the same effect in the development of structural analysis, there is ample evidence to negate the stereotype that describes it as "consensual sociology." After all, "it is no accident" (as one says) that Lewis Coser, a continuing exponent of the variant tradition of structural analysis, adopted for investigation the twin foci registered in the title of his early book, *The Functions of Social Conflict* (1956); then went on to develop *Continuities in the Study of Social Conflict* (1967); and, most recently, focused on structural sources of social conflict in his *Greedy Institutions* (1974).

Pluralistic Cognitive Structure of Sociology

So much for one substantive aspect of this variant of structural analysis as a theoretical orientation. As we have briefly noted and will now consider at length, this orientation has been associated in its metatheoretical aspect with a particular image of the cognitive map of sociology.

In that image, sociology has a plurality of theoretical orientations —distinct paradigms and theories of the middle range—rather than a single actual or soon-to-be-attained comprehensive theory. This imagery relates to the general question of the form of various models of the structure and growth of scientific knowledge generally which has more recently re-entered the domain of sociology through the gateway provided by the philosophy of science. Popper, Kuhn, Lakatos, Feyerabend, and Naess are among the principal (in some cases, charismatic) figures in the renewed debate between theoretical pluralism and theoretical monism.

The issue is examined here for several reasons. For one thing, it is in direct line of cognitive if not historical continuity with the debate taking place in sociology since the 1940s. That debate contrasted the ideal and prospect of an overarching theoretical system with the image of a multiplicity of occasionally consolidated paradigms. For another thing, the issue is relevant because muddled versions of the Popperian and the Kuhnian doctrines have been seeping into sociology particularly through that neighbor of the philosophy of science, the sociology of science. Not least, inquiry into the issue will help us to locate structural analysis on the cognitive map of sociology.

I begin with the seemingly paradoxical judgment that Talcott Parsons (at least the Parsons of the 1940s) and Thomas Kuhn (at least the Kuhn of 1962), though usually taken to be poles apart, have in fact been nearly of a kind on the question of the cognitive structure, if not the processes of change, of scientific disciplines. They have both been theoretical monists, setting out the image of a single, all-encompassing paradigm in mature sciences: Parsons principally in the context of advocacy; Kuhn in the context of his descriptive conceptualization of "normal science."

The grounds for this judgment need to be filled in with a little detail because of the triple relevance of the subject and because it is especially the moving antepenultimate past of a rapidly growing discipline that becomes opaque to successive cohorts of recruits. The more distant past is known to them through prescribed study of the doctrine while the institutionally prescribed focus on the moving frontier of investigation leads to studied neglect of the sources of ideas and findings which have been obliterated by incorporation into canonical knowledge.[16]

During the 1940s, when he was plainly emerging as the leader of a school which, as he saw to it, was chiefly made up of critical followers rather than disciples, Talcott Parsons was anticipating and advocating theoretical monism. As he put it, "there is every prospect" that the then-current diversity of theories advanced within the "professional group"—the collectivity of trained sociologists—would "converge in the development of a single conceptual structure" (Parsons, 1948: 157). Even in those remote days, as no doubt to excess since, one of Parsons's students countered this monistic orientation by observing the actuality, and advocating the uses, of a plurality of theories. The clash of opinion was no less deep-seated

---

[16] Historians and sociologists of science are obliged to take note of this pattern of "obliteration of source of ideas or findings by their incorporation in currently accepted knowledge." (Merton, 1968: 28, 35, 38) *Obliteration of source* in the strict sense of erasing every trace of origins is the limiting case in the lineage of scientific knowledge and even then holds primarily for the journeymen of science. Every scientific discipline has some practitioners who take pleasure in keeping green the memory of developers of ideas though none, to my limited knowledge, more so than Paul Samuelson, master constructor of those freight-trains of eponyms which instantly catch up main lines in a genealogy of ideas ("an exact Hume-Ricardo-Marshall model of international trade" can serve as the example of the hyphenated variety though a longer search would surely uncover as long a freight-train as the adjacency type exemplified in "the economic theory of index numbers associated with the names of Pigou, Könus, Keynes, Staehle, Leontief, Frisch, Lerner, R. G. D. Allen, Wald and my own theories of revealed preference"). As I have had occasion to note in *On the Shoulders of Giants* (1965), obliteration of scholarly or scientific source often occurs in the form of palimpsests in which later writings efface earlier ones.

for being expressed in would-be forceful but civil terms such as these:

> . . . when Mr. Parsons suggests that our chief task is to deal with "theory" rather than with "theories," I must take strong exception. The fact is that the term "sociological theory," just as would be the case with the terms "physical theory" or "medical theory," is often misleading. It suggests *a tighter integration of diverse working theories than ordinarily obtains in any of these disciplines.* Let me try to make clear what is here implied. Of course, every discipline has a strain toward logical and empirical consistency. Of course, the temporary co-existence of logically incompatible theories sets up a tension, resolved only if one or another of the theories is abandoned or is so revised as to eliminate the inconsistency. Of course, also, every discipline has basic concepts, postulates, and theorems which are common resources of theorists, irrespective of the special range of problems with which they deal.
>
> Of course, distinct theories often involve partly *overlapping concepts and postulates.* But the significant fact is that the progress of these disciplines consists in working out a large number of theories specific to certain types of phenomena and in exploring their mutual relations, and not in centering attention on "theory" as such.
>
> To concentrate solely on the master conceptual scheme for deriving all sociological theory is to run the risk of producing twentieth-century equivalents of the large philosophical systems of the past, with all their suggestiveness, all their architectonic splendor and all their scientific sterility. [Merton, 1948: 164–65; italics inserted]

In view of the various pluralistic doctrines now filling the journals of the philosophy of science, it is even more in point that this rudimentary proposal for a plurality of middle-range theories described actual sociological theory as consisting largely of gross, loose-knit "general orientations" rather than having the fine-grained, tight-knit fabric of the "hypothetico-deductive theory" then being widely bruited. For example, it was noted that:

> . . . much of what is described in textbooks as sociological theory consists of *general orientations* toward substantive materials. Such orientations involve broad postulates that indicate *types* of variables which are *somehow to be taken into account* rather than specifying determinate relationships between particular variables. Indispensable though these orientations are, they provide only the

broadest framework for empirical inquiry. [Merton, 1945: 465; italics inserted]

That was why, from the 1940s onward, some of us took to proposing the terminology of "paradigms" and "theoretical orientations" to refer to the actually operating theoretical structure of sociology. Those were the days when I touched upon the character and functions of paradigms in sociology (Merton, 1968: 69–72, 109, 514; Friedrichs, 1972) and worked out paradigms for functional analysis and for the sociology of knowledge designed to identify basic assumptions, concepts, problematics, and types of pertinent evidence. But it remained for Raymond Boudon (1970) to clarify and explicate the distinction between sociological theory properly so-called and paradigms and, through his typology of paradigms, to indicate their distinctive uses and limitations.

One reason for the ready acceptance of the notion of a plurality of paradigms immediately suggests itself. It depicted the actual state of things, if not the remote ideal, in social science. Although good-sized regions of economics and even of psychology were then taken as having developed fairly tight-knit theoretical systems, social scientists generally were chastened enough by actual experience to acknowledge the truly modest character of their theoretical achievements. The notion of paradigm, loose in construction but far better than the bottomless pit of sheer empiricism, provided both description and rationale for what was going on, while not leading one to abandon all hope of developing paradigms into broader and more exacting theoretical constructions.

As mini-structures of basic ideas, concepts, problematics, and findings, paradigms were held to represent unpretentious but organized claims to a limited kind of scientific knowledge. They were taken as intermediate to what Leontief had described in those days (1937) as "implicit theorizing" with its absence of theoretical control, and hypothetico-deductive theorizing, with its elaborate sets of logically interdependent and empirically grounded propositions. Finally, in contrast to the scientism of the time deriving from logical empiricism and the "unity of science" movement, the notion of a plurality of loose-knit paradigms insulated sociologists against adopting the comparatively mature sciences of physics, chemistry, and biology as realistically appropriate models rather than as, in many ways, contrasting reference models.

Kuhn and Structural Analysis

This condition of sociologists diversely working at their lasts in a state of reality-enforced modesty recognizably continued through much of the 1940s and 1950s (as, in spite of some current views to the contrary, it has continued since). Then came 1962 and the public appearance of *The Structure of Scientific Revolutions* by the physicist and historical philosopher of science, Thomas Kuhn. The result of almost fifteen years of slowly crystallizing thought, the monograph began to take final shape, appropriately enough, during Kuhn's stay in 1958–59 at the interdisciplinary Center for Advanced Study in the Behavioral Sciences. It was there, as he reports in the preface to his consequential book, that he was struck by the multiplicity of overt disagreement over fundamentals among social scientists of a kind that seemed to him unlike the controversies in fields such as astronomy, physics, chemistry, or biology. As Kuhn noted, it was:

> . . . attempting to discover the source of that difference [which] led me to recognize the role in scientific research of what I have since called "paradigms." These I take to be universally recognized scientific achievements that for a time provide model problems and solutions to a community of practitioners. Once that piece of my puzzle fell into place, a draft of this essay emerged rapidly. [Kuhn, 1962: x]

In several respects, the fate of Kuhn's book is self-exemplifying. It exemplifies the influence and the occasionally commanding authority exercised by a well-selected though loosely constructed paradigm of the pre-Kuhnian variety. It provides an array of basic assumptions made explicit, fundamental concepts, an array of problems, and a tacit typology of pertinent evidence, all drawing explicitly upon and also significantly recombining and developing earlier ideas in the historical philosophy and sociology of science. It was, as Kuhn has often remarked since, an effort at codification in this sphere of knowledge.

Kuhn's own concept of "paradigm" was multivalent enough to yield twenty-one discriminable senses to a sympathetic analyst.[17]

---

[17] As is well known, it was Margaret Masterman who carried out the considerable feat of distinguishing these numerous senses. As is the way with such exercises,

Understandably enough, the multiplicity of meanings was no bar to the wide diffusion of Kuhn's informing idea. If anything, that great variety of meanings may have contributed to its rapid spread. For as the variegated literature making use of it attests, Kuhn's paradigm about paradigms was taken to mean all manner of things to all manner of practitioners in all manner of scientific and philosophical groups and communities requiring him, on occasion, to disown ideas imputed to him by his more enthusiastic self-appointed disciples. (Confronted with the imputations of these disciples, Kuhn must periodically be tempted to exclaim, after the fashion of that Victorian scholar who spent much of his long exile in the British Museum: "je ne suis pas Kuhniste.") Above all else for our immediate purposes, the Kuhnian paradigm could be interpreted as asserting that at least the "mature" sciences in their prolonged "normal" puzzle-solving periods were characterized by full consensus on a paradigm. Thus, apparently without Kuhn's intent, though with his powerful inadvertent assistance, the book advanced, if it did not launch, the Doctrine of the Single Paradigm.

Kuhn afforded ample opportunity for this selective reading of his 1962 book. Quickly told examples will serve (especially since they are deliberately taken out of the contexts evidently ignored by critics and, even more significantly, by would-be adherents): "Normally, the members of a mature scientific community work from a single paradigm or from a closely related set" (Kuhn, 1962: 161). Or again, Kuhn refers more than once to "the reception of a common paradigm" by "the scientific community" (e.g. 162). It is no doubt this sort of statement [18] strewn throughout *The Structure of Scientific Revolutions* that led the invincible Imre Lakatos to observe with a doubly redundant emphasis on Kuhn's singularity that "In Kuhn's 1962 view major fields of science are, and must be, always dominated by one single supreme paradigm. My (Popperian) view allows for simultaneously growing rival research programmes. In *this* sense—and I am sure Professor Koertge will agree—no

---

they could be reduced to only a few classes: metaphysical paradigms, sociological paradigms, and artefact or construct paradigms. For this careful, even loving, analysis, see Masterman (1970). As Kuhn himself notes, "The most thoughtful and thorough negative account" of this multiplicity of senses in which he uses the term is provided by Shapere (1964).

[18] Yet those wanting to read otherwise can find a plenitude of statements in the 1962 Kuhn (e.g., p. 165) alluding to multiple paradigms even in presumably "mature" scientific communities during their "normal" state given over to "puzzle-solving."

Popperian approach is 'monotheoretical' " (Lakatos, 1971: 177; also 1970: 91–195).[19]

That was the Kuhn of 1962—or, at least, it was the 1962 Kuhn widely perceived. In a style exemplifying institutional norms of science, Kuhn has since gone to some pains to re-examine and clarify his earlier ideas and to communicate—or, put more cautiously, in light of the reciprocal misunderstandings pandemically alleged by philosophers of science, to state—his current ideas (Kuhn, 1970a, 1970b, 1974). He has done so in response to the strong critical impulse among colleagues of differing (though overlapping) theoretical persuasion who were themselves behaving in accord with that institutional norm of science known for some time as "organized skepticism" which calls for mutual criticism and less easily achieved self-criticism in the process of proposing or publicly assessing claims to knowledge (Merton, 1973: 264–66, 277–78, passim; Storer, 1966: 77–79, 87–88, 116–26).

The vigorous multilateral debates about the Kuhnian paradigm have generated a good-sized library in the recent philosophy of science—and the end is not in sight. But this, surely, is not the place to examine in detail even the sociologically relevant ingredients in those discussions involving Popper and Kuhn, in almost the first instance, but also a goodly company of others including Lakatos, Quine, Feyerabend, Toulmin, Putnam, Agassi, Ayer, Naess, Watkins, Wisdom, Scheffler, Shapere, Musgrave, and Jonathan Cohen, as well as an unitemized number of still others, all arguing their finely differentiated views in today's tumultuous philosophy of science. That examination must wait for another time. Still, it must be noted that the ideas in these discussions have been adapted, often in distorted versions, by sociologists who would find aid and comfort for their total relativism and subjectivism in what they regard as the Kuhnian doctrine, and even in the Popperian and Lakatosian doctrines. Foreclosing discussion at this time, I can only claim that neither the self-described Kuhn$_1$ of 1962 nor the Kuhn$_2$ of the early 1970s but only the reconstructed Kuhn$_3$ wishfully imagined by subjectivistic sociologists can be taken to provide that

---

[19] Lakatos is replying here to the "charge" by his onetime student Noretta Koertge that his account of the growth of science is "mono-theoretical," i.e., that it claims that "the most important critical processes take place within the context of a *single* theory or a *single* research programme" (Koertge, 1971). It is symptomatic of course that the alleged theoretical monism is treated as untenable by both critic and criticized.

wanted authoritative support.[20] Beyond that, I note only that Kuhn's recent iterations and reiterations seem to me to be in their sociological aspects, as they evidently seem to him (Kuhn 1968: 80–82), of a piece with modes of structural analysis developing in the sociology of science over the years.

In place of the much-needed detailed examination of the matter, it may be useful to set out some of the principles (and, most spottily, just a few of the principals, Popper and Kuhn being of course ubiquitous) caught up in the developing debates. So far as I have been able to discover, these would include at least the following variously linked problems and sub-problems:

    1. *Theoretical monism and theoretical pluralism* [21] (Popper, Kuhn, Feyerabend, Naess, Lakatos, Radnitsky, *op. cit.*).

[20] This differentiation of selves and of ascribed images of selves only continues what threatens to become a traditional practice among philosophers of science. Lakatos seems to have started it all when, in 1968, he distinguished three Poppers: $Popper_0$, "The dogmatic falsificationist who never published a word"; $Popper_1$, "the naive falsificationist"; and $Popper_2$, "the sophisticated falsificationist" (Lakatos, 1968; also, 1970: 181). $Feyerabend_2$ picked up the practice in "ironical criticism" of Lakatos in referring to $Feyerabend_1$ (a "$Popperian_3$" author) (Feyerabend, 1970a: 214–5). Kuhn then went on to distinguish $Kuhn_1$, author of the essay "Reflections on My Critics" and of a book of now familiar title published in 1962 by $Kuhn_2$, "the author of another book with the same title . . . here cited repeatedly by Sir Karl Popper . . . &c . . ." (Kuhn, 1970b: 231). On at least one occasion, Popper himself would have none of this differentiation of selves: " . . . I do not want to enter here into Professor Lakatos's distinctions between $Popper_0$, $Popper_1$, $Popper_2$" (Popper, 1974: 1186, n. 70a).

    As expositional and polemical tactic, this multiplication of entities is reminiscent of Korzybski (1949); as behavior, it invites the attention of sociologists of science to the recurrent syndrome, in scientific controversy, of *having been misunderstood*—or, at least, of having been misrepresented. The recurrence of this common complaint among scholars and scientists invites sociological reflection beyond the short work made of it by Merton (1967: 21–22). A related problem needing investigation by sociologists of science concerns the operation of "organized skepticism." The various disciplines apparently differ in their patterns of cognitive competition and conflict. Sociologists themselves appear forever engaged in hot dispute. Perhaps they are, beyond the generality of other scholars and scientists, but surely no more so than the internecine tribe of today's philosophers of science, each of its members engaged in vigorously announcing his own claims to knowledge while cheerfully denouncing the claims of most others.

[21] The term "theoretical pluralism" is adopted here in the broad sense of a plurality of hypotheses, ideas or, for that matter, theories and paradigms involved in the growth of a scientific discipline. The term is not being employed in the special sense most emphatically and extensively used by Feyerabend (1970b; Klima, 1971, 1972) which not only advocates the "proliferation of hypotheses" but as Naess, Lakatos, and many another point out,

2. *Incommensurability of paradigms, disciplinary matrices, exemplars (Kuhn); research programs (Lakatos); images of science (Elkana); themata (Holton); paradigms, general theoretical orientations (Merton).*
3. *Selective accumulation of scientific knowledge (including problem of progressive and degenerating problemshifts)* (Childe, 1956; Lakatos, 1970; Agassi, 1963; Kuhn, 1962, 1968; Radnitsky, 1971; Elkana, 1974) .

    3a. *Whig, anti-Whig and anti-anti-Whig perspectives on the growth and development of science* (Butterfield, 1951b; Samuelson, 1974:76).

    3b. *Continuities and discontinuities in scientific development* (D. T. Campbell, 1970, 1974; Toulmin, 1972; L. J. Cohen, 1973).

4. *Demarcation of science and non-science (in particular, pseudoscience)* (Popper, [1935] 1959, 1962, 1972, 1974; Lakatos, 1974; Musgrave, 1968).
5. *Theory-laden facts and scientific instruments* (Kuhn, passim; Norman Campbell, 1920: 101–112; Henderson, 1932; Parsons, 1937: 28, 41–42; Hanson, 1958).
6. *Falsification and confirmation in scientific inquiry* (Popper, passim; Watkins, 1964; Lakatos, 1970; Musgrave, 1973).
7. *Subjectivism and relativism* (Kuhn, Popper, Lakatos, passim; Scheffler, 1967, 1972) .
8. *Social substrate of science ("the scientific community")* (Polanyi, 1958; Kuhn, 1962, 1970a; Price, 1961, 1963; D. T. Campbell, 1969).

Clearly, a tempting array of problems for sociological and not only philosophical investigation.

The Uses of Diversity

Reverting to my observations on the announced crisis of sociology, I propose that, while the unified consolidation of paradigms

---

argues a kind of methodological dadaism. As Popper himself observes, "The idea of theoretical pluralism is no novelty. Under the name 'The Method of Multiple Hypotheses,' its methodological importance was stressed by the geologist T. C. Chamberlin at the end of the nineteenth century" [Popper (1974: 1187, n. 80)].

remains a useful but distant ideal of the Pareto T-type, a plurality of paradigms has its own uses in an evolving discipline. For as some of us have been monotonously reiterating for decades, paradigms have diverse cognitive functions just as they have diverse social functions for the collectivities of scientists engaged in developing them. Among these uses, I touch upon only two.

First, a plurality of paradigms institutes a variety of problems for investigation instead of prematurely confining inquiry to the problematics of a single, assumedly overarching paradigm. That is one reason, for example, why Keynes deeply regretted that Malthus's unpublished line of approach to the connections between savings, outputs, and profits was ignored while Ricardo's prevailed, describing that century-long domination as no less than "a disaster to the progress of economics" (Keynes [1933] 1972: 98–99). The disaster lay rather in the failure to ask certain questions than in the answers to the questions that were raised. Or, turning from great matters to small ones, it was in the difficult 1940s (not the difficult 1960s or 1970s) that a paradigm included this observation under the caption of "Concepts of Dynamics and Change":

". . . functional analysts *tend* to focus on the statics of social structure and to neglect the study of structural change. This emphasis upon statics is not, however, *inherent*." And further, "the concept of dysfunction, which implies the concept of strain, stress and tension on the structural level, provides an analytical approach to the study of dynamics and change." And, still addressing itself to the focus of a particular line of thought, this statement of the 1940s continues with the basic query focussed on preemption: "does the prevailing concern among functional analysts with the concept of *social equilibrium* divert attention from the phenomena of *social disequilibrium?*" [Merton (1949) 1968: 107–8]

In cases such as this, the question is not one of detecting substantive contradictions between paradigms but of considering their problematics. Paradigms differ in focussing upon distinctive ranges of problems for investigation. As a result, the exclusive adherence of a scientific community to a single paradigm, whatever it might be, will preempt the attention of scientists in the sense of having them focus on a limited range or problems at the expense of attending to others. Through such preemption, monistic theory becomes dysfunctional for the advancement of other types of knowledge in that field. Manifestly, therefore, conscientious advocates of theoretical monism will heed the warning: *caveat præemptor.*[22]

This formulation leads directly to a second use of diverse paradigms with their more-or-less differing problematics: they direct the attention of research workers to differing kinds of *phenomena* through which each array of problems can be investigated to good advantage. This is no small or incidental matter. It is not happenstance, for example, that structural analysis of the Marxian variety elects to center on historical change in class structures rather than on routines of everyday social interaction just as it is not happenstance that ethnomethodology centers on tacit rules exhibited in the routine interactions of individuals getting through their day rather than on the dynamics of changing class structure. The set of problematics imbedded in differing paradigms directs attention toward differing "strategic research sites, objects or materials" which will best exhibit the processes, mechanism, or structural arrangements to be investigated. Thus, knowledge becomes unwittingly confined to the understanding of limited materials exhibiting the phenomena of theoretical interest.[23] To the extent that the paradigms are intellectually disciplined and not merely an adventitious

[22] A current investigation by Joshua Lederberg, Harriet Zuckerman, Yehuda Elkana, and myself has identified this process of the preemption of interest as probably involved in patterns of "prematurity, maturity and postmaturity" of contributions to science. On the dysfunctions of monopolistic orthodoxies in science resulting in "accumulative imbalances" of research attention and on the functions of regulated cognitive conflict for correcting those imbalances, see Merton, 1973: 57–58; Radnitsky, 1973b: 136; for analysis of "the imbalance between psychological and sociological orientations to the subject of ambivalence," see Merton and Barber, 1963: 93–94.

[23] As Frank Beach (1950) has reported, for example, for a time more than half of American experimental psychologists had focussed on one species, the rat, as their experimental organism. Ernst Mayr (1974: 657) writes of certain implications of such a focus on research-objects and research-interests: "Much of the recent controversy in the literature on animal behavior can be better understood now that we are aware of the important differences between behaviors controlled by closed and by open genetic programs. Ethologists have been primarily interested in species-specific signals and in their evolution. Comparison of different species has been of great concern to them. The classical experimental psychologists, who were principally interested in the neurophysiological and developmental aspects of behavior, almost invariably worked only with a single species. Their primary interest was in learning, conditioning, and other modifications of behavior. They approached behavior with the interests of the physiologist, and the phenomena thus studied were, to a large extent, aspects of noncommunicative behavior, such as maze-running or food selection."

assortment of personal interests generating little cognitive power, diversity leads to the illuminating of quite distinct aspects of human action and society, including aspects that a single paradigm would leave unnoticed.

The diversity of aspect requiring investigation provides another reason why paradigms are often in social rather than cognitive competition. Exponents of particular sociological paradigms compete for the interest ·of new cohorts of recruits to move ahead with their line of work just as they compete, one surmises less effectively, for old cohorts of veterans who have been using other paradigms to transfer their allegiance. In short, exponents of paradigms compete in the allocation of all resources that affect the distribution of attention by sociologists to the broad spectrum of sociological work. More often than might be supposed, coexisting paradigms, conspicuously so in a laboriously evolving discipline such as sociology, involve competition for cognitive *attention* rather than cognitive contradictions and confrontations, although the disagreeable and, to some, alluring noise of polemics may suggest otherwise. (On the general process, especially that of cognitive agreement and value disagreement, see Merton, 1973: Chapter 3.)

Though often obscured by polemics, the cognitive problems of coexisting paradigms call for discovering the capabilities and limitations of each. This involves identifying the kinds and range of problems each is good for (and noting those for which it is incompetent or irrelevant), thus providing for potential awareness of the respects in which they are complementary or contradictory. It is within this sort of context that the stipulations for one variant of structural analysis have indicated a range of problems for which it seems particularly suited; the detailed expansion of those hints is hardly the work of an evening. But even in condensed form, the stipulations may suggest why this kind of structural analysis continues to hold a certain interest and why, at the same time, even sociologists dedicated to structural analysis must recognize that it remains only one, albeit a most inviting one, among the plurality of sociological paradigms now being energetically developed.

Examining this same circumstance from the perspective of the sociology of science, I must report that variations in the number and variety of paradigms in scientific disciplines remain poorly understood. So far, no model of the growth of science has managed to account for the extent of doctrinal pluralism in different disciplines or in the same discipline at differing times. Long before the subject of growth of knowledge became a renewed focus for inquiry, the older metaphors carried with them suggestions of one or another model. The metaphor of a "marketplace of ideas" suggested processes of production, distribution, and exchange under conditions ranging from monopoly to open competition; the "forum of ideas" suggested an image of free discussion subject to processes of persuasion and the exercise of types of authority; the "arena of ideas" conveyed the image of combat to the desperate end, rejecting the possibility, except for rare indulgent moments, of coexistence or complementarity of paradigms; and, to go no further, the metaphor of "a population of ideas" suggests a population-genetics model of variation and selection in evolutionary development. But whether one adopts Popper's falsification model or Kuhn's matrix model or Lakatos's model of research programs or the evolutionary models of Donald Campbell, Gerald Holton, and Stephen Toulmin, the models of scientific growth are all as one in maintaining that a plurality of paradigms in competitive and sometimes conflictful interaction are subject to more or less common criteria and rules of evidence which transcend other differences among the contending intellectual traditions.[24] Thus, after Kuhn had rejected the total relativism that many held to be implicit in the 1962 version of his doctrine, Radnitsky taxed even his far more restrained version with being unable to deal with the strategically important issue of whether shifts in paradigms represent, in given instances, "an advance" or "a retrogression," a question which Imre Lakatos makes central to his concept of "research programmes" (Radnitsky, 1974: 110–11; Lakatos, 1970, 1974). Once again, the exponents of the total subjectivism which is here and there finding its way into today's sociology, who expressly seek legitimation in today's philosophy of science, are being left behind to fend for themselves. Even in the last third of the twentieth century, pushpin is not as good as poetry.[25]

It should be plain, then, that in describing and advocating a plurality of theoretical orientations in sociology in the form of a "disciplined eclecticism," I neither describe nor advocate a kind of

---

[24] In any case, the strong impression of substantial underlying agreement on this assumption is gained from long-continued examination of the vigorous debates which I have barely touched upon in the preceding part of this chapter.

[25] The allusion is, of course, to Bentham's almost unforgettable affirmation: "Prejudice apart, the game of push-pin is of equal value with the arts and sciences of music and poetry" (*Rationalist Review* 1825: 206).

theoretical anarchism in which anything goes (cf. Feyerabend, 1965, 1970b, 1975; Naess, 1972). Nor does this stance rest upon the dictum from Peking: "Let a hundred flowers bloom and let a hundred schools of thought contend." After all, as the concept of hyperexis teaches us, there really can be too much of a good thing (Chairman Mao has evidently concluded as much since his pronouncement of 1957). It is among a much smaller plurality of theoretical orientations that structural analysis in sociology must find its evolving place. It seems safe to conclude from what has gone before that, in the interactive process of cognitive and social selection among sociological ideas, structural analysis will continue to link up with complementary ideas in other paradigms and thus continue to make modest theoretical consolidations toward the ultimate and still very remote ideal of a unified comprehensive theory.

3

What Do We Mean by Social "Structure"?

George C. Homans

FEW WORDS do sociologists use more often than "structure," especially in the phrase "social structure." Yet we seldom ask what we mean by the word. I shall begin by trying to elucidate some of the meanings. In this job I shall not have to do much of the work myself. I shall rely heavily on a thoughtful little book by Professor Raymond Boudon of the Université René Descartes, *A Quoi sert la notion de "structure"?* (1968). Indeed the first part of my paper will be little more than a commentary on his book. Later I shall spend some time going beyond the question of definition to ask how "structure" comes into our efforts to explain social phenomena, that is, how it comes into social theory.

As used by sociologists, "structure" seems to refer first to those aspects of social behavior that the investigator considers relatively enduring or persistent. What is relatively enduring may include a number of different kinds of things. It may include formal organizations, such as the Church of Rome. The Church certainly changes, but some of its features change relatively slowly. What is relatively enduring may include within both formal and informal organizations a complex of positions and roles. It may include institutions, such as marriage, which are not organizations, but which are subject to organizational control, for instance, by the courts. It may include a certain distribution of occupations and incomes—a stratification system—which, though certainly related to organizations and institutions, is not itself institutionalized at all in Western societies but which may manifest for many decades a surprising tendency to persist. It may include a certain pattern of interaction and activity among the members of a small group. I myself use the word "structure" for such a pattern.

My mentioning different time spans within which what the scholar takes to be permanent, his social structure, persists indicates that the persistence in question must always be relative. It can never be absolute, for no social structure remains unchanged forever. Structure is what the scholar considers to be somehow *more* persistent than some other aspect of social behavior he is interested in. He cannot decide what is structure by reference to itself alone. Perhaps we should all adopt the rough distinction the French make between *structure* and *conjuncture*. In a familiar example, the former might be represented by a relatively enduring pattern of world trade, and the latter by the particular circumstances obtaining at a particular point in time, such as an Arab oil embargo. The example ought to teach us that some conjunctures may lead to enduring changes in structures.

Second, many sociologists, and indeed many social scientists, call structural those characteristics of the phenomena they study which appear to them more fundamental than other more superficial characteristics. This definition overlaps the first, as the more fundamental characteristics are often just the ones the investigator believes to be least subject to change. Thus Boudon (1968:72) mentions Gurvich's distinction between "structure" and "organization": "The 'organizations' by which a 'social class' expresses itself can be changed without changing the structure of the latter." This particular statement carries the suggestion that what is structural pertains to the larger social unit, because its characteristics change more slowly than those of the smaller units that make it up. It is far from clear that this assumption holds good generally. Thus family organization may in some cases change more slowly than other features of the social structure to which the families belong. A more interesting assumption is that what is structural in the sense of fundamental is somehow hidden, only to be revealed by research and analysis carried out by adepts, while the nonfundamental is what is visible to the ordinary damn fool. I do not believe that this assumption holds good any more often than the earlier one.

Third, many sociologists use "social structure" to refer to some kind of social whole, which can be divided, at least conceptually, into parts, and in which the parts are in some way interdependent, at least in the sense that a change in some of them will be associated with changes in some of the others. In this meaning, a structure is distinguished from a mere aggregation. Sometimes sociologists make a stronger and less easily demonstrated claim that a change in any one of the parts will produce changes in all the others. As with the definition of structure as relative persistence, the parts in question and the nature of their interdependence may both be of very different kinds: the individual members of a group and the interrelations between them, the co-presence within a society of certain institutions, or even the entries in the cells of a matrix of quantitative data, when the matrix is of the sort in which a change in the figures in any one of the cells requires changes in the others (see Boudon, 1968: 43). No matter how far the degree of interdependence of the parts is pursued, a social structure in the present sense does not appear to refer to anything different from what used to be called a social system. Moreover, this definition also overlaps the first, since some sociologists appear to believe, more as a matter of intuition than of explicit statement, that the interdependence of the parts is just what maintains the relative persistence, or equilibrium, of the structure: the interrelations of the parts with one another dampen the variation that is possible in any one of them. Again, I am not sure that this is generally true. But then the older I get, the more skeptical I seem to become.

Finally, the use of "structure" in the present sense sometimes carries with it the implication that the whole in question is greater than the sum of its parts. Now it is, to say the least, difficult to attach any meaning to this famous proposition that is both unambiguous and illuminating. Of course if its parts are such that they can be kept physically separate or disassembled, an organism is dead or a machine inoperative. This does not reveal to us anything we did not know before. Don't tell me, as one of my teachers was fond of doing, that half a sheep is mutton. This sort of illustration of the proposition is interesting only to a butcher. If they are organisms or machines at all, societies are not the sort of organisms or machines for which the truth of the proposition can be tested. In this connection I like Boudon's remark (1968:26) that some of the words used to define "structure" are at least as obscure as what is being defined.

This point leads up to my next. Though I can think, for instance, of particular mathematical techniques that have been used to analyze certain kinds of phenomena called structural, none of the definitions of "social structure" listed so far entails or implies the use of any general method of research or analysis that can be distinguished from other methods of social science as specifically "structural." As Boudon puts it (1968:86), "Certain structural analyses are structural only to the extent that they use the word 'structure' like an incantation."

What is more important, none of the definitions entails any special kind of structural explanation of what features particular social structures exhibit or why social structures should exist at all. I am not sure that Peter Blau has always understood this point, though he must by this time, as I have drawn his attention to his error. He once wrote as if what he called "structural effects" could not be explained by a particular kind of theory but required a different kind. His words were (Blau, 1960:180):

> If we should find that, regardless of whether or not an individual has an authoritarian disposition, he is more apt to discriminate against minorities if he lives in a community where authoritarian values prevail than if he lives in one where they do not, we would have evidence that this social value exerts external constraints upon the tendency to discriminate—structural effects that are independent of the internalized value orientations of individuals.

The error here, as I pointed out (Homans, 1964:971):

> . . . consists in Blau's assuming that this individual holds only one "internalized value," whereas he certainly holds many, and they are in competition with one another. We need consider only two: anti-authoritarianism and social acceptance. . . . If an individual cannot get acceptance from other members of the community except by discriminating against minorities, which is apt to be the case when the other members hold authoritarian values, the probability will increase of his forgoing the rewards of anti-authoritarianism in favor of those of social acceptance, and Blau's "structural effect" will be produced.

That is to say, the effect in question does not in the least require for its explanation a theory that excludes propositions about the values of individuals. Indeed Blau would have done much better to call his "structural effect" a "collective effect": it concerns the influence of a collection of individuals—but if a collection, still individuals—on another individual. It is, of course, an example of what statisticians call an "interaction effect" (Boudon, 1968:62). But if you wish to savor one highly specialized use of the word "structural," here it is.

The definitions of "structure" cited so far do not imply anything distinctively structural in either method or theory. That is why Boudon (1968:85) calls them "intentional" definitions. A scholar who uses one of them is stating a bit vaguely what he intends to study—some relatively enduring, relatively fundamental social phenomenon made up of interdependent elements. But he is stating nothing about how, in method or theory, he intends to study it.

Boudon then passes from the first class of definitions of "structure," the intentional definitions, to the second class, which he calls "effective" definitions. Unlike the first, a definition of the second class associates the notion of structure with a logical construction which, applied to a particular social system as an object, specifies the structure of that object (Boudon, 1968:90). In his discussion of the first class of definitions I am wholly in agreement with Boudon. In his discussion of the second, I am not; or rather I believe he does not sufficiently consider some of the further implications of this class.

It will serve no purpose to discuss further in general terms the characteristics of effective definitions in the absence of an example. Boudon gives several examples of structures as effectively defined. I shall consider only one of them, which I choose because it concerns a subject I once used to know a great deal about: the rules stating who is permitted or forbidden to marry whom in certain nonliterate societies (see Homans and Schneider, 1955). Hereafter I shall refer to them as "marriage rules" for short, though they are certainly not the only rules applying to marital behavior.

Many anthropologists have written about these rules. Boudon follows the formal analysis made of them by Kemeny, Snell, and Thompson (1956). Their procedure begins by stating a set of "axioms," which can also be formulated in mathematical terms. The first few axioms have to do with the very general notion of a "type" of marriage. Later I shall consider what that means concretely. At present I only want to get the axioms on the record. They are (Boudon, 1968:128–29):

 a. Each member of a society S belongs to one type of marriage.
 b. Two individuals may marry if and only if they belong to the same type.
 c. The type of marriage of an individual is determined ex-

clusively by the sex of this individual and by the type of marriage of his (or her) parents.

d. Two men or two women whose parents are of different types are themselves of different types.

e. Whether marriage between two individuals of different sex is allowed or forbidden depends only on the kinship relation between them.

f. No man may marry his sister. (We recognize this, of course, as part of the so-called incest taboo.)

g. It is always possible for certain descendants of two individuals to marry one another. (Note that this condition offers us our first hint that this set of axioms cannot provide the general propositions of a theory of marriage rules, for in a regime of strictly endogamous castes the descendants of two individuals belonging to two different castes could never marry one another.)

I do not propose to get into discussion of particular axioms. I only wish to elucidate what Boudon and others do with them. Here the first question is what is meant by "type" of marriage. Theoretically it is defined in such a way that the axioms are satisfied by the marriage rules of the societies in question. But if we use the language of ordinary anthropological fieldwork, the word refers to the rules of descent that determine what groups (or categories) members of the society belong to, as far as these rules relate to marriage. They are usually also related to other matters such as residence.

Let me take two examples. The first is that of the Kariera of Western Australia as described by Radcliffe-Brown (1913). The tribe was divided into two patrilineal moieties, subdivided in turn into two crosscutting moieties, membership in which was determined by the principle of alternating generations. (The system may also be described as one of patrilineal moieties intersected by matrilineal ones.) Such a system is called a four-section system, and the Kariera gave the sections names. The rules were that a Banaka man married a Burung woman; their children were Palyeri and married Karimera. A Burung man married a Banaka woman; their children were Karimera and married Palyeri. The children of Palyeri and Karimera men became Banaka and Burung respectively, and the cycle repeated itself indefinitely. Thus the rules meant that a Banaka man or woman was required to marry a Burung woman or man respectively, a Palyeri man or woman a Karimera woman or man. Members of these pairs belonged to the same type of marriage, as the word *type* is employed in the axioms. Accordingly, by axiom

(b) they were allowed to marry. But a Burung man or woman was not allowed to marry another Burung, and so forth.

It can be shown that, provided "marriage type" is defined according to the Kariera rules, Kariera marriage satisfied all the axioms. It can be shown further that a Kariera man was allowed to marry a woman who, so far as the kinship relationship between them was concerned, was his mother's brother's daughter or his father's sister's daughter—she could be both at once—but *not* his mother's sister's daughter or his father's brother's daughter. That is, he was allowed to marry either of his immediate cross-cousins but not his sister or his parallel cousins, and accordingly the Kariera are said to have practiced bilateral cross-cousin marriage. (A Kariera man was also allowed under the rules to marry genealogically more distant cousins, but we need not go into that.)

Another example is provided by a number of societies that practice one of the forms of unilateral cross-cousin marriage. (See Lévi-Strauss, 1949; Homans and Schneider, 1955.) These societies are divided into lineages, at least three in number, membership in which is determined by either patrilineal or matrilineal descent but not by both. Suppose that there are only three lineages. The rule is that a man of lineage A must marry a woman of lineage B, and only a woman of that lineage; a man of lineage B, a woman of lineage C; and a man of lineage C, a woman of lineage A. The women marry in the opposite direction. In terms of the theory, each member of society belongs to one type of marriage; in this case a man of A and a woman of B etc. belong to the same type of marriage, and so are allowed to marry.

It can be shown that, provided "marriage type" is defined according to these new rules, marriage in these societies satisfies all the axioms. As in the Kariera system, a man is not allowed to marry his sister or any parallel cousin. But the system differs from the Kariera one in that a man is allowed to marry only one of his immediate cross-cousins. He is allowed to marry a woman who stands in the kinship relationship to him of mother's brother's daughter but not father's sister's daughter. For this reason the system is called matrilateral cross-cousin marriage.

There are other marriage systems that can be treated in the same way, though not many. Still, two will be enough to illustrate what Boudon means by an "effective definition" of structure. In the procedures carried out, three elements have been isolated. First is a set of axioms (A), more general, that is, less variable within the scope of the phenomena to be explained, than the other two elements. Second is a set of rules specifying different types of marriage, which, as Boudon does not point out but I do, are in fact rules specifying how members of a society are assigned to different groups or categories by unilineal descent, alternation of generations, etc., so far as the assignment is related to marriage. These rules are more variable than the axioms, and I have suggested the variation by considering two different sets of rules. Third, also variable, is the set of rules indicating the different close relatives with whom marriage is allowed or forbidden. These rules satisfy the axioms and follow from them in conjuncture with the second element.

Boudon (1968:134) proposes to call the second element the "structural description" of the social system in question, and the third element the "apparent characteristics of the system." He then adopts the following notation to indicate the relations between the elements:

$$A \text{ (Axiomatic)} + \text{Str (S)} \xrightarrow{\text{calculation}} \text{App (S)}$$

That is, from the axioms in conjunction with the structure the apparent characteristics of the system can be logically derived. According to Boudon, a structure is "effectively defined" by its place in such a logical construction.

At this point I shall begin to make some critical comments, gradually increasing in their scope. First, Boudon (1968:134) says of the structure of a society as now defined that it consists of "an ensemble of propositions that only make sense [*n'ont de sens que*] in relation to an axiomatic and that must be compatible with this axiomatic." It is not altogether clear what this statement means, and there may be a problem in my translation from the French, yet some of the features of the structures in question, such as patrilineal or matrilineal descent-groups and a division of persons by alternating generations, certainly make sense apart from the axiomatic. That is, there are societies in which similar features exist without being related in these ways to mariage rules, and reasons for their existence can be offered quite apart from any connection they may have with marriage.

Second, it is difficult to find a criterion whereby the second element should be called structural but the third element not. Boudon refers to the third element as "the apparent characteristics of the system." In our examples these are the rules whereby persons whose relationship to ego is defined in terms of kinship are permitted or forbidden spouses. To call these rules apparent is to suggest that those included under structure are somehow less apparent. Boudon seems to have in mind some distinction such as the Chomskian one between the "deep structure" of a language and its surface or manifest characteristics. But in the examples considered, what Boudon calls the "structural description" of the system—the existence of institutions such as lineages and alternating generations and the way persons are assigned to membership in them—are just as "apparent" as the "apparent characteristics" in any sense in which I can conceive of that word's being used. I mean that an ethnographer can discover them equally easily: the natives can be brought to talk about both. This is also true of some of the axioms, such as the rule forbidding marriage between brother and sister, though not of all of them. Moreover, both the second and the third elements are equally structural by the intentional definition: they are relatively permanent features of the social organization.

The second and third elements are also equivalent in logical status. As Boudon (1968:138) recognizes, if from the axiomatic in conjunction with the structure the apparent characteristics of the system can be deduced, it is also true in the examples considered that from the axiomatic in conjunction with the apparent characteristics the structure can be deduced. Or, in terms of the notation:

$$A + App\ (S) \xrightarrow{\text{calculation}} Str\ (S)$$

I turn now to the relationships between the analysis of the intentional and effective notions of structure and a subject that is dear to my heart, explanation in social science. For me explanation, not only in the social sciences but in all the sciences, consists in the construction of deductive systems in which the propositions to be explained, the *explicanda,* follow in logic from a set of more general propositions under different specified given conditions (see especially Homans, 1967). This is sometimes called the "covering law" view of explanation. It should be obvious how Boudon's example of effective definition of structure fits into this pattern. His first element, the axiomatic, corresponds to the general propositions, more general than the others in the sense that the axiomatic cannot be derived from the logical combination of the other two. The second, the structure, corresponds to the different given conditions to which the general propositions may be applied. And the third, the apparent characteristics of the system, corresponds to the propositions to be explained. The interesting thing about the example, which may not hold good of all explanations, is that either the structure or the apparent characteristics can take the place of either the givens or the *explicanda,* respectively. Thus a further definition of structure is "what is taken as given in a certain kind of deductive system in social science."

Yet I must utter a warning that we should not take the fact that the example meets the formal requirements of an explanation as evidence that it provides us with an adequate theory of marriage rules.

First, it is at best a far from general theory. The full set of axioms is simply not applicable in the explanation of the marriage rules of most societies. I have already pointed out that axiom g is always violated in the case of caste endogamy. The axiom that requires each member of a society to belong to a single "type" of marriage does not apply to by far the largest number of human societies, far less to the largest number of all marriages, unless it is restated in such a way as to be meaningless, as in the form: the single type of marriage is one that excludes brother and sister, mother and son, and father and daughter as possible spouses. That is, only the incest taboo within the nuclear family stands up as very general, and even that has its exceptions. Boudon (1968:137) claims that the theory explains why marriage between parallel cousins is "generally forbidden." But even if it is forbidden in many societies, the exceptions to the rule are of the greatest importance. Thus one form of parallel cousin marriage, marriage of a man with his father's brother's daughter, is not only an allowed but a preferred form of marriage among the Bedouin and other societies that have come historically under the influence of Bedouin society through Islam. A general theory ought to be able to explain regular exceptions to general tendencies as well as these tendencies themselves. It is both interesting and remarkable that the marriage rules of a few societies can be explained by deductive systems of the sort considered. Yet the theory remains what Boudon (1968:137) calls a "segmentary" theory. And as he goes on to say: "One may always, in effect, ask oneself to what degree a segmentary theory is not simply an *ad hoc* representation of, and without real explanatory value for, the fragment of reality to which it applies."

Not only does the theory explain the marriage rules of only a limited number of societies, but also it takes as given a very large number of features of social organization that themselves cry out for explanation. For one thing it deals with rules, with norms, and never asks to what extent or for what reasons the rules are obeyed. But we know that the members of these societies, like the rest of us, discover all sorts of ways of getting around the rules if they find it to their net interest to do so. Sometimes they manage to establish fictitious ties of kinship between persons who otherwise would not be allowed to marry, and in this way preserve the letter of the system intact while sacrificing its spirit. Sometimes they break the rules directly, and if they do so often and in the same way the system itself will turn into a different one. If we are looking for a general theory of marriage rules, much less a general theory of kinship ties, we need to explain conformity to norms.

Not only do sociologists assume too easily that they have explained behavior when they can point to a norm to which it conforms, they also do not ask often enough why the norms themselves are what they are. The reason why the theory in question seems peculiarly formal is that it uses norms, both in the axioms and the structure, to explain other norms in the form of "apparent characteristics." Under the name of structure it takes for granted that the members of a society may be organized in patrilineages or matrilineages and may be further subdivided by alternating generations. But why should they be so organized? Technology appears to have something to do with the answer. Thus the societies of hunters or herdsmen tend to be patrilineal. Some of the axioms themselves cry for further explanation. Why should some societies have organizations that can be interpreted as allowing each member to belong to only one marriage type? The theory seems formal because it offers no efficient causes in the characteristics of human behavior to account for these features. Even the incest taboo, I believe, will yield to this type of explanation and will not always have to be explained, as it usually is today, by pointing to various final causes, such as its function in producing links between groups through the exchange of women (see Lévi-Strauss, 1949:65).

To speak very crudely, moving from intentional to effective definitions is in one sense a regression. Structures under the intentional definitions are what we at least intend to explain, but those under the effective definitions are what we are prepared simply to take for granted.

That is, the problem implied by the intentional definitions remains. Structures are the relatively permanent features of societies and groups whose characteristics and interrelations we intend to describe, analyze, and explain. Structures are the subject-matter of sociologists of many different methodological and theoretical persuasions, and in sociology there is no method that can be distinguished as specifically structuralist. Indeed for explaining structures we shall need axioms that are not themselves structural in any sense in which that word has been used so far. I do not even like to call them axioms. The axioms of geometry are arbitrarily chosen; they are noncontingent. The mathematician who chooses one set will derive from it a different geometry from the one who chooses another. The general propositions we shall need are, even though discovered by men and women, still not arbitrary but rooted in the nature of things, that is, in the nature of humanity.

Working in the field of small groups, I always say that the first theoretical question sociologists should ask is one that takes precedence intellectually over the one asked by Boudon. It is: Why should things recognizable as social structures exist at all? In answering the question I have tried to show how relatively enduring structures, a status-system for instance, can be created and maintained by the actions of individuals, actions of course taken under the influence and constraint of the actions of other individuals. That is, I have tried to explain the properties of certain simple structures using as general propositions the propositions of behavioral psychology (see Homans, 1974). For reasons I shall not go into here, because I have gone into them so often elsewhere, I believe that this kind of work promises to provide the soundest intellectual foundation for sociology.

But once I have explained—to my own satisfaction, not always to that of others—some of the elementary features of a social structure, I take these as given for the time being and show how under these conditions the propositions of behavioral psychology will also explain, for instance, why persons occupying different positions in the structure will further differentiate their behavior, notably in the degree to which they conform to group norms (see Homans, 1974: 319–39). By following this procedure I return to the Boudon model in so far as I relate to one another three elements analogous to his three, thus:

$$\text{General Propositions} + \text{Structure} \xrightarrow{\text{Calculation}} \begin{array}{c}\text{Further Differences}\\ \text{in Behavior}\end{array}$$

These further differences in behavior may themselves become structural, that is, may tend to persist.

The analogy fails only in that the axiomatic I use is different from his. (Not that my axiomatic is any more mine than his is his: both of us use propositions first formulated by others.) This constitutes a big difference in the content of the argument but not in its form. I believe that the theoretical work of many sociologists takes this form implicitly: in the process of explaining certain structural relationships we take others as given. When I say that our theoretical work takes this form implicitly, I mean that many sociologists and other social scientists leave the equivalent of the axiomatic, that is, their major premises, unstated. But if unstated they are still there, like ghosts waiting to materialize.

4

Homans' and Merton's Structural Approach

William J. Goode

IN THIS BOOK we are all being challenged to take a position on a major intellectual issue. We are also being asked—though that may be somewhat more difficult than just taking a position—to understand that issue. To will such a book is an assertion that even if we do not wish to take a position, or understand the issue either, we should at least be able to talk about "social structure," for it will be a major theoretical topic in sociology for years to come.

In evaluating these contributions we may reject as extreme what may be correct or consider dull and trite what may contain the seeds of future sociology. We take a position even if we ignore the debate. We can calculate, but we have no way of guessing the odds that we may be right. We have limited intellectual capital and must decide where to put our investment. Will it be fruitful to espouse a structural approach? Peter Blau has given his answer, in organizing this collection of papers around that theme. In the preceding chapters, two distinguished sociologists have affirmed their versions of a structural approach.

I would venture the guess that most of the sociologists at these meetings learned with some astonishment that theorists have been arguing for some years, with great heat, about structuralism, that dozens of books have been published on the topic, and that it has become a major issue in sociology. They have, to be sure, been using the term "social structure" without embarrassment, but they had not supposed that in order to use it they needed to be re-educated in a whole new literature.

We are now being told that a new concept has arrived on the scene—not a new term and not a new hypothesis, but a new concept, idea, or notion. This always causes us some discomfort, and certainly we were comfortable with the old one. As George Homans has reminded us, there are few terms that we use more often, and our comfort with the old term and concept is proved by our not bothering to ask what they mean or how we could make the idea more fruitful.

However, in considering any new concept, we should remember that in all sciences, and especially sociology, the rate of infant mortality among new concepts is very high. Far more are rejected than survive. Survival is not mainly a function of etymological precision or even clarity of reference, though both do help somewhat, but of how much fruitful research a new concept generates. Most concepts new or old are not killed by attack but by neglect.

This one is now thriving, as these papers attest, but the very attention they give to it may alert us to the problems it contains when we depart from our former comfortable relationship with the older version. Indeed, on my bleaker days I ponder the chances of our drifting into the sterile polemic about it that marked our relationship with the notion of functionalism. As I pointed out in some detail in my book, *Explorations in Social Theory* (1973), those who have most vociferously attacked "functionalism" not only assaulted a set of doctrines that no one defended, but also practiced the same functionalism in their empirical research that almost everyone else did. If that occurs with the new notions of "social structure," we shall waste another decade in an intellectual desert.

Homans has pointed out the underlying meanings or referents of the term "social structure," as it has ordinarily been used, and I shall add a bit to that. For the most part, I agree with his statement, and indeed I have made it myself many times over the past two decades. Usually, when the term had any meaning at all, it referred to social patterns that appear to be relatively persistent or enduring; that seem more fundamental—here, I would say: That have more causal influence, or explain more of the variance, or are what we call an "independent variable"; that seem to contain parts that constitute a kind of social unity or whole, i.e., are interdependent;

and (a meaning that Homans appears to reject) that make up a unity or whole that is somehow greater than the sum of the parts.

I would only wish to go one step beyond his comment on the second attribute of a social structure. I agree that it is viewed as somewhat more "fundamental," for in the actual usage of "structure and function" in the past, "functions" were usually effects, or consequences, while structures were independent or causal variables or behaviors. In any continuing analysis, however, it was always possible to challenge that independent or causal status and ask, with reference to any social pattern that was called a "structure," what caused *it* in turn, i.e., to view it as caused, as dependent, as a "function" of something still more fundamental. For example, one could assert that the day-to-day economic decisions of employers and workers are a function of the relations of production, the more fundamental structures of a society; but one could (reversing Marx) argue that these in turn are a function of the juridical and political structures. How far one would go in such an alternation of focuses on structure and on function is perhaps a matter of intellectual taste.

Homans has also expressed some of his salutary scepticism by noting that though the usual meaning of social structure suggests a "larger social unit" because it changes more slowly, some smaller units actually resist change more than larger ones. He points to the example of the family, and ethnomethodologists have also brought to our attention the regularities to be encountered in microsocial behavior, where formerly we had supposed great lability and even whimsy were more common. Lomax and Arensberg (1968) have presented an array of data, too, to show that folksong styles may persist through generations and over thousands of miles of travel, while kingdoms crumble and empires fall.

Indeed, one might mark this point as still more far-reaching than those casual examples might suggest. It is likely that in the history of all fields a similar pattern may be found: Scientists uncover some larger wholes or parts that make up a system, and only much later come to discover that those larger regularities are created by still deeper microregularities and persistences. The parts of the body that were described in classical anatomy owe their persistence and durability precisely to the equally persisting microphysiological events that continue to recreate those bones and muscles. Structure and function may well merge at a later stage of knowledge, as may statics and dynamics.

Even if I am correct about those later stages of inquiry in developed sciences, the current scene is rife with polemics against synchronic studies and arguments for diachronic ones; attacks on statics and praise of dynamics; calls for conflict analysis and rejections of analyses of social order; and denials of functions but affirmations of structures. Why has structuralism suddenly become intellectually chic?

A classical rebuttal has always been available for any new intellectual orientation; it is iterated often in Sorokin's *Contemporary Sociological Theories* (1928). It may be phrased thus: What seems to be fruitful in it was always known or done by excellent sociologists; what is new is simply wrong. That view may yield us some solace, but it is incorrect. Robert K. Merton's precise stipulation of a newer, more sophisticated form of structuralism aids us somewhat in perceiving, amidst the complex flow of research findings we daily confront, which key elements we need to accept or reject now. We may wish to deny some parts of it, but he has helped us to know which are the important parts we must evaluate. He has also brought to our attention the historical roots of structuralism, especially in his typically graceful and apposite footnotes, with the particular reminder that the sociological version does not derive from the Prague school of linguistics, from Piaget's developmental psychology, or from Lévi-Strauss's cultural analyses.

But though that derivation is correct, it does not explain the growing popularity of the terms "structuralism" and "structural analysis," and certainly not the increasing flow of articles and books on the topic itself. I assert that both are mainly caused by the apparent success of what seems to be a new meaning of structuralism, quite different from the version stipulated by Merton and with only a metaphorical connection with our older, unchallenged concept, "social structure." This last, Homans reminds us correctly, simply refers to "what used to be called a social system."

Like other fields, sociology has frequently borrowed its metaphors from more successful intellectual disciplines—and not the least of those was Herbert Spencer's appropriation in 1858 of the concepts of "structure and function" from biology. When the word began to spread recently that linguistics was being transformed by creative people who discovered "structures" in ordinary language, that endeavor seemed to be analogous with our frequent efforts to find structures in ordinary social behavior. If locating structures could be intellectually revolutionary, perhaps we too could do it, and we certainly believed we needed an intellectual revolution! Numerous book reviews and articles have proclaimed the brilliant success of the Lévi-Straussian structuralism, in which once again an underlying cultural or perhaps even psychological structure seemed to explain a diversity of labels, oppositions, relationships, and even social behaviors. Again, the formula seemed clear: Uncover a structure that will generate the social phenomena we observe.

True enough, some of these anthropological analyses seemed almost uncannily to ape the style of salon Freudianism in the 1920s: comparisons and analogies that seemed only literarily persuasive, incantatory utterances with great resonance but obscure meaning, quick jumps in reasoning when one hoped for a precise methodology or at least a clear proof, and so on. Nevertheless, their success among the intelligentsia, and even some anthropologists, is apparent; and if we have been wistful for so much acclaim, and hopeful that we might use a similar method creatively, or at least become stylish by adopting structuralist terms, that is understandable.

Thus, I do not believe that the present widespread attention being paid to structuralism comes from its great success in our own field, or from an examination of neoclassical structuralism as Robert Merton has stipulated it, but from the success of structuralism in other fields. I believe, with Raymond Boudon and George Homans, that the new structuralism is different from any that we have developed in sociology; I also agree that it is a much more sophisticated scientific creation than any we have achieved in sociology.

I depart from both of them in one minor point, and from each of them separately in a major point to which I shall devote my last remarks. My minor disagreement is with their implicit concession that Lévi-Strauss has in fact uncovered or created a set of axioms and rules that will generate precise descriptions of real kinship behavior—in short, that he has discovered a set of laws that explain the form or structure of family behavior. Of course, I may be doing Homans an injustice, for his disbelief in grand social science architectonics is substantial, and his key footnote in his paper at that point is to a sharp attack that he once wrote on Lévi-Strauss' analyses. Moreover, later he does warn us of two gaps in the Lévi-Strauss formulation: (a) it seems to be segmentary, not general, for it fails to explain the marriage rules of most societies; and (b) it offers no set of efficient causes that ultimately create those regularities. Nevertheless, we cannot both deny the validity of that set of so-called discoveries and also use it as an example of the new structuralism that would be worth emulating.

Both Boudon and Homans agree that if "structural method" means "the very general approach which consists in envisaging the analysed object as a whole, as a set of interdependent elements whose coherence must be shown, then such a method does exist," for all of us are structuralists in that sense, and all social analysts since Plato have been structuralists. Used in that sense, the term is at best magical, a yearning for order in one's data. If our data show that workers vote less radically in middle-class neighborhoods, that hardly calls for the term "structural effects." We can of course *call* that a "structural effect" if it pleases us to do so, but it has little to do with the new structuralism, and we have never lacked for terms to describe that effect. Such usages are at best cabalistic, and they are applied in the hope that the persuasiveness or prosperity of structuralism will somehow be granted to our propositions and findings.

If we use the term in that traditional sense, and we are all structuralists, then there is no method or theory to emulate and, worse yet, nothing even worth arguing about. If on the other hand, we use the term in the newer sense, it still refers to no special method of discovering theories. It is not comparable to the experimental method in science (Boudon, 1971:140). We cannot, then, go to another field, learn that method, and return to our own work with a magical wand that will transform the opaqueness of our observations into valid hypotheses. It is for this reason that Boudon (1971:141) argues that sociology and economics "cannot expect much from 'structuralism' as such."

The new term does, nevertheless, refer to an intellectual form that is different from our traditional structural analyses. In what Boudon calls its operative definition, "a structure is always the theory of a system of appearances." It is a " 'testable theory of a system of apparent characteristics' " (189). It can, if valid, generate or predict the observables or data that we seek to explain. To that extent, it is different from Merton's structural stipulations, but it is not very different from an ordinary theory in the mature sciences.

Here, Homans believes, if I read him correctly, that a deeper understanding of structuralism will disclose that its form is ultimately that of all good science; and that if it fails it does so because the axioms it uses (at least in the instance of kinship analyses) contain norms, but they are used to explain other norms, whereas our axioms must contain other factors, forces, or efficient causes that "are not arbitrary but rooted in the nature of things."

It is especially at this point that Homans differs from Merton, for the latter restates a position he has held over many years, that in sociology no unitary or monistic theory is to be expected. His form of structuralism accepts warmly the wide variety of loose-knit general orientations or of mini-paradigms that we encounter in our fields, "rather than the fine-meshed, tight-knit fabric of 'hypothetic-deductive theory'" that Homans sees as the dominating characteristic of real science, and as the core of the new structural method.

Since theorists are the intellectual gad-flies of their fields, constantly nagging their colleagues to rise above the present reality of their field and to aim at still better science, it is not a sufficient answer to Homans that in fact sociology is not only intellectually loose: One might argue that it is not put together at all. Some of its domains seem to be entirely disconnected from many others. For example, a tiny band of hardy adventurers do follow a hypothetico-deductive quasi-mathematical method, but most of us would be terrified of a high school algebra test. Nevertheless, we need not be satisfied with that state of affairs, and if we could achieve great science by working out a set of axioms and defined operations, by which we could deduce and predict the social behavior we observe, surely that is a noble aspiration.

Such a yearning after the Holy Grail of science probably does us little harm, and perhaps some good. We may, as a result, try to formulate our hypotheses more precisely, and to test them more rigorously. But we should not doom ourselves to a self-created failure by believing that form of science will come to us in the near future even if we work hard to accomplish that end. I would go much beyond Merton's mild statement that the "notion of a plurality of loose-knit paradigms (has) insulated sociologists against adopting the comparatively mature sciences of physics, chemistry, and biology as realistically appropriate models rather than as, in many ways, contrasting reference groups." In fact, the familiar textbook version of scientific thought, expressed neatly by Homans, has not characterized even those relatively mature sciences during most of their history over the past three hundred years.

I am not, of course, referring to the fact that real scientists often do not proceed from axioms and rules of calculation to predictions of reality, and instead frequently jump first to their final conclusions and then go back to construct a logical or mathematical basis for that prediction. I am rather asserting that only one science, physics, followed that model with much consistency. Until its later invasion by twentieth-century physics, for example, chemistry was not mathematical in its thought system; and it would be stretching reality even to claim that it was a set of logical derivations from axioms, except in the trivial sense that we all use deduction in our thinking. Biology did not have any overarching theory at all, and strictly speaking it does not yet. Prior to the twentieth century, its one grand theory was evolutionism, which was not axiomatic or mathematical. Its first approximation to that form occurred in the subfield of genetics, a development that is hardly a generation old. Its second took place in the 1950s in molecular biology, when it became possible to apply modern physical theory to intracellular phenomena. Within the two most advanced sciences, physics and chemistry, there are two subfields, crystallography and structural chemistry, that have grown less—and it is always a matter of degree —from an axiomatic, mathematical base than from observed regularities in the real physical structure of the objects observed. For example, the actual spacing of atoms in different rows and planes of a crystalline compound determines many of its physical and chemical properties, such as light transmission, elasticity, or how it reacts with other compounds.

One might, of course, counter that strong assertion by arguing that eventually, when a science becomes sufficiently mature, it does begin to approximate the thought form of physics, but surely that will help us but little in our contemporary quandary, when those of us who practice sociology exhibit even less faith in our field than outsiders do, and thus have little confidence that we can become a science by donning its outer trappings.

Nevertheless, even if I believe that Homans' optimism about what we can do next seems premature, I wish to close by referring again to part of his analysis of the structural method, where he notes how important it is that the general propositions or axioms with which we begin our deductions must be rooted in the nature of things. What *is* the nature of things that seems most susceptible to a structural analysis in the new sense?

I believe that the best sociology for the next fifty years will be made up of numerous nodules or theory fragments, each constituted by precise descriptions and predictions that apply to only limited areas of social behavior. These little islands of valid knowledge will be much like those encountered in biology through most of its modern history, e.g., the systematic relations between the Isles of Langerhans and the oxidation of sugar; the response and recovery of the retinal rods, as light changes in intensity; or the differentiation of species when animals enter a new ecological niche. If you really do not believe we, too, have been moving toward such a body of real knowledge, I urge you to spend some time examining the sociological journals and monographs of, say, fifty years ago. Our generation does know more, and more precisely, about social behavior than did our intellectual forefathers. To paraphrase Mark Twain, an excellent sociologist who was rooted in the nineteenth century, they knew a great deal, but much of it was not so.

However, some of those theory fragments will be harder to create than others. More significantly for our purposes here is that not only do some bits of reality yield more quickly to Homans' ideal form of science, but some will also fit more easily into a structural formulation in the new sense. Some pieces of physical, biological, and social reality, I believe, do approximate more closely to genuine structures in the strict sense that the *arrangement of the parts* controls much of the variance in the phenomena. Wittgenstein said in this connection that we should pay attention to the network, the geometry of its arrangement, and not the characteristics of the things that net describes; if a field has so progressed that it can create such an intellectual structure, perhaps that advice is wise. However, it is not true that an examination of all social relations, all biological phenomena, or all cultural patterns will easily disclose an underlying structure in which the arrangement of the structure is the most central set of variables to be considered.

Lest it be thought that I am imposing a too-stringent requirement, let me first point out that sociologists have hardly made the attempt to carry out structural analyses in this sense, and so we have not ascertained whether they might be more widely possible than we know. Most of sociology has not aimed at structuralism in that sense. It has not even studied group behavior very much. Instead it has mainly shown how group memberships and group norms affect individual behavior. On the other hand, a moment's thought will inform us that there are some areas of social behavior which might be good candidates for this kind of analysis.

One is communication systems, where the structure of the network affects the flow of information and social interaction among human beings, e.g., a wheel with a leader at its center has different effects than does a system made up of a single line, and so on. A second type is authority systems, e.g., a T-structure, especially common in factories of the past, has different consequences than does an L-structure, which is more commonly found in organizations in which a large percentage of professionals work. A third type of problem is paths of travel. It is not thrifty to make a direct path from everywhere to everywhere; total redundancy in route-making is costly. It is also unproductive, or costly to human wishes, to build only one path, linking only two social centers. Paths and routes must permit many different options of linking more than one need or goal. Consequently, paths that human beings work out, for purposes as diverse as friendship and submarine patrols, are likely to be complex, overlapping, and not made up of straight lines. As it happens, this interaction between paths and social interaction *has* been investigated with the aid of sophisticated mathematics, including topology, for it exhibits structural similarities with many other phenomena, such as circuit networks, the structure of trees and their roots, cell geometry, and the vascular system of the body (for a good summary, see Haggett, 1967).

A fourth possibility is one that Merton himself suggested many years ago: how the physical layout of housing affects social interaction.

Doubtless, many of you will have your own nominations for this kind of structuralist endeavor, for you have perceived an inner structure within some social patterns that determines those patterns more fully than traditional individual or group variables have done.

I have avoided the temptation to sketch out either my hopes or predictions about the immediate future of sociology. Instead, I have focused on the two versions of structuralism that my distinguished colleagues have presented. Both are ideals, whose achievement would challenge our talents, skills, and energies. Moreover, those programs cannot be viewed as hollow calls for others to do their duty. In fact, over the years both men have staked their own careers on the fruitfulness of their vision, and have proved by multifaceted researches that we are not likely to go far wrong if we try, albeit with modesty, to emulate their example in the future, as so many of us have done in the past.

Their works have illuminated our thinking, and I assert that their research will continue to serve as wise guides in the future, when all these metatheoretical comments about the structural method will have been forgotten.

5

Social Structure and a Theory of Action

James S. Coleman

A FEW MONTHS AGO, I was engaged in a conflict with a body much larger and more powerful than I. As I frequently do, I began to reflect upon the conflict, attempting to conceptualize it in sociological terms. I began to describe it, as follows. There were two actors in the conflict: I and my more powerful opponent. There was a single event in which we both had an interest: I an interest in one outcome of the event, and my opponent an interest in the other outcome, which was mutually exclusive with the first. My opponent held full control over the event and thus could exercise that control to bring about the outcome it desired. Furthermore, I held no control over any event which was of interest to this more powerful actor. Yet my interest in obtaining the outcome I desired was exceedingly great. What did I do? I searched two lists of actors: first, those who had some control over events of interest to my opponent, attempting to select out those to whom I might have some connection; and second, those who had some interest in events over which I had some control, attempting to select out those who might have some connection, direct or indirect, to my opponent. The latter included persons with whom I had some generalized mutual obligations that ordinarily go under the heading of friendship.

By these means, I located five points of entry into my opponent, that is, five actors who might have some control over an event of interest to the corporate body in control of the event I was interested in. For one of these points of entry, I had direct contact. For the other four, my contact was one or two steps removed. For three of the five, there was a single contact with the actor who was a point of entry to my opponent. For one, there were two contacts. For one, there were five contacts.

After all these new actors and events were brought into the conflict and exercised the control, or threat of control, that they held, the structure of the relevant system was enormously different from its structure at the outset. The interests and control of the principals to the conflict had not changed, but by bringing in a large number of new events and actors, I had changed the structure of the system enough to bring about a change in the outcome of the event at issue.

This is the way I describe the conflict now. Some years ago, when my interest in the sociology of conflict began, I would have described the conflict in very different terms. I would not have used the concepts actors, events, interest, control. Instead, I would have focused on the mutual polarization that took place, the proliferation of issues, the acceleration of activities, the enlargement of the circle of active participants, as the conflict came close to the point of final decision. I would have seen the conflict more nearly as an autonomous process, self-sustaining and with an internal logic and dynamic, which worked itself out. In short, my description of the conflict some years ago would not have involved the concepts of purposive action, but would have described the properties of the conflict through time as a dynamic observable phenomenon, much as one would describe the properties of a tornado or other physical phenomenon over time.

The description I might have made then is no more incorrect than is the description I just gave. It merely attends to different aspects of the conflict. But it uses a conceptual framework that is strikingly different from the one I've used now. The description I have used, with its terms actors, events, interest, and control, views the conflict as inhabited by purposive actors, whose action is predictable from their interests and control and whose joint action gives rise to the dynamic phenomena of proliferation of issues, proliferation of actors, and the like that I might have observed some years ago.

Related Changes in Four Social Sciences

The change of conceptual framework that I've just described would be of little interest if it were merely a change in one person's way of viewing the world. But just as I have modified my way of viewing the social world, others have changed as well. Indeed, there are points in the history of a discipline at which certain unexamined postulates are held up for inspection, certain assumptions looked at anew. The present time may be such a point in the history of sociology, at which the postulates and assumptions that govern sociological research and discourse must justify themselves or be replaced.

The possibility that this is so is increased by the fact that changes have begun to occur in psychology, political science, and economics that are to some degree parallel to those beginning in sociology. In psychology, the change is most like the one I've described: There are fewer new positivist or behaviorist conceptual schemes, more frameworks in which the terms goal or purpose play a part, and an acceleration of work in cognitive psychology. Examples of the change are Miller, Galanter, and Pribram's *Plans and the Structure of Behavior* (1960), work by Newell and Simon (1972) and others in using computer programs as models of purposive action, and a new book by William T. Powers, *Behavior: The Control of Perception* (1973), in which goal-directedness is the organizing principle of action.

In economics, the change has not been in the introduction of a purposive model of behavior, for that has already been central to the economist's armamentarium, in the form of the rational man of micro-economic theory. It is, rather, the extension of this framework beyond the confines of traditional economic variables and beyond the confines of traditional forms of economic exchange transactions. Using the framework of rational action borrowed from classical economic theory, economists such as Gary Becker (1964) and Theodore Schultz (1963) have begun to account for different levels and patterns of education, variations in birth rates, and variations in marriage rates, to give a few examples. Using the same framework of rational action, other economists such as Kenneth Arrow (1959), Mancur Olson (1965), and James Buchanan (1968) have examined forms of relationship other than production or exchange of private goods, involving public goods, polluting activities, and collective decisions.

In political science, this change is more confused, because the discipline has been without direction for some time. But the newly developing direction is that of a theory of purposive action applied to political processes such as political party structure, coalitions, and legislative behavior. It is perhaps best exemplified by Riker and

Ordeshook's book, *An Introduction to Positive Political Theory* (1973).

The developments in all three of these related disciplines have resulted in application of theories of purposive action to an increasingly broad range of behavior. Along with this has come the beginning of greater convergence among the social sciences than has been true for some time.

In sociology, the idea of rational or purposive action as the core of a conceptual framework is hardly new. Talcott Parsons in 1937 outlined in *The Structure of Social Action* a paradigm for purposive action (see pages 77–82). But then he never applied this paradigm in any systematic way, and for a long time held the discipline enthralled with a classification scheme of pattern variables that diverted attention away from these important initial contributions. Paul Lazarsfeld has reviewed and analyzed early work in the study of purposive action by the social psychologists Karl and Charlotte Bühler and their colleagues (1972). George Homans (1974; originally published 1961) introduced more explicitly than had been done before by sociologists the idea of social exchange, emphasizing the necessity of beginning sociological theory at the level of individual persons; but then he moved into a behaviorism incompatible with the purposive action at the base of exchange theory. Peter Blau, in his *Exchange and Power in Social Life* (1964), and a few other sociologists have moved exchange theory forward in sociology, by applying the economic exchange paradigm to a wider variety of commodities and activities.[1] S. N. Eisenstadt has begun to incorporate ideas of exchange into his most recent theoretical work on cultural codes.

Tasks in the Development of a Theory of Action

However, if such developments in sociology are to be more than sporadic and stray gestures toward a purposive theory of action, in-

---

[1] Most of the work in sociology has not used the power of economists' generalizations about declining marginal utility and increasing marginal cost. As a result, the exchange theory of sociologists has provided a way of describing certain observed phenomena in a way that makes them appear sensible, but has not led to predictions in the same way that economists' application of purposive theory to non-economic behavior has done. See later sections of this paper for further discussion.

frequent departures from an otherwise uniform continuity with the past, it is necessary that certain tasks be accomplished.

First, it is necessary to examine the forms of relationship among persons through which a theory of action can mirror social structure. One of the barriers to extensive use of a theory of action in sociology has been that the only form of interpersonal interaction considered has been that of exchange. In this paper, I will indicate other forms of relationship necessary to a broad use of purposive action theory in sociology.

Second, if such a theory is to be more than a new way of looking at the social world, that is, if it is to be specifically useful as a theory, it must generate some predictions or deductions. Without making specific predictions here, I will attempt to show how one can expect such a theory to make predictions and what elements must be introduced into the theory in order to do so. Related to this is the establishment of specific connections to research. Research in sociology has been almost wholly inductive explanation of observed social phenomena; yet the use of theory implies some deductive elements as well. How are deduction and induction to be related in the use of a theory of action in research?

There is a third task as welcome as it is important. This is the task of reestablishing a connection between social theory and social and moral philosophy. Much has been written in sociology about a "value-free" science, but there has been some confusion between two senses of that phase, leading to disagreements about whether sociology should, in fact, attempt to be value-free. A theory of action, appropriately applied, allows for evaluation of social systems, not in terms of the sociologist's values but in terms of the levels of satisfaction a system provides for its members. This fourth task, then, is to show how a theory of action can appropriately allow for evaluation of social systems and social organization, how it can provide the base for a normative theory of society.

In the remainder of this paper, I will sketch how each of these three tasks may be accomplished. This will of course be no more than to point out a direction of activity; but sometimes to point out such directions can itself be useful. In doing this, I will sometimes introduce the elements of a particular form of a theory of action that I have begun to use in my own work. At other times, I will, in an eclectic way, take examples that illustrate the points I wish to make, from other people's work. All of these examples will use as a basis the conception of rational action found in economic analysis and statistical decision theory. For the moment, it is the only well-developed conception of rational action that we have; and though it may well be replaced when cognitive psychology is more fully developed, there is nothing to replace it now.

This conception of rational action is deceptively simple. It begins by assuming that for a person each state of the world has a particular *utility* level, where utility is that which the person seeks to maximize, through his actions. In statistical decision theory, the model of rational action is slightly more complex. The decision maker's action does not lead with certainty to a partciular state, so we say there is an *event* with different possible outcomes each of which has a utility level for the decision maker and over which he has partial control. He takes that action which will give him the outcomes with the highest expected utility. If the outcomes of an event have different utilities for a person, we may say that he has an *interest* in the outcome of the event. Thus we may think of persons (or actors, as I shall sometimes refer to them) and events, with actors both interested in and in partial or total control of the events.

If a person is faced with a mutually contingent environment, then the definition of rational action becomes more complex, and it is this complexity for which the theory of games has been developed. For most of what I will describe here, it will not be necessary to introduce this double contingency, though in a more fully worked out theory, this will be necessary at a number of points.

The simple notions of rational action that I have described underlie all the examples I will use. It is the essence of this approach that the complexity lies not in the model of man that it uses, but in the structural configurations within which this simple man acts. Of particular importance to sociologists are the various forms of relation among persons that generate these structural configurations, and it is to these that I now turn.

Forms of Relationship and Interaction

Several of the forms of relationship can be described by use of the concepts actors, events, interest, and control, as previously introduced.

There is first a distinction between two forms of relationship which has been long noted in sociology. The two were probably most clearly distinguished in a brilliant paper some years ago by Theodore Abel (1930), in which he distinguished between *interest* and *sentiment* relations. This distinction of Abel's pointed to the fundamental difference between a case in which a relation is a means to an end for a member of it (an interest relation, in Abel's terms) and a case in which the relation is an end in itself (a sentiment relation, in Abel's terms). Other sociologists have described social structures that tend to generate these two kinds of relation. George Herbert Mead was one, in discussing forms of social organization with complementarity (generating interest relations) and those in which all persons were in common position (generating sentiment relations). Durkheim's distinction between organic and mechanical solidarity, Toennies' *Gesellschaft* and *Gemeinschaft,* pointed to the same two forms of organization.

In the theory of action I want to describe here, these two kinds of relation enter not as relations *per se,* but as two kinds of orientation of one actor toward another. This is, of course, implicit in Abel's formulation, because a relation could be an interest relation for one actor and a sentiment relation for the other. In the theory of action we describe Abel's "interest relation" as a case in which an actor has an interest in an event over which a second actor has some control. This leads naturally to exchange of control, if the second also has an interest in an event over which the first has some control, and indeed is the basis for exchange relationships. If the "events" are private goods, then the exchange is a pure economic exchange; if not, it is a more general social exchange. In either case, the actors are beneficial to one another—by "accident" if you will, because each is interested only in his own welfare; yet each, in using the other as a means to his own ends, must aid the other's welfare in order to benefit his own.

The other form of relation, Abel's sentiment relation, is one in which the second actor's welfare enters more directly into the actions of the first. In the absence of this form of relation, then only if an event has consequences for himself personally will the first actor have an interest in it. But if he has a sentiment relation to the second, then he will be interested in an event if it has consequences for the second. The precise way this may best enter the model is not clear. Gary Becker (1973), in a slightly unorthodox economist's formulation, has made the first actor's utility dependent (positively or negatively) upon certain characteristics of the second actor. Thus not only his own state, but that of other actors, determines the utility that an actor experiences. In my own work (Coleman, in press), I have introduced something roughly equivalent, but with a slightly different conceptual structure: We conceive of each actor having an "object self" and an "acting self," corresponding to the "me" and the "I" of Mead. The acting self takes actions on the basis of perceived consequences of events for the object self. But this separation of selves allows the acting self to have psychic investment not only in its own object self but also in the object selves of other persons.[2] When an actor has in Abel's terms a sentiment relation to another actor, then the first actor's acting self has a psychic investment (positive or negative) in the second actor's object self. Thus he becomes interested not only in events that have consequences for himself (i.e., his own object self), but in those that have consequences for the other as well.

These, then, are two fundamentally different ways in which actors are related: first, through events for which control and interest are distributed among different actors, leading to exchange; and second, by a direct interest of one actor in whatever events have consequences for another. I will continue to use Abel's labels for these for convenience, and call them interest and sentiment relations, respectively. There are important variations among the first of these two, and it is to these I now turn. The variations turn upon certain properties of events: their "internality," their "divisibility," and their "alienability."

INTERNALITY

If an event has consequences for only one actor, it can be said to have the property of internality. Otherwise, it has externalities, to use the term from economics. Suppose an actor has control over an event. If, no matter to what other single actor control of the event is transferred, it has consequences for an actor not in control of it, then the event has externalities. All polluting activities are by definition of this type. The fundamental difference between an event without externalities and one with externalities is that in the latter case no simple exchange can put control of the event into the

---

[2] This is another point at which a purposive theory of action constitutes a valuable theoretical aid: We expect such investments to be made or withdrawn rationally, based on expectations of psychic returns. Thus one can make predictions about what psychic investments will be made and the conditions under which they will be made or withdrawn.

hands of a single actor who experiences its consequences. As the event has consequences for more than one actor, it naturally leads to forms of relationship other than those of simple exchange, such as coercion or joint control.

The externalities of an event may be positive or negative. Negative ones, called external diseconomies by economists, are exemplified by pollution or by the undesirable side effects of an airport on the residents who live nearby. Positive ones, called external economies or spillover benefits, are exemplified by the increase in surrounding property values when more expensive houses are built in a neighborhood or, to use less economic examples, the psychological benefits experienced by all in a community when one of its members becomes famous or the benefits to all candidates on a ticket when one candidate is very popular.

When these benefits are widespread and have this property of non-excludability just described, they are called by economists public goods. Various problems are associated with public goods, the most important of which is motivating persons to pay the costs of producing them, since they can experience the benefits if another pays the cost.

DIVISIBILITY

Just as internality has to do with multiple consequences of an event, divisibility has to do with multiple control. While some events are under the control of a single actor, others are under the control of more than one. A special form of exercising control over these latter events is necessary. Voting, with a particular decision rule, is the most common; but sometimes one actor has the right to initiate an event, and another the right to exercise a veto over it. Or, as in the case of dual kingships in early Rome, both may have rights of initiation and veto.

The essential aspect of this form of interaction is that, because of the joint control, unilateral action by one party does not determine the outcome of the event. Many social structures include events of this form, and in order to develop a theory appropriate to them, the theory of action must be adapted to the study of collective decisions. Such work was stimulated some years ago by Kenneth Arrow (1959), who showed the impossibility of a wholly satisfactory decision rule for arriving at a collective decision by aggregating votes. It has been carried on by a number of political scientists and economists providing the beginnings of an economic theory of collective decisions.[3]

ALIENABILITY

There are other properties of events that affect the form of relationship among persons, but I will only briefly mention one of these. This is the alienability of control over an event. If control over an event is alienable, as is control over private goods, then physical exchange can take place. If it is not alienable, as in the case of an action one takes which uses his own skills, then nothing can be exchanged beyond a promise to act in a given way. Such events, then, generate networks of trust and trustworthiness, and networks of obligation and expectations, in contrast to alienable events.

Movement among Levels

But rather than to elaborate the different forms of relation among persons in a theory of action (and I make no claim to have been exhaustive), I want to turn to perhaps the most crucial form of relationship. Most scientific disciplines must deal with the problem of shifting between levels of organization. In sociology, this shift manifests itself in the movement from persons as units of analysis to groups or organizations that have persons as members, to organizations or social systems that have groups or organizations themselves as members. Robert Merton (1968) has pointed to the critical character of the problem of making the shift in a conceptually satisfactory way in sociology and has taken some steps toward doing so; but in general, the problem has been ignored, with the analyst or theorist of macro-social structures taking as given the level at which he chooses his units and not grounding his analysis at the level of individual persons, and the theorist of micro-social structure never moving beyond the level of interpersonal relations.

This shift between levels must be intrinsic to a theory of action, for the theory does not afford itself the luxury of beginning with

[3] See, for example, Anthony Downs (1957), James Buchanan and Gordon Tullock (1962), and the journal, *Public Choice*.

already-formed units of social organization. Instead, it must begin with persons, and move up from there, or if, in an application, it begins at a level above persons, it must be ultimately analyzable into relations among persons. I will describe how my own version of this theory does so, to give an idea of what is involved (for a full discussion, see Coleman, 1972, 1973a).

Considering the *interest* form of relation (around which most of social structure is built), I propose that we think of an organization as a *system of social exchange,* with a delimited set of events and a delimited set of persons as actors. The system is defined by the actors, the events, the structure of control of actors over events, and the structure of interest of actors in events. Then because this is in fact an articulated system of social exchange, there will develop a continuing process of exchange, with each satisfying his interest subject to his initial control over events of interest to others.

If this system of exchange operates as a perfect market the theory allows calculation of the value of each of the events and the power of each of the persons to realize his interests through action in this system. Furthermore, a shift of levels is possible: If we conceive of this system as an actor at the next level (which I shall call a "corporate actor"), then its interests are given by the values of events at the lower level. In such an integrated system, the organization acts as if it were a single actor, and the directions in which it acts are given by the values of events generated at the lower level. In other words, as we shift between levels, the values of events at the lower level give the interest of the corporate actor in actions at the next level. The control by this corporate actor over events at the next level is determined externally by the structure of the situation. The control in turn of the corporate actor's actions is shown by the relative power of the different persons that are members of it.

Now such a conception would be of little use if it did not accord with what we see around us. But in fact everyday experience does tell us that organizations are actors in the social system, just as are individuals, and that we conceive of the social world as consisting not only of persons as actors but of these corporate actors as well.

Thus the shift between levels in this theory is accomplished by conceiving of organizations as continuing systems of action, subject to internal analysis, and also as corporate actors, with interests derivable from that internal analysis. It thus becomes possible either to carry out an analysis wholly at one level, with no actors subject to internal analysis, or to carry out an analysis that covers two or more levels.

For example, consider a simple ideal-typical system of legislative representation, in which it is assumed that members of a legislator's constituency control his actions through their votes for or against him at re-election. Then in each constituency, it is possible to generate the *values* of the constituency (considered as a system of action or a corporate actor) from the interests and power of the constituents. These then become the *interests* of the constituency as corporate actor, and indirectly of the legislator as its agent; and the predicted outcome of legislation is derived from these interests, in conjunction with knowledge about control of specific events (i.e., issues) by legislators through their votes or committee positions. Such analyses have not been carried out extensively, but in at least one case, the Norwegian Parliament, such an analysis with empirical data has been carried out (Hernes, 1971), and in another, the American Senate, a similar analysis has been initiated.

Turning to the other kind of relation between persons, the sentiment relation in Abel's terms, it is again possible to establish a relation between levels. Once an organization or other corporate acting unit is conceived as an actor, then persons may make psychic investments in it, just as they make psychic investments in another person. Thus whether it is IBM, the Boy Scouts, the United States of America, or the Communist Party, a corporate actor may be the object of psychic investment, positive or negative, so that those persons with such an investment feel its fortunes as their own (or if the investment is negative, as the opposite of their own). We are all familiar with the everyday experience and observation of these psychic investments; and in other branches of social psychological theory, the term "reference groups" in one of its uses refers to this relation of a person to a corporate body.

This is the second kind of relation between levels in the theory under discussion. The one of primary importance, however, is the first, discussed earlier, because it provides a way of creating actors at one level from stable structures of control and interest among actors at the level below.

Besides the shift between levels of social organization that occurs in this theory, macro-social structure is mirrored in a second way. This can be illustrated by the example of social conflict that I used at the beginning of this paper. In that example, I conceive of the situation in just the way I have been suggesting for systems of action: actors and events, connected by the control of actor over events and the interest of actors in events. But in that example, there was no "system of action." Unlike an ongoing institution, group, or organization, there was a single event that temporarily brought two actors together: a corporate actor with full control over it and some interest in it, and a person with no control over it and strong interest in it. In such situations, there is no set of events and actors in a system with boundaries, but only the single event and the two actors. What happened was that interest in the event led the actor with no control over the event of interest to construct an *ad hoc* system of action by bringing in new actors who were interested in events he controlled or with whom he had some credit. In short, the interest led not to a social exchange in order to satisfy one's interest but to a use by the person of other control he held to bring into play control held by other actors over events of possible interest to the corporate actor in question.

Thus according to this theory, there are, in addition to ongoing stable systems of action that can be conceptualized as corporate actors, relationships of control and interest among actors and events that remain dormant until they are temporarily brought together for a specific purpose by one or more actors. This is one extreme of a continuum of which the other extreme is a stable system of exchange, functioning very much as does an economist's perfect market. In between are various imperfect, incomplete, and partial exchange systems of which much social structure consists. The development of the theory consists in part of developing theories of imperfect, incomplete, and partial systems of social exchange to mirror the particular forms of social structure that exist.

Use of a Theory of Action in Empirical Research

One of the greatest difficulties of sociological theory has lain in moving from a theoretical or conceptual framework to a theory that provides testable predictions and can be useful for empirical research. The fact that a theoretical framework fails to do so does not make it useless; such frameworks can often lead one to see new possible relationships or to get new ideas simply by providing a new way to look at the world. It is important, however, if the principal value of a theory is to be realized, to drive toward specific predictions and to drive toward use of the theory in research.

It is helpful to look at micro-economics, which uses the same purposive actor model as under discussion here, to ask how its deductions or predictions are made. There are several points to note. The first is that nearly all the deductions are qualitative, rather than quantitative, despite the extensive use of mathematics in arriving at the deductions. The second point is that the deductions all stem from a combination of two elements: the logical structure of the theory and one or more empirical generalizations, which are usually qualitative and usually based on general experience rather than specific research. One of the most central empirical generalizations is the declining marginal utility of any normal good: The more one has, the less he wants an additional amount of the same good. A second is the declining marginal productivity of a factor of production: the more of a factor that is used in combination with a fixed amount of others, then after a certain point, the less productive will an additional unit of that factor be. But many of the empirical generalizations are merely conditional, and the resulting deductions are conditional as well: If income increases, then there will be a given effect, say on the pattern of consumption. It is from these conditions or from the weak generalizations, in conjunction with the logical structure of microeconomic theory, that a remarkably large quantity of qualitative predictions can be made. For example, in an extension of the theory to incorporate social interaction due to Abel's sentiment relation, Gary Becker (1973) is able to make qualitative statements such as this: "Consequently, the larger the share [of his full income] contributed by his social environment [through respect or admiration from others], the smaller would be the average percentage change in his own full income [due to a change in his money income] " Put in other terms, this says that the more important their evaluations are to him, the less effect a change in his money income would have on his consumption patterns. Such statements that make predictions use the theory to connect changes in two or more observable variables: in this case, the share of his psychic income contributed by his social environment, changes in income, and changes in expenditures. Ordinarily, no single one of these predictions is massively illuminating; it is their cumulative and combined quality that makes the theory of value.

I suggest that theory in sociology will come to have the same kinds of predictions as the example given above: qualitative predictions that connect changes in two or more observable variables. For example, using a form of the theory of action, one can predict that in a legislature, for an issue on which geographically-concentrated special interests are opposed by geographically-dispersed general interests, the greater the time for negotiations before voting, the greater the likelihood is that the special interests will win.

The testing of such predictions is one way in which systematic research relates to this kind of theory. Note that systematic research appears to play a small and insignificant part in formulation of the theory; rather it is used later, in testing the theory, to decide whether one must reject the theory and begin again.

There are other ways in which such theory is used in relation to research besides use of research to test the theory. The theory in its turn provides benefits for research. A simple example from an application of the theory of rational action to human capital formation is this: Jacob Mincer (1974) argues, from the theory (in which human capital is created through on-the-job training) that income growth and other job-related phenomena that change over time should show greater regularity as a function of years of labor force experience than as a function of age. Such a prediction serves as a guide for research. Possibly this guide seems self-evident; yet in most studies of income changes over time for given cohorts, time has been measured by age rather than labor force experience, and age rather than years of experience has been used as an independent variable in explaining income. Thus it was not self-evident to these researchers, both economists and sociologists.

Perhaps, however, the most important way a theory such as those under discussion is used to guide research is as a framework for design of research and analysis of results. Before the theory of human capital, no one thought of attempting to estimate the "rate of return to education," considered as an investment. Since the theory was developed, rates of return for a number of countries for differing subgroups within country and for differing educational levels have been estimated from empirical data. Or before the theory, no one thought of estimating, nor had a way to estimate, the value of a woman's time spent in childrearing and thus the costs expended in the home on childrearing. Now that can be and has been done (Mincer and Polachek, 1974).

An example can be provided more directly in sociology. Suppose we have two categories of persons in a relatively closed social system, for example, males and females. They express interest in various members of the opposite sex, as is done in sociometric choice, doing so first shortly after formation of the system (as for example in the first month of high school) and then again later. Use of a theory of action, which specifies the functional forms through which interests of two persons in one another are linked, together with these data will allow calculation of the degree to which the system moves toward an equilibrium between the interests of the males and those of the females. It will also allow measurement of the degree to which males are the dominant actors and females merely passive objects of their will versus females the dominant actors and males merely passive objects of their will (Coleman, in press).

It is important to keep in mind these points; to recognize that a theory of action can comprise more than mere definitions, as has so often been the case in sociology. It can generate testable predictions that will allow it to be rejected or revised, and it can provide a framework for the design of empirical research and analysis of data. To make it do so, however, requires attention on the part of the theorist, who may otherwise be inclined only to develop a neat logical system without specific connections to observable data.

Developing Evaluative or Normative Social Theory Alongside Positive Social Theory

Recently, a major work in moral philosophy has been published: *A Theory of Justice,* by John Rawls (1971). Rawls in this theory attempts to specify the conditions under which inequality in a society is compatible with justice in that society, and thus to provide a normative theory for inequality in society. The core of his argument is that if and only if an inequality makes the least advantaged person in society better off is it compatible with a just society. In stating this principle, Rawls attempts to provide a criterion for social policy other than the criterion of efficiency that derives from economic analysis, for the criterion of efficiency pays no attention to inequality. Yet it is important to note that the normative theory of justice which he develops is based upon the same conception of rational action used in economic theory.

Rawls appropriately, given his dependence upon the economist's conception of rational action, has hundreds of references to works in economics, but only three incidental ones to contemporary sociologists (two to Homans and one to Runciman) and two to classical social theorists (one to Durkheim and one to Max Weber). He found no necessity (nor presumably even the possibility) to review theoretical literature in sociology relating justice to inequality. The irony in this lies in the fact that sociologists carry out more empirical research on inequality than do members of any other discipline, and sociologists' values lead them on the whole to be more concerned about inequalities in society than are most other scholars, certainly more on the whole than are economists. Yet in their theoretical work, there is little or no normative content concerning inequality. They may through use of functional analysis describe the functions of inequalities as found in a stratification system, or they may declare on ideological impulse without theoretical rationale that all inequalities are bad, but they have not developed normative theories concerning inequality. They have not attempted to answer the question, "What is the optimum level or structure of equality in society?" based on particular theoretical assumptions and certain conceptions of social welfare.

Some sociologists would argue that this is as it should be; that normative statements have no place in sociology; that social theory should be wholly positive theory without a place for normative theory.

I believe this position is incorrect—that with an appropriate theory of action, normative theory follows quite naturally. Further, I would point to economics, where in welfare economics there is the attempt, though far from successful at present, to provide normative theory.

My argument is simple and straightforward. A theory of action has at its base individual preferences or subjective well-being. It then becomes possible to evaluate social arrangements, social structures, or even whole social systems on the basis of their satisfaction of preferences. The task is not simple, and there will be many undecidable comparisons. Rawls provides one principle for judging inequalities, a principle having to do with the well-being of the least advantaged. There is another principle more widely applicable. This is the principle of Pareto optimality, named for Wilfredo Pareto in his capacity as economist, not as sociologist. The principle of Pareto optimality states that if one social arrangement or one policy is preferred to a second by at least one person in society, and the second is preferred by no one to the first, a move from the second to the first is a desirable move for the society—a move toward "Pareto optimality."[4]

This is not a strong principle, but it provides a foothold for

_____

[4] Rawls' principle can be viewed as an interesting variation on the Pareto principle. Whereas the Pareto principle examines each person's preferences between two social arrangements, Rawls' principle examines only the least

normative evaluations of society by the degree to which they satisfy the preferences of their members. The possibility is intrinsic to any theory which begins with individual preferences. In the theory of action involving corporate actors discussed earlier, there is an additional possibility for normative statements: Because the theory includes both corporate bodies and persons as purposive actors in society, we can evaluate social systems according to the degree to which persons' interests and the interests of corporate actors are satisfied. If, between two social systems, all persons' interests are more fully satisfied in the first than in the second, even though some corporate actors' interests are better satisfied in the second, we can say the first is more desirable to persons than is the second. This may turn out to be a rather strong principle for evaluating social systems or organizations that differ structurally.

As I indicated earlier, I do not expect all sociologists to agree that normative social theory is possible. I can only reiterate, however, that it appears to me as a sociologist eminently possible and to me as a person eminently desirable. It is possible, I believe, using the approach I have sketched above. It is desirable, because it constitutes an intellectually satisfactory way of bringing our values as persons and our theoretical activities as sociologists closer together.

Altogether, what I have attempted to do in this chapter is to sketch the outlines and the potentialities of a purposive theory of action in sociology. This theory of action borrows much from economic theory, and indeed, some economists are already moving forward in the development of such theory. But economists cannot be expected to build sociological theory. If a theory of social organization and social structure is to be built, it is sociologists who must begin to address the task. I believe they can successfully do so through a purposive theory of action like that I've discussed here.

In early days, sociology and economics were very close, hardly constituting separate academic disciplines. The last major sociologist to examine seriously social and economic theories together, thus emphasizing these common roots, was Talcott Parsons in *The Structure of Social Action*. It was also Talcott Parsons who was the last major sociologist to begin to lay out a framework for a theory of action, in that same work. It would indeed be a fortunate realization of that early program of his if at last sociology were to move forward in the development of a theory of action.

---

advantaged. This makes his principle much stronger as a basis for comparing social arrangements, but at the expense of the voluntarism inherent in Pareto's principle.

6

Social Structure and the Symbolic Media of Interchange

Talcott Parsons

IN RESPONSE to Peter Blau's invitation to me to participate in this major symposium on the theory of social structure, it seemed to me that it would be appropriate to take as a subtopic within that field an outline of a development which has been of very great importance to me and a few other associates for a number of years now. This is the analysis of what we have been calling generalized symbolic media of interchange as components of social systems and other systems of action.

The Properties of Media

For me, the primary model was money (Mill, 1909), but another which has been conspicuous in recent years and has recently been much further studied by Victor Lidz (1974 and in press), is language. There has, however, been a tendency to treat each of these phenomena as unique in itself and not related to other phenomena in the action system. This postulate of the uniqueness of money on the one side, language on the other, is one of the traditions which some of us have been challenging. Our attempt has been to treat each of them as members of a much more extensive family of media. So far we have explored intensively the family, which is anchored in the social system, where, in addition to money, we have dealt at some length with political power, influence, and value-commitments as such media (Parsons, 1969: Chapters 14–16). We have also extended the analysis to the level of a general system of action where the anchor concept has been intelligence, unconventionally conceived not as a trait of personality but as a generalized medium. We have tentatively worked out a four-fold scheme for the general action level. We have also made beginnings with respect to the personality of the individual, but this is only a beginning and will need much further work.

The foundations of this development lay in two major steps of my own theoretical development, specifically, of the four-function scheme. Its first version was published in *Working Papers in the Theory of Action* (1953), in which I collaborated with Robert Bales and Edward Shils. The second, somewhat later foundation was the substantially revised version of my views of the relation of economic and sociological theory which was published in the small book *Economy and Society* (1956), in collaboration with Neil Smelser. Subsequent to these works, however, the development of the idea of generalized media took a few years. The first venture beyond money was the analysis of the concept of political power (Parsons, 1963a) and the second the concept of influence (Parsons, 1963b). It was in connection with the latter that I first encountered James Coleman in this context, when at the meeting of the Association for Public Opinion Research at which I presented my paper he was one of the main commentators (Coleman, 1963).

With respect to money, three of its functions which were clearly stated by the classical economists relatively early in the last century stood out as salient. Money, that is to say, was (1) a medium of exchange which had value in exchange, but in the pure type case, no value in use. (2) Money functioned as a measure of value, as they put it, in that it makes goods and services and factors of production, which in other respects such as physical properties are incomparably heterogeneous, comparable in terms of an economic measure, that of utility. And (3) money served as a store of value in that if it were accepted in exchange for possession of concrete commodities or access to concrete services, apart from phenomena of inflation, retaining possession of money does not lead to loss over time; on the contrary, it leads to gain in the form of interest.

The endeavor in extending the theoretical model of money as medium to other media was to match these traits with cases which,

though formally similar, had a different content. The first criterion
or property of a medium was the symbolic character which was
stated by the classical economists for money in the proposition that
it had value in exchange, but not value in use. Such a criterion
applies to linguistic symbols, e.g., the word "dog," though signifying
a species of mammalian quadruped, can neither bark nor bite,
though the concrete dog can do both. Under this general rubric of
symbolic character, we have stressed four further properties of such
a medium as money. First comes *institutionalization,* especially in
relation to property. We thus held such a medium to be characterized by a state of institutionalization, one aspect of which for the
case of money is its backing by governmental authority through the
status that is technically called legal tender. In the case of power
this criterion led us to focus on what Weber (1947a:152–53) calls
legitimate use of power as distinguished from a Hobbesian capacity
to gain one's ends through having "what it takes" (Hobbes, 1651).
Money can, of course, be used illegitimately through such channels
as political bribery, and similarly power and influence can be used
illegitimately; but these are special cases rather than constitutive
criteria of the phenomena.

Second, there must be *specificity* of meaning and efficaciousness
in both evaluation and interchange. As we put it in the case of
money, it is the medium which can operate in economic exchanges,
but many other interchange relations among humans cannot be
mediated by money.

The third property may be called *circulability.* Money, like
possession of commodities, changes hands. Any other medium should
be subject to transfer of control from one acting unit to another in
some kind of interchange transactions.

A fourth property, which proved of particular importance in
bringing political power within this context, was the contention that
a medium *could not have a zero-sum character* attributed to it in all
contexts. Most political scientists dealing with political power had
either explicitly stated or tacitly assumed that it was a zero-sum
phenomenon, that is, that an increase in the amount of power held
by one group in a system *ipso facto* entailed a corresponding de-
crease in the amount held by others (Friedrichs, 1963; Lasswell and
Kaplan, 1950; Mills, 1956). This patently was not the case with
money because of the phenomenon—well known to economists—of
credit creation. And we went to considerable trouble to show that it
need not be assumed to be a characteristic of power systems (Parsons,
1963a).

The Institutional Contexts of Media

It is an exceedingly important point that the theoretical articulation of social system media with the social structure should be conceived at what I should call the institutional, precisely as distinguished from the collective, level. Unfortunately, sociological terminology has almost from the beginning tended to confuse the two. We speak of organizations and other collectivities as institutions (note McGill University or the Université de Montreal), but we also speak of property, contract, and authority as institutions. In the collective sense, of course, the concept of membership in an institution makes sense; in the latter context, membership is simply nonsensical—one simply cannot speak of being a member of the institution of property. Institutions in the latter sense, the one relevant here, are complexes of normative rules and principles which, either through law or other mechanisms of social control, serve to regulate social action and relationships—of course, with varying degrees of success. Each medium then is conceived to be articulated in a functionally defined institutional complex.

For the economic case, it would seem that the central institution is that of property. The underlying concept of property rights centers on rights of possession, which in turn can be broken down into disposal-acquisition, control, and use. In legal history there has been endless discussion and analysis of the nature of property. The objects of rights of possession are broadly classifiable into the three categories of commodities: (1) physical objects; (2) services, that is, human performances evaluated as having utility in the economic sense; and (3) financially significant assets where the economic value is abstracted from any particular characteristics in other respects, such as corporate or government securities, bank accounts, or insurance policies, all of which constitute rights to money payments under specifiable conditions.

The other principal economic institutions are occupation and contract. I conceive occupation essentially to be the institutionalized rubric under which rights to services as an output of the economic process, as distinguished from goods or commodities, are, as rights, transferable from performers to recipients. Seen in this context, a commodity is a physical object of output, possession in which can be transferred without the involvement of human agency beyond the settlement of terms; whereas services require that the performer stand in continuing relation to the recipient throughout the duration of the process.

We think it exceedingly important to make a distinction between services and their occupational organization as categories of economic output on the one hand and labor as a factor of production in the sense of economic theory on the other hand. Labor becomes service only when it has been combined with the other factors of production, and thereby its value has been added to.

Contract we conceive to be the primary integrative reference of the institutionalization of the economic complex. It is the institutional nexus which defines the conditions of legitimate exchange and possession in a sociological as distinguished from either a specifically economic or a legal context. I would consider Durkheim (1964: Book 1, Chapter 7) to be the preeminent sociological theorist of the nature of contract.

Other media, of course, function in complexes of institutional norms which are different from those of primarily economic significance. In the political context the paramount institutional complex is what we call authority. This may be defined as the legitimized capacity to make and to contribute to the implementation of decisions which are binding on a specifiable collective unit or class of them, where the holder of authority has some kind of right of speaking in the name of the collectivity. A typical case is that of a duly legitimized official of a unit of government. The principal modes of institutionalization under authority are the familiar executive, legislative, and judicial categories.

Even within the restricted framework outlined so far, it can, I think, be seen that the conception of generalized media and their articulation with structural components at the institutional level introduces an element of dynamic into the analysis of social relationships and processes. The broadest formula is that, in sufficiently highly differentiated systems of interchange, the principal processes, whether they be those of equilibration or of structural change, are mediated by the interchange of media for intrinsic outputs and factors and conversely of intrinsically significant outputs and factors for media. In this process the media provide or perform regulatory and integrative functions in that the rules governing their use define certain areas of legitimacy and the limits of such areas within which extension of systems of transaction can develop and proliferate. The introduction of a theory of media into the kind of structural perspective I have in mind goes far, it seems to me, to refute the frequent allegations that this type of structural analysis is inherently plagued with a static bias, which makes it impossible to do justice to dynamic problems. Let me, then, again insist that under the category of dynamic I mean to include both equilibrating processes and processes of structural change.

Having reviewed certain features of money as a medium and its institutionalization, let us now say something about the first major extension beyond money which we undertook, namely, fitting a revised concept of political power into the idea of media of interchange. This was substantially more difficult than the analysis of money because in the latter case we were aided by the fact that the economic theorists have handed us a monetary concept which, with certain adaptations, could be treated as ready-made for sociological purposes. As I have noted, this has not been the case for the concept of political power, most conspicuously owing to the explicit or implicit assumption of a zero-sum condition. There are, however, also certain other difficulties. One of the most important of them has been the lack of specificity of the concept of power. This goes back to the great tradition of Hobbes, which most political theorists have followed, as have such sociologists as Max Weber. Hobbes' (1651) famous definition will be remembered: "The power of a man . . . is his present means to obtain some future apparent good." Power, this is to say, is *any* capacity for an acting unit in a social system to "get what it wants," as Weber (1946a:180) said, with or without opposition, in a nexus of social relationships. By this definition, money clearly is a form of power, as also are influence and a number of other entities.

A theoretically satisfactory solution of this problem proved difficult, but I think it was finally arrived at. Two essential features of this solution are its collective reference and its rooting of power in legitimacy. It is first our contention that the concept of political power should be used essentially in a collective context to designate capacities to act effectively with reference to the affairs of a collective system, not necessarily of government. The Hobbesian version of individualism, to talk about relations among individuals independent of their collective affiliations, has been one source of lack of specificity.

The second essential ingredient is the concept of *bindingness* (Parsons, 1963a: 381–82). This bindingness definitely rests on a conception of legitimacy. That is, people who have power have legitimated rights to make and implement collectively binding decisions. The role of coercion can be dealt with from this point of view in that coercive sanctions are important in the follow-up of binding decisions. The most general formula is that in the case of a decision which is politically binding in the present sense, noncompliance on the part of those to whom it applies will in general evoke coercive sanctions. Physical force is not so much the prototype of such sanctions as the limiting case whereby the symbolic elements of social interaction are reduced to a minimum in favor of measures which either compel or strongly motivate to submission independent of questions of legitimacy.

It is assumed throughout this analysis that the category "political" is analytically defined and not the label for a concrete set of phenomena. In this respect it is parallel to that of "economic," which deals, at a technical theoretical level, with an analytically defined set of aspects of concrete behavior, and not, except secondarily, with a concrete type of behavior. Thus, to cite an example, Chester Barnard's famous book *The Functions of the Executive* (1938) deals overwhelmingly with action in business firms. This, however, does not make it a theoretical treatise in economics; I would consider it one of the classics of political theory. The firm as collectivity, that is to say, performs political functions in the analytical sense, even though, since it is a firm, these functions are subordinated to economic organization, purposes, and goals—in Barnard's case, the purveying of telephone service under the imperative of financial solvency and profit.

Before leaving the subject of political power, a few further words should be said about the zero-sum problem in that context. As I mentioned, there was a particularly sharp difference of opinion between economic theorists dealing in the monetary area and political theorists dealing in that of power to the effect that, of course, money was not subject to zero-sum conditions, whereas power almost "of course" was. This dichotomy did not seem to make sense, and I think the claim can be made that the issue has been resolved, at least in principle, in favor of the economic non-zero-sum model, as generalizable to the power case (Parsons, 1963a). The essential question seems to me to be whether there are processes, and what they are, by which power, as defined, can be newly introduced into a power system without a corresponding dimunition of the power in the hands of other elements.

In the case of money the classical instance is the creation of new money in the form of credit by banks. This is to say that bankers lend funds which are the property of their depositors to borrowers on terms that involve an inherent risk to the depositors' financial interest but are nonetheless both legally legitimized and relatively safe under "ordinary" circumstances. There is a fundamental asymmetry in the relations of a bank to its depositors, on the one hand, and its borrowers, on the other. Depositors are entitled to the return of their deposits in full on demand; the bank, however, makes loans which are not repayable before the expiration of the stated terms of the loans. In a certain technical sense, therefore, any normally operating bank is inherently "insolvent," but entering this condition of insolvency is a condition of its being an economically productive institution in a sense other than being only a custodian of deposited funds.

We would contend that the—or one—political analogue of the banking function in the lending context is to be found in that of political leadership. Political leadership will make promises, fulfillment of which is dependent on the implied consent of the constituencies of the political leaders who have given them a grant of power under institutionalized authority, most obviously in cases of election to office. Once in office, however, such power holders may introduce extended plans which can be implemented only through new political power. As in the case of bank loans regarded as funds for investment, it is expected that they will pay off over time, but any immediate stringency which calls for immediate repayment can ordinarily not be met. Essentially, what this type of leadership is doing in our opinion is to use its fiduciary position to extend credit to politically significant enterprises which are not at the time of these decisions in a position to present complete pay-off in political effectiveness. We think that this is a process which is rather strictly analogous to that of credit creation on the part of bank executives.

In the case of credit creation through the legal bindingness of loan contracts, power is mobilized in support of economic investment. Similarly in the case of power creation, the influence of leadership may be mobilized in support of the expansion of power. In both cases this support comes from calling on the medium next higher in the cybernetic order. It need not, however, follow that *only* this next higher medium is involved in such cases. It seems more likely that various cybernetically higher forces, in combinations that vary from case to case, are mobilized in such a way that the total effect is "funneled" through the next higher medium.

The next step beyond establishing, in what seemed to us to be a relatively satisfactory theoretical manner, a status of the concept of political power as a symbolic medium, was to explore the possibilities of finding still other members of the family of media anchored in social system functions. The obvious focus of this next step concerned a medium which was primarily anchored in integrative functions of the system. This led into a complex set of ramifications of considerations of sociological theory. The paths were even less clearly marked than in the case of political power. An index of this indeterminancy was the fact that there was no obvious single term such as power, to say nothing of that of money. We, however, thought that the use of the concept influence in much sociopolitical discussion made it worth exploring as a possible symbolic label appropriate to this particular context (Parsons, 1963a). As the crucial differentiating criterion between power and influence, we took that of collective bindingness in the one case and its absence in the other. The essential problem was what was going on in the context of a unit or class of units trying to get something of collective significance "done," and what, if anything, was the difference between the two cases. In the case of power we used the criterion of the bindingness of their decisions on the collectivity as a whole as the primary criterion. If, however, they were using influence, their decisions and recommendations would not in this sense be binding, that is, noncompliance with them would not result in coercive sanctions. We have treated influence as a medium of *persuasion*.

Persuasion here should be regarded as only a partially adequate term. The place assigned to it in the sanction paradigm (Parsons, 1969: 412, 413, 415 ff.) is to our mind clearly justified by the contrast with the relevance of the two categories of negative sanctions, namely, deterrence and activation of commitments.

The mode of persuasion that is particularly relevant for influence entails invoking collectively relevant *justifications* of the course of action recommended by the agent of influence. This in general invokes considerations of *collective* interest transcending those of the particular units involved and usually includes the call to what is at some level defined as a matter of moral obligation.

There are a number of different contexts of social interaction in which this problem could be worked through. One that has turned out to be particularly important to me and my colleagues is that of the performance of professional services, which for us came to a head in the medical world. When, however, such a term as "doctor's orders" is used, it clearly is not binding on the patient to comply with those orders at the penalty of some kind of coercive negative sanctions. The penalty will probably be health disadvantages to the patient, but he can make his own decision without exposing himself to "punishment" for noncompliance, that is, punishment administered by the physician or by some collective agency of health care which he represents. Thus a heart attack is not imposed by the medical profession on patients who disregard warnings about overexertion.

At the same time, it was difficult to clarify the implications of the fundamental distinction about media that influence should not be interpreted to be a matter of conveying specific information but rather of using a position of prestige which might be based, among other things, on specialized knowledge and experience, to persuade objects of interaction, in the medical case patients, that it was in their interest and that of the relevant collective groups to accept what was often called the "advice" of a physician (Parsons, 1969: 430–38). The costs of such non-acceptance, however, would be assumed directly by the patient and not imposed through the means of coercive sanction. We came to feel that influence in this sense is a deeply important mode of the regulation of communication in systems where neither economic interests nor politically binding considerations are paramount.

A particularly significant empirical finding came in some of the work on academic systems in which I have participated (see Parsons and Platt, 1973). We felt that we were able to make a pretty clear discrimination between positions or the components of positions predominantly involving power in our technical sense and involving influence within the academic context. For example, in an as yet fragmentarily published study of academic roles, we used the question whether the respondent would prefer to function as a department chairman or as an influential senior member of the department (Parsons and Platt, 1968a, 1968b). We found our respondents, on the whole, highly sensitive to this distinction and, especially at the institutions of higher prestige, a substantial majority preferred to be influential members of their departments. We thought we could draw the line between the fact that the chairman, by virtue of his office, exercises certain capacities to make power decisions binding on the department and the fact that an influential member cannot do this except through the collective process of departmental decision-making through voting or "persuading" the chairman and other colleagues. We suggest, therefore, that, independently of specific expertise, which, after all, cannot be generalized in a highly differentiated system, persons occupying positions of prestige in the system could function effectively to persuade their colleagues and the collectivity without having coercive sanctions at their disposal.

Parallel to property and authority we conceive prestige to be the primary institutional category focussing on the integrative system, or societal community. It operates primarily under the legitimation of the value-pattern of solidarity, similar to utility in the economic sphere and collective effectiveness in the political.

Under the authorization of relative prestige, then, we postulate the institutionalization of capacity, through influence, to mobilize commitments of units to what we have called valued association, and to regulate the interplay between political support and identification through membership in (plural) solidary involvements.

Intelligence and Affect

The roster of primary media anchored in the social system is conceived to consist of the three that have been briefly discussed, namely, money, political power, and influence, and a fourth we have called value-commitment, which is anchored in the fiduciary system (Parsons, 1968). It has, however, become increasingly evident that the same general mode of analysis ought to be extended to other systems of action than the social. The example that has been most fully worked out is that of what we have been calling the general system of action. This is interpreted to comprise the social system, the cultural system, the personality or motivational system of the individual, and what currently I have started to call the behavioral system, omitting earlier reference to the organism. (This change has been under the influence of an as yet unpublished paper by Victor and Charles Lidz (in press) which relates the conception to the cognitive psychology of Jean Piaget.)

To my mind, an important line of development of the theory, which has occurred essentially since my original book, *The Structure of Social Action* (1937), has sought to clarify the nature of the general action system. The first major step in this direction was achieved in the volume *Toward A General Theory of Action* (Parsons and Shils, 1951), but it has been quite substantially extended and revised since that time (Parsons and Smelser, 1956). A particularly significant distinction—on a strictly analytical level, of course —is that between the social system and the cultural system, in our technical sense of the terms. The recent program of study on the university in which I have collaborated with Gerald Platt (1973) involves these problems, because one cannot deal theoretically with the university without taking into account systematically both its characteristics as a social system and its involvement with a cultural system.

The focus of the university's involvement in the cultural system lies especially in its concern with knowledge. This concerns the transmission of knowledge, notably from faculty members to students through the processes of teaching and learning, but also the advancement of knowledge which is particularly concentrated in the research function. From the point of view of researchers and their collaborators, research is also a learning process since a research program whose outcome is known in advance would be pointless. The researcher has to *learn* the answers to the problems posed in a research project.

Knowledge we have treated as the primary cultural component of a larger complex involving all of the subsystems of the general system of action. In this connection we have treated rationality as predominantly a phenomenon of the social system, as competence is anchored in the personality system; and we have adapted the concept of intelligence to the role of a generalized symbolic medium as anchored in what Lidz and Lidz (in press; see also Parsons and Platt, 1973: 33–102) call the behavioral system. The most important link between the cultural and the social systems we treat as the commitment of the university as a whole to the value of cognitive rationality. Rationality, as noted in this context, we conceive to be basically a social category, whereas the term "cognitive" formulates the relation of rationality to the prevailing concern with knowledge in the two primary modes of transmission and advancement just mentioned. The individual's capacity to handle cognitive problems we have called competence, which we conceive as established in the personality through processes of socialization which constitute an essential part of the experience of participation in academic communities, especially, though far from exclusively, in the role of student, whether graduate or undergraduate.

Let me now elucidate a bit how we have tried to adapt the concept of intelligence to the rubric of generalized medium of interchange. The simplest definition we would give is that intelligence may be considered to be the capacity of an acting unit, usually an individual, effectively to mobilize the resources requisite to the solution of cognitive problems. This definition is conventional enough. The unconventionality of our treatment lies in our conception of the conditions and processes involved in its operation as such a capacity. First, we conceive of intelligence, though of course greatly affected by genetic components, to be predominantly acquired through socialization and learning processes. However, we conceive it not only possible to acquire intelligence but also to spend it through use in problem-solving activity.

Perhaps it will be helpful to explicate what we mean by the circulation of intelligence. If the human individual be taken as the primary point of reference—as seems appropriate for most purposes—we conceive that the level of intelligence of such an individual as an adult, let us say, is the outcome of combinatorial confluence of factors which have operated on him in the course of his life history. Among these factors clearly must be included the relevant aspect of the genetic constitution with which he was born. But the genetic factor does not stand alone. It is combined with cognitive learning experience and with a primarily noncognitive framework of socialization expectations.

Intelligence as cognitive capacity may then be conceived as capable of growth for long periods. Once available it can then be "used" in a wide variety of ways, notably in the solution of specific cognitive problems. The question then becomes whether and how such an actor of reference can recoup the expenditure of intelligence on problem-solving activity. The answer seems to be that he "learns from experience" and the next time around can—on a certain average—do better than he could have without the experience.

Thus, rather than treating a person's intelligence as something he simply "has," we treat it as a fluid resource which can be acquired and enhanced in the course of action and effectively used by being "spent" (Lidz and Lidz, in press; Parsons and Platt, 1973:33–102).

There is a primary line of distinction between intelligence as medium and intelligence as trait. Our model here for intelligence as medium is that of other media, notably, money. We can speak of an individual as wealthy and in one linguistic usage his level of wealth is a trait of the individual; on the other hand, we know that his wealth was not part of his hereditary constitution, in the organic sense, and that the possession of wealth, that is, of economically valuable assets, places the individual in a network of interchange transactions where he can not only acquire such assets but also use those he has in the further interchange system.

We therefore posit that intelligence, considered as a medium, must meet the criteria of circulation. Its relative specificity seems scarcely to be in question, and the fact of the mode of its involvement in the cognitive complex, including the various levels of education, points to the primacy of the factor of institutionalization, which we also have stressed for media in general. I will not try to enter into an analysis of the non-zero-sum properties of intelligence conceived in this way, but will assert most emphatically that it fits the model of money as essentially a non-zero-sum phenomenon, and not the more traditional one of power as bound by zero-sum limitations. Indeed, I think one of the most serious objections to the conventional psychological conceptions of intelligence lies in the tendency to subject it to the zero-sum condition.

The relation to social structure comes from the fact that we think of the entire cognitive complex as institutionalized at the social system level. Without this state of institutionalization there could be no such thing as the modern university. As institutional type, we think of the university as belonging to a distinctive category of social organization which, unfortunately, has not in our opinion been adequately stressed in most recent sociological writing. The technical term we choose to refer to it by is a "collegial association." This should clearly be distinguished from a market system on the one hand, from a bureaucratic type of organization on another, and within the broader category of associational types, from purely democratic associations. It is distinguished from the last by a fiduciary component, in this case responsibility for the complex of cognitive interests and their involvement in certain respects in the larger action system, and a related pattern of stratification.

As concrete organization, the modern university has, of course, a bureaucratic component of considerable magnitude; and it is involved in the market nexus through its multifarious economic transactions. But the core, in our opinion, consists in the faculty-student collectivity which we define as predominantly a collegial association. Perhaps the most telling structural criterion of this is the fundamental equality of the status of membership at each of a number of graded prestige levels. The highest we conceive to be senior faculty status, which has traditionally come to carry full tenure; we have, however, extended the concept of tenure to include not merely senior faculty but also junior time-limited faculty membership and membership in student capacities, both graduate and undergraduate. At any given level of tenure we conceive members

of the same university to be equals of each other, but the system
as a whole is stratified on the basis of levels of commitment to and
competence in the implementation of the value of cognitive
rationality. Thus it can scarcely be conceived that the average undergraduate freshman is the equal in these two respects to the
career-committed senior professor. We thus treat the tenure levels
as the main framework of its stratification pattern (Parsons and Platt,
1973:103–62).

The academic version of the collegial association belongs to a
larger family of such associational structures in modern society. To
us the most notable others are the kinship association, especially in
the form in which it has developed in the more recent phases of
modern society, the national or societal community, and the predominantly religious association. If space permitted, the similarities
and differences among these four types could be considerably
elaborated.

All of these major types of fiduciary association tend to have a
collegial character and some concept of membership of which in a
certain sense prototypical is that of citizenship, as that idea has been
defined and developed by T. H. Marshall (1965). All are social
structures within which certain functions can be performed with
relative success and which are to important degrees insulated from
the generally recognized "play of interests" which in a society like
ours focuses at the economic and political levels. From the point of
view of the more simplistic conception of the determination of social
phenomena by interests in this sense, they are relatively useless from
a utilitarian point of view. Perhaps a classic statement of this point
of view is the one attributed to Stalin, I believe at the Yalta Conference, in which there was some reference to the Pope. Stalin's query
in evaluating the importance of the Pope was alleged to be, "How
many divisions does he have?" Quite clearly neither the military nor
the economic significance of universities, of families, of religious
bodies, and indeed, of communities in the sense of this discussion
are the primary criteria of their importance. They are not primarily
characterized by sheer control of means of coercive sanctions by
political power or wealth.

This, however, is not a criterion of their lack of importance as
components of the social structure. As I have several times said in
print (Parsons and Platt, 1973: 1–7; Parsons, in press), I concur with
Daniel Bell (1973) in the judgment that the university has become
strategically the most important single category of structural collec-

tivity in modern society, especially in what Bell refers to as its post-industrial phase. This is not because it has become the center either of wealth or of power, though it must participate in both of these interchange systems. It is rather because it is the center of the mobilization of a type of resource which has acquired a quite new level of significance in the more recent phases of social development which Bell characterizes, correctly I think, as focusing on the importance of "theoretical knowledge."

In order not to leave the concept of intelligence as a generalized medium functioning at the level of the general system of action entirely alone, perhaps it would be appropriate at this point to introduce a brief discussion of another medium which I have been calling *affect* (Parsons and Platt, 1973). Whereas I conceive intelligence to be anchored in what the Lidz brothers (in press) call the behavioral system, I conceive of affect as anchored in the *social* subsystem of the general action system. It is, however, conceived to circulate not only within the social system but between it and the other primary functional subsystems of action, namely, the cultural, personality, and behavioral subsystems. Affect thus conceived is the generalized medium most definitely concerned with the mobilization and control of the factors of solidarity in Durkheim's sense.[1]

Solidarity as a primary property of social collectivities grounded in a value category is dependent on factors mobilized from all four of the primary subsystems of action. These factors include the cathectic commitments of individual persons to participation in solidary collectivities; the moral standards which underlie social order as this concept was employed by Durkheim, which is a contribution from cultural sources; and, finally, rational grounds for the allocation of affect as between the societal and nonsocietal commitments and within the latter as between plural memberships in different societal subcollectivities.

Back of this way of looking at affect as a generalized circulating medium lies a Durkheimian conception of the social system as playing a dual role in action. On the one hand, from the point of view

---

[1] Among those concerned with media theory at the general action level there has been a disagreement with respect to the placement of affect. Notably, Mark Gould and Dean Gerstein have opted to use it as the medium anchored in the first instance in the personality system and to introduce an alternative concept for the social system medium. My own preference is definitely to use it in the social system context, but I do not feel dogmatic about it and hope that it will eventually prove possible to reach terminological consensus in this important area.

of the acting individual, it is an environment which constitutes the focus of the individual's primary adaptive orientations. On the other hand, it is not part of the "natural" environment, which is analytically separate from the field of human action, but is itself part of the system of action and a creation of past processes of action. As such, its constitution consists of action components, of which a particularly important aspect is provided by the element of moral order which is a primary regulator of solidary relationships within the same social system (Parsons, 1973).

Affect we conceive to be the medium through which the stabilities essential to the moral order of a social system are adjusted to the ranges of variation that occur in the more concrete social environment in which the individual acts. We have stressed that the level of the general system of action must be intimately articulated with that of the internal imperatives of the social system. We would like, therefore, to draw a parallel between the functions of intelligence and the functions of affect as media which are involved in these processes of articulation. In fact, affective attachment of individuals to the collectivities which are constitutive of the structure of the social system and to the other individuals who share membership status with them are at the center of the mechanisms by which general action factors can achieve the status of institutionalization in defining the structure of social units. We have already illustrated this in the case of the modern university considered as a social system. These considerations can and should be generalized to a wide variety of other types of collective structure which play a part in social systems, particularly of the modern type characterized by an advanced division of labor.[2]

---

[2] We consider the process of institutionalization as previously referred to to be the action-system equivalent of natural selection as that concept has come to be an integral part of biological theory, that is, the theory of the nature and functioning of organic systems. The general action system, and particularly its cultural component, we conceive to be analogous to the genetic constitution of species and the primary source of genetic variation. As such, the cultural system promulgates patterns of what at the value level may be characterized as desirable modes of action. By no means all of these, however, become institutionalized as operative characteristics of going social systems. The intervening process is one of selection according to which some such patterns prove to be favorable in meeting the conditional exigencies of more concrete societal functioning, whereas others prove to be less successful. There develops, that is to say, a differential survival probability among those that are better and less well adapted to coping with such exigencies.

Social Stratification

In this last section, I want to return to the social system level to outline briefly a use of the conception of generalized media of interchange in relation to social structure in dealing with a very central problem which has concerned sociological theorists for a long time, namely, the nature of social stratification.

Perhaps as good a starting point as any is to make clear that the older organization of stratification systems about the institution of aristocracy may for most practical purposes be considered to be dead. It has not, however, been replaced by a pattern of flat equality, though pressures in the direction of equalization have been very powerful in recent times. What we seem to have, however, is a complex balance between trends to equality on the one hand and the kinds of opportunities and freedoms that make for considerable inequality on the other.

It has frequently been noted that modern society has been characterized by a growing trend to pluralization which is very much in accord with Durkheim's (1964: Book 1) conception of the progressive growth of the social as distinguished from the purely economic division of labor. Of course, the scale of organization has continued to grow; and many observers, particularly those with a neo-Marxist bent, seem to feel that the nineteenth-century characterization of the stratification structure of industrial society, especially in the Marxian tradition, is still fully adequate. There is a sense in which this characterization has been held to be reinforced in the later stages of "capitalism" by the concentration of managerial authority and power in large organizations and by the growth of big government which has maintained close liaison with the private-enterprise business world.

We would like, however, to direct attention to a somewhat different aspect of development. Bell has strongly emphasized the growing importance of the university in modern society, and this growing importance cannot be explained mainly by the transfer of very large shares of the control of economic resources and of political power to it. As Bell (1973) puts it, it rests mainly on the university's role in the mobilization of a newly important resource, namely, theoretical knowledge. Another straw in the interpretive wind has been the contention of Jencks and Riesman (1968) that the line between the college-educated sector of the population and those who lack this level of education has come to be the most important single line in the stratification system. We may perhaps put these two sets of considerations together in their relation to another phenomenon, which, for example, has recently been emphasized by Eliot Freidson (1973a, 1973b), and which he refers to as the trend to professionalization of modern society. Many social scientists have been aware of the major shifts that have taken place in the nature of the labor force, notably through the relative decline of agriculture, the decline of the role of unskilled labor, and the concurrent rise of what are ordinarily designated as service occupations. Freidson in particular stresses the rise of the technical and professional occupations in relative size and importance and their requirements of specialized training in institutions of higher education, that is, institutions that are by and large outside the spheres of control of the employing organizations and their managerial components. Freidson, quite correctly I think, strongly emphasizes the penetration of large organizations both in government and business as well as in the private nonprofit sector by professional components and in particular the impact of this on the position of management in the traditional sense. One way of putting it is to suggest a substantial decline in the relative importance of bureaucratic authority of the traditional sort in modern organizations and a far greater autonomy in the hands of the trained and technical occupational groups. Such groups, however, have been organized more according to associational than to bureaucratic patterns.

It was Durkheim (1964: Book 1) above all who, in sharp disagreement with Spencer (1925–29), held that the concomitant development of an economy made up of independent units, in something like a so-called free enterprise system, and of the state and government, could be regarded as a normal development. It seems to me that in some of the developments we have just mentioned, still a third more or less independent set of structural components has risen to a new order of prominence, namely, those having to do with a certain cultural primacy. The case of the system of higher education, which should be understood to include the research function, is probably only the most conspicuous single case. Again, as Freidson (1973a; 1973b) points out, professionalism permeates the structures of large business enterprise and government, but its significance is by no means confined to this penetration. Besides institutions of higher education, we can think of the immense proliferation of health care organization and the other so-called helping professions, and as another particularly important case that of the mass media, in which we would include the press, television and radio, book publishing, and a variety of other modes of organizing broadcast communication.

I would like to suggest that a structural pattern which Gerald Platt and I (1973) utilized in our analysis of the university can be generalized to help understand the nature of the changes that have been occurring in the general stratification system. For the case of the university we were struck by the persistence under the same organizational tent, as it were, of a number of apparently heterogeneous elements. Thus, for example, universities have come to include the whole range of intellectual disciplines, the teaching function and the research function, both graduate and undergraduate versions of the teaching function, and professional schools, along with the core arts and sciences faculties. We called this combination the "bundle" (Parsons, 1974; Parsons and Platt, 1973: 346–88).

We think that the wide scope of this conspicuous bundle, which stands in contrast to the much touted tendencies to specialized separatism, has to do with an analogy to Adam Smith's (1904) conception of the relation of the division of labor and the extent of the market which clearly includes level of productivity as well as quantitative extension. We think, however, that the effectiveness of the combination of academic functions through their being in this sense "bundled" together is highly dependent on new levels of the development of generalized media. In the case of the university we have stressed two levels, intelligence as we have outlined its nature operating at the general action level, and influence operating internally to the social system aspect of the organization of higher education and mediating its relations to other sectors. We suggest that such coherence as exists in the upper sectors of the modern system of stratification might also be considered to be integrated especially through bundle mechanisms.

In order to make clear what we mean by such a statement, it would seem best to outline very briefly what components go into such a bundle and how they are related. The two most obvious dimensions are a "horizontal" one (for purpose of diagramming) and a "vertical" one. The former may for our purposes be designated as the "range" of extension of a bundle, whereas the latter may be designated to refer to the "levels" at which various components of the bundled complex are held to stand. In the academic case referred to previously the range is constituted by the spectrum of intellectual disciplines, which ranges from mathematics and physics through the biological and the social sciences into the humanities, perhaps ending with the critical analysis of the arts.

What, in *The American University*, Platt and I have called the "cognitive complex" involves in the first instance a cultural level which comes to focus about valid and significant knowledge, considered as a primary output of cognitive processes (notably research) but, at the same time, as a central condition for the further development of cognitive processes. At another level the cognitive human interest comes to be embodied in a variety of social organizations— in higher education, colleges and universities, faculties and departments, administrations, research organizations, and schools for professional training. We hold quite specifically that it is not fruitful to confuse the cultural and the social organization levels. Finally, at both levels, the cognitive endeavor is one actively participated in by various categories of human individuals, as personalities and as behavioral systems. At the sociological level they are in such roles as faculty members, graduate and undergraduate students, research workers, and administrators.

Two further ranges, related to but not identical with the primary academic one of the intellectual disciplines stand respectively above and below the latter in level terms. The first of these may be called the range of "research problems," which often stretch across parts of several disciplines.

The second range arises primarily for the applied professions. Platt and I (1973:225–66) have called it the "clinical focus." The prototypical example is the frequently referred to "science of medicine," which is not a discipline in the Arts and Sciences sense at all but a way of mobilizing knowledge in terms of its practical bearing on the tasks of the health professions in dealing with problems of health and illness.

For the case of a stratification bundle, clearly the principal range axis concerns the variety of what in a broad sense are "social" types which have some standing in the higher prestige levels. Though kinship heredity has not altogether disappeared—*vide* the Kennedys and the Rockefellers—by and large eligibility is gained mainly by achievement, not kinship ascription. There has been, in the middle third of the present century, an enormous access of new groups, such as Jews and more recently Blacks. We may conceive a continual process of competition for prestige status, among those already "there" and between them and aspirants for inclusion.

The weakening of the hereditary principle is conspicuous, but even more so perhaps is the wide variety of types which must now be included. It used to be said that the businessmen were the "natural leaders of the community." That a good many prominent businessmen are among such leaders today few would doubt, but equally few would doubt that a considerably broader group, or rather set of groups, would now need to be taken into account. I would not conceive such a set of "upper" groups to constitute a neatly structured symmetrical pyramid but rather a variegated complex of types of "influentials" who would be regarded, with an approximation of consensus, as having relatively high prestige.

In a rough way these groups can, I think, be arranged along a spectrum which is not as such a rank order of prestige. At one end of the spectrum I should place groups whose claims to prestige could be grounded in cultural—shading into moral—bases of status. This "wing" of the spectrum would include, first, the academics, the more professional types rather than top administrators such as presidents; second, that rather vaguely defined category called "intellectuals" who are found both inside and outside academia; third, the clergy of various denominations; and fourth, the artists, including the literary contingent. The final, fifth, principal subgroup I would assign to this wing are the "professionals" in the traditional sense, distinguished from the academics. This group comprises those engaged in "practical" pursuits but with major academic training, such as lawyers, physicians, increasingly some "para-medical" health personnel, engineers, and representatives of some of the newer professional groups (Parsons and Platt, 1973).

In what may be called the "middle" sector of the spectrum I would include some of the higher reaches of the political and the business worlds. There is, however, an important if not fully clear line which cuts across these categories, namely, that between proprietors or politicians "in their own right" and "administrators" who, at least nominally, are "employed" by the former. It is here that most of what has sometimes been called the "power elite" is to be found, but it is itself a mixed bag and internally very heterogeneous. Also, though less prominent, I think the leadership of labor unions should be included here.

Finally, the third sector will include the leadership of movements which have gained some importance and usually some "political clout" but which are not yet fully integrated in the larger stratification system. Most conspicuous among these are leaders of various "rights" movements, of which two of the more massive recently have been "civil rights" and women's rights. Certainly such leaders are very much in the public eye, and some of them have become national heroes.[3]

It should be made clear that most of the occupational categories mentioned above comprise a range of prestige status such that only their higher-prestige subgroups can qualify for inclusion in an "upper" stratum of the society. Thus members of the faculties of small community colleges have clearly a different status from those of leading universities, officers of small local businesses from those of major national and international firms, politicians in minor local offices from national political figures, and so on. The cutting points, however, are by no means rigidly defined.

Another relevant basis of differentiation is that defined by Merton (1957), Gouldner (1957), and others as that between "locals" and "cosmopolitans," which has to do with the range of salience and influence.

The second major dimension of variation is that which we have called *level*, using that term to refer to the cybernetic hierarchy of components of systems of human action. We have referred above to the increasing prominence, within the present century, of groups the prestige of which is grounded in primarily *cultural* competence and achievements, such as the rise in relative standing of scientists and other masters of "theoretical knowledge" as compared to the prominence of "practical" men of business at the turn of the century. Another example is the rise in the relative prominence of the arts and the groups involved with them. The relations between academic intellectuals and the arts are highly complex. I think Bell (1973, esp. last chapter) goes too far in speaking of a nearly

---

[3] There is something to be said for the view that some students should be included in this higher-prestige range, not so much because of high academic achievement, to say nothing of kinship ascription or eliteness of institution attended, but by virtue of leadership in one or a set of "movements." Certainly in the disturbances which culminated in the late 1960s a good many student leaders gained national prominence. The great structural difficulty of including such a group in a national "elite" lies in the age-boundness of student status and hence the short period in which any given individual remains a student. High academic achievers will have a chance to become prominent academics or professionals, especially, but the future of student leaders, after their student days are over, is more problematic.

total dissociation between the "cultural," as he calls it, and the institutionalized aspects of culture in science and technology.

A further prominent shift is in the rise of a very diverse category of predominantly secular "intellectuals," writers and communicators on many different levels on many subjects, among which subjects problems of public policy figure prominently. There is a partial but by no means simple sense in which these have displaced the more traditional clergy as the intellectual-moral leading element.

By contrast to the just-listed groups, with the practicing professions standing somewhat in the middle, we may place the groups with leading positions in practical affairs—in the business, labor, and political worlds, including those in administrative rather than proprietary or elective positions who work at rather high levels of responsibility in organizations in these sectors.

Finally, as noted, the more prestigeful elements identified with "movements" should be placed in a somewhat different category because of their only partly institutionalized status. For individuals and subgroups of course this status can shift. Thus Thurgood Marshall as lawyer made his primary reputation as attorney for the NAACP in the legal phase of the black movement's battle for improved civil rights. On his elevation to the Supreme Court, however, Mr. Marshall came to occupy one of the most fully institutionalized statuses in the higher echelons of the society.

The two dimensions which we have called range and level have never stood alone in bundle phenomena. Thus in the academic case we have stressed the importance of what we have called the socialization function, analysis of which Platt and I (1973: 163–224) concentrated on in our chapter on the undergraduate aspect of the university system. There is a sense in which socialization is a set of processes which helps to integrate a complex and tension-prone institutional system along the age gradient of the life course. In this case the primary reference points are the generation groups incorporated in the statuses of student and faculty member respectively. We have stressed that, though necessarily faculties exercise more "influence" on their students than vice versa, the process is clearly not merely a one-way affair but a two-way one with built-in reciprocities. The primary interacting groups, however, are not simple "equals" of each other because of the double difference of stage in the life course and levels of competence and commitment in the academic culture.

Perhaps the most closely analogous function of the stratification bundle concerns the part it plays in the integration of the society across lines of actual and potential conflict. That such lines should be both "vertical" and "horizontal," in our metaphorical language, is, of course, commonplace. They of course include but are not confined to "class" conflicts, latent and overt, which I conceive as vertical in the sense that they concern different statuses within given sectors of what we have called the relevant ranges. For present purposes, however, I should place greater stress on the other axis of conflict, namely, that of qualitative differentiation, which has arisen in the course of the division of labor as well as certain "historical" factors such as religious and ethnic diversity grounded (for the United States) in the history of immigration. This is to an important degree the context which has often been referred to as the "pluralism" of modern societies, especially perhaps the American. Much more circumstantial investigation of the range dimension and that of levels, as well as that of lines of conflict, is greatly needed but cannot be undertaken within the confines of this rather brief paper.

In conclusion only two more topics can be all too briefly dealt with. The first concerns the probability that, in spite of the growing pluralism to which reference has just been made, one or a few particular groups may acquire a special salience in the stratification and integrative functions of such a society. I should like to suggest that this is the case in the recent and present junctures, for certain leading elements of what may be called the legal complex in American society. In the recent dramatic processes leading to the forcing of a President from office for the first time in American history, a special role has been taken by lawyers, in and out of public office. In the latter context the courts of law have, of course, played a special role, both the Federal district courts as the trial courts for grand jury investigations and actual trials of indicted persons, and the Supreme Court, especially in its unanimous decision on Presidential prerogative.

Legislative bodies have always had a major participation of lawyers, and in both Houses of Congress recently they have played an especially prominent part, notably the House Judiciary Committee, the whole membership of which consists of lawyers. Then, in spite of their vicissitudes, the role of two special prosecutors and their staffs should not be forgotten.

Of course these "in office" actions of lawyers could not have taken place without the existence and position in the society of a much larger pool of lawyers who have shown a special concern for the "public interest," as it has often been called. There is a sense in which the current era has been one of resurgence of the significance of "the law," including not only the body of norms but also the groups with special responsibilities for their implementation. It seems to us that this special role of the legal complex operates in part because it can mediate between the normative and cultural orders which have become so important to a complex society and the vast complex of especially economic and political interests which are the primary focus of centrifugal pressures. This is a topic meriting much more sociological attention than it has received.[4]

The final topic for brief mention is the role in this integrative process of the media themselves. Because of the complexity of the problems only a few bare indications can be given here. First, it seems to me that the central role must be given to *influence* as a medium and that this connects especially with the role of the legal complex, but also the intellectuals and the media people, as I have called them. Lawyers, through legislative enactments and court decisions, articulate with the power system and its coercive sanctions, but its main members are not primarily "men of power" but rather of influence, as trustees of an especially important aspect of the normative order of the society. In such capacities their role is much more to define, interpret, and advise than it is to issue "orders." They are, above all, regulators of the power system and, in somewhat different ways, of the economic system.

In the other cybernetic direction, "upward," the influence complex is articulated with that of values, which overlaps especially into the constitutional aspects of the legal system itself. Here one of the most important functions of the members of the legal complex is to activate the consideration of the relevance of general moral and institutional principles which have been central to our societal history and to help bring them to bear on the specific problems of the day. Here the academic branch of the legal profession is of paramount importance and, through it especially, the articulation in the larger university system and the culture of intellectuals.

[4] This is partially remedied by the dissertation of John L. Akula (1973). "Law and the Development of Citizenship," unpublished dissertation, Department of Sociology, Harvard University, 1973.

Finally, one generalized medium operating at the level of the general system of action, affect, belongs in this context. If we are right about its special relation to solidarity, we may suggest that it functions above all to help to mobilize the factors in generation and renewal of the larger solidarities which have been imperiled by recent developments. This, however, opens up complications which far transcend the scope of this paper; the problem could only be mentioned.

I hope it has been possible to present a brief outline, in this concluding section, of how, through a recently emerging "stratification bundle," a set of integrative mechanisms has begun to take hold in our society, which can easily be overlooked because of our preoccupation with the more specific phenomena of economic and political interests. If this is indeed developing, its understanding will centrally involve what we have been calling the generalized media of interchange in relation to the social structure.

7

Structure and Action in the Theories of Coleman and Parsons

Walter L. Wallace

My DISCUSSION WILL BE LIMITED to explicating the two papers that immediately precede this one. For reasons of space, however, I will not discuss many of their specific components—including the conceptualizations of "power," "influence," "value-commitment," "intelligence," and "affect" that Parsons proposes, and the conceptualizations of "actor," "event," "outcome," and "control" that Coleman proposes. So my remarks will only compare Parsons' and Coleman's theories with respect to (1) purposive orientation; (2) levels, media, and interests; and (3) the evaluation of social systems.

Purposive Orientation

As background for what I shall say about Parsons' and Coleman's approaches to purposive orientation, let me indicate what I take to be the crucial difference between social structuralist theory and social actionist theory: social structuralist theory treats purposiveness and other subjective orientational factors as at least secondary and at most irrelevant in explaining social phenomena, while these fac-

☐ I wish to express appreciation to Peter M. Blau for his helpful queries during preparation of my comments for publication.

tors are primary in social actionist theory. It seems to me that this is the real significance of Peter Blau's point that the social structural view emphasizes "differentiation" and "heterogeneity" and that "value orientations are taken into account only indirectly." I believe the differentiation and heterogeneity to which Blau gives primacy refer to variability in the things people do, and objectively can do, to each other, rather than variability in the things they think or feel about each other.

For Parsons, on the other hand, despite the many changes that his published thought has undergone, one feature has persisted: it is the indispensability of subjective orientation to his definition of social phenomena. Thus, as early as *The Structure of Social Action* (1937:732–33) he declared that essential to the action frame of reference is "a normative orientation of action, a teleological character . . . [and] the normative elements can be conceived of as 'existing' only in the mind of the actor." In a publication dated 33 years later, he defined "acts" as "behavior to which their authors and those who significantly interact with them attribute, in Weber's phrase, a 'subjective,' which is to say cultural or symbolic meaning" (1970b:29). Moreover, Parsons has consistently held that the purposive orientations that define action are themselves explained by purposive orientations, insofar as the latter guide socialization and the social control of role expectations. This double theoretic role is reflected in the paper before us in its treatment of subjectively understood symbols (more precisely, "symbolic media of interchange") as partly definitive of social systems in general and as partly explanatory of social stratification systems in particular.

Coleman also places purposive orientation in a central position through the title of his paper and through his attention to "interests." But in my judgment, despite this initial appearance of theoretic congeniality, several contrasts between Parsons' and Coleman's usages of purposive orientation persist and divide them. Coleman clearly would like to use interest to explain other things— things such as how he "changed the structure of the system" described in his opening illustration (and he does not mean the system of subjective interest and purposes, but the system of objective control relations between himself and his opponent). It is equally clear, however, that Coleman does not raise the explanation of interests as being of any theoretic concern and does not attribute any essential variability to interests (with one important exception that

I shall come to in a moment). Although his views may have changed since then, three years ago one of Coleman's publications contained a striking expression regarding his view of the nature of human interests. There he said "I will start with an image of man as wholly free: unsocialized, entirely self-interested, not constrained by the norms of a system, but only rationally calculating to further his own self-interest" (1971:273). (One has to notice and then overlook, in the present context, the persistent masculinity of his, and all of our, nouns and third-person pronouns.) From this statement, it is clear that Coleman wished at that time to treat interests as fixed within individuals, universal across individuals, and prior to the social experience of individuals.

Parsons, however, does not seem ever to have treated interests, purposes, orientations, and the like in this way, as it is largely variation in the content and stability of actors' purposive orientations that he has wanted to explain and to which he has also turned for explanation. Moreover, Coleman allows us to believe that he believes the origin of human interests lies in the genetic inheritance of the species, or at least somewhere outside the social system. Parsons, admittedly with some qualification regarding the extrasocial constraints imposed by "situation" and "need dispositions," has explained interests through socialization, the normative specification of role relations, social deviance and social control—all of which locate the origin of actors' orientations neither in their selves nor in their ancestors but in their social relations.

Now, one might think Coleman adopted a view of interests as fixed, universal, and prior to social experience merely as an heuristic device, as a matter of convenient theoretic presumption, without any necessary factual truth attached to it. But it is one thing to say axiomatically that "I will start with an image of human beings as unsocialized, entirely self-interested," and so on, and quite another to evaluate such persons as "wholly free." The latter statement indicates that the image in question is not to be viewed merely as an heuristic device but as a real (though perhaps obscured) fact of nature in whose existence Coleman is philosophically, if not empirically, convinced. Therefore, Coleman may be interpreted as not merely supposing but positively claiming that human beings can only be free when they are unsocialized and outside any social system and as positing that when people are free, they are entirely self-interested and seek rationally to maximize this interest. The special significance of this philosophical, rather than merely heuristic, point of departure becomes clear, I think, in Coleman's evaluative theory of social systems, which I will examine in the last section of this discussion.

Nevertheless, it should be borne in mind that the quotation I read to you is now some three years old, and Coleman tells us that the paper we have just heard marks a turning point in his thinking about purposiveness. All the returns on this change may not be in yet. Indeed, the publication three years ago described human interest as exclusively selfish; in the paper we have just heard, there is a major effort to introduce unselfish, altruistic interest, which undoubtedly marks an important, and perhaps intermediate, step in Coleman's developing thought.

The present paper does not, therefore, give explicit evidence on whether Coleman continues to view interests as fixed, universal, and prior to social experience. But it does provide some implicit evidence to this effect insofar as it shows that Coleman still thinks of two other subjective orientational features of social life in this way. Thus in the opening illustration of the present paper, he says that "there was a single event in which [my opponent] and I both had an interest: I had an interest in one outcome of the event, and my opponent had an interest in another outcome." Coleman thus overlooks the possibility that his opponent and he defined the situation in different ways, such that there was involved not "a single event" but two events (that is, two actor-defined events) and also two sets of outcomes. In obvious contrast, Parsons' theory of action has always stressed variability in the subjective definition of the situation and has always stressed the systematic sociocultural determination of that definition.

It is true that Coleman acknowledges, in a general way, his own inattention to such sociocultural determination and thus may seem to move toward closing this gap between Parsons and himself. But consider his argument in this respect: Coleman says that in his opening illustration "there was no 'system of action.' Unlike an ongoing institution, group, or organization, there was a single event that temporarily brought two actors together." There are two fundamental contrasts here with Parsons. First, Coleman's emphasis is on objective duration as the underlying difference between "*ad hoc*" systems and "stable" systems, while Parsons' emphasis would be on subjective moral factors as the underlying difference. Thus, where

Coleman stressed the temporariness of the *ad hoc* interaction in his illustration, Parsons would have stressed its lack of purposive orientation, in the sense that neither actor had clear expectations regarding the appropriateness of alternatives open to it and open to its opponent. Second, it seems significant that Coleman begins with an *"ad hoc,"* "temporary" system and then adds something about other systems. This seems to reflect the persistence of his view that "it is not norms, and individuals socialized to them, which are the starting points of a fruitful theory of social systems" (1971:286). Obviously, Parsons has long adhered precisely to this starting point that Coleman so explicitly rejected three years ago and may still reject.

Now why should all these contrasts in the treatment of purposive orientation exist between Coleman and Parsons, both of whom pledge allegiance to a purposive theory of action in sociology? It seems to me that the answer can be found in Coleman's statement that "It is the essence of this approach that the complexity lies not in the model of man that it uses, but *in the structural configurations within which this simple man acts"* (emphasis added). Thus, it seems that despite Coleman's deliberate emphasis here on purposive orientation and despite his expressed desire to identify with social action theory, what he really wants to do is simplify, fix, and thus dispense with the complexities and instabilities of purposive orientations in favor of the complexities and instabilities of "structural configurations." He would like to rid his theory of interests rather than infuse his theory with them. But these days (and largely as a result of Parsons' entire life's work so far) it is hardly feasible completely to ignore purposive orientations. Therefore, instead of ignoring them, a moderate social structuralist (like Blau), might argue that subjective orientations are only second-order explanatory factors, since they are themselves generated by the objective things people do and can do to each other. But a more extreme social structuralist than Blau might argue that purposive orientations are fixed, universal, and prior; on this ground dismiss them as invariant; and then turn full attention to "structural configurations"—that is, again, to the objective things people do and can do to each other. This latter, in my judgment, is the route Coleman has chosen. Thus Coleman seems to take up interests only in order to put them down and then get on with what I think he really wants to do, namely, advance social structuralist theory, and not social actionist theory.

Levels, Media, and Interests

LEVELS

Parsons and Coleman both use the term "levels" in their paper, and obviously they converge in meaning that something is hierarchically ordered, but perhaps not so obviously they diverge insofar as the "something" is one thing in Parsons' case and quite another in Coleman's. Parsons speaks of a "cybernetic control hierarchy" and by this he means that the "something" is control or causal dominance. Thus the cultural subsystem is said to be on a "higher" level than the social subsystem of the general action system because the cultural subsystem controls the social subsystem. Note that it is not the case (despite an ambiguous recent illustration by Parsons, 1970b: 44) that the higher levels include, in the spatiotemporal sense, the lower levels. Although it is higher, the cultural subsystem does not include the social subsystem; instead, Parsons instructs us to view these two subsystems as referring to two "analytical" properties or "theoretical abstractions" of the same concrete action system (1959 and 1970b:44).

Coleman, however, speaks of "levels of organization," rather than levels of control; it seems clear that what he has in mind is a hierarchy of concrete entities rather than abstract properties, because "the shift [from lower to higher levels] manifests itself in the movement from persons as units of analysis to groups or organizations that have persons as members, to organizations or social systems that have groups or organizations themselves as members." Thus Coleman proposes a hierarchy in which the constituents of any given entity are "lower" because they are spatiotemporally smaller entities.

The juncture between the first and second ideas discussed here, namely, purposive orientation and levels, generates important, but quite different, theoretic consequences in Parsons' and Coleman's thought. Parsons' focus on orientation leads him to place its producers—the cultural subsystem and the pattern-maintenance or fiduciary sub-subsystem—at the top of the control hierarchy of the general action system and at the top of the control hierarchy of the social subsystem, respectively. (In my judgment, it is just at this point where the substantive generality of the concept "purposive orientation," employed as definitional of social phenomena, seems identical with the substantive generality of the same concept employed as explanatory of social phenomena—that is, where the thing-to-be-explained seems identical with the thing-that-explains-it —that Parsons' theoretic scheme reveals a short-run circularity.)

In Coleman's argument, the conjunction of the concept "levels" with his idea that "interests" are fixed in individuals is reflected in his location of causal dominance at the bottom, rather than the top, of the entity hierarchy, such that "as we shift between levels, the values of events at the lower level give the interest of the corporate actor in actions at the next level." Thus Coleman appears to deny or ignore the reverse possibility that the values of events at the higher level may "give" the interest of the individual actor; he also appears to overlook the possibility that genuinely new interests may emerge from a new arrangement (especially a hierarchical arrangement) of individual actors.

Coleman's rejection of corporate determination of individual interest and his apparent choice of interest-aggregation over interest-emergence between the individual and the corporate levels seem clearly to constitute psychological reductionism. Indeed, such reductionism is logically derivable from Coleman's apparent conviction, mentioned earlier, that human interest is fixed in every individual, universal across individuals, and prior to the social experience of individuals. Under these conditions, no matter how such individuals are arranged, the interests of the arrangements would remain more or less simple additive aggregations of the interests of the individuals they contain, and these interests would remain impervious to all outside (including corporate) influence.

Parsons, however, partly because he originates control in an analytical property rather than in a concrete entity of the action system, can allow both for system-determination of individual orientation (1967:193–97) and for the nonaggregative emergence of new orientations in new arrangements of individuals. His recent attention to "symbolic media of interchange" expresses this latter concern insofar as new variants in the media are said to develop out of new arrangements (Parsons' case in point here is the university) and to constitute manifestations of new symbolic orientations.

MEDIA

In addition to such theoretic problems regarding the dimension along which hierarchic ordering takes place in social phenomena, there are also problems of integration within and between levels. How are the component parts of a given level held together? How are different levels held together? How is disintegration, either within or between levels, to be explained? Parsons' discussion of "generalized symbolic media of interchange" seems directly addressed to these theoretic questions.

I shall not attempt to examine here the specific media that Parsons proposes, nor shall I address the distinct theoretical problems implied by the concept of mediation between levels that are analytically defined in terms of theoretical abstractions versus mediation between levels that are concretely defined in terms of entities. But consider the more general idea of a "medium." What exactly is meant by this term? I was not able to find an explicit definition of "medium" (or of "generalized symbolic medium"), either in those of Parsons' writings with which I am familiar or in a quick scanning of some of the communications literature. So I made up my own definitions: A "medium" is any phenomenon that translates some other phenomenon from one context to another. A "symbolic" medium refers to a process wherein the phenomenon whose meaning is to be translated is first represented by something else (which thus becomes a "symbol") in the sending context and then the symbol is transported or transmitted to the receiving context, where it is attached to some new phenomenon whose meaning is thereby made equivalent to that of the first phenomenon. And a "generalized" medium is one that translates a relatively wide variety of phenomena between a relatively wide variety of contexts. Obviously, I intend "translation" to include physical transportation and transmission of entities, as well as psychical translation of meaning. I intend also that the mediated contexts may differ in any conceivable way— for example, either hierarchically or not and either concretely or analytically. Finally, I intend (in explicit difference with Parsons but in accord with classical physics) that the medium itself need not "circulate" as it translates.

There are several implications of this definition, but perhaps the most important one is that any phenomenon may be considered to be a medium depending on how the observer frames the contexts and the phenomena to be translated between them. Thus, in one frame of analysis, money mediates between different commodities and services, but in another frame, commodities and services mediate between different monies, that is, between different beliefs in the stable translatability or "negotiability" of money (see Parsons,

1967:275). The theoretic status of media therefore appears as a function of analytic choice rather than existential fact, in the identical way that the same variable may be independent, dependent, or intervening in different frames of analysis.

Closely related to this implication is a second: that a medium between two contexts may operate either as a one-way translator or as a two-way translator. Applying Parsons' terminology, a given medium may mediate change in either direction or interchange in both directions.

Third, a medium may be more or less generalized. Thus, Parsons' references to "barter" and to "ascriptive role expectations" as being incapable of mediating double interchanges between subsystems (1967:348) may actually refer to their usually greater specificity than money with regard to the phenomena that each may translate and the contexts that each may translate between.

A fourth implication of my definition of "medium" is the possibility that media may be thought of as varying in their degree of reliance on symbol, rather than as being exclusively symbolic. This consideration, together with the others, suggests that (to use, roughly, Parsons' ideas) whereas money may be treated as a symbolic, two-way, and generalized medium between the adaptive subsystem and the pattern-maintenance or fiduciary subsystem (1967:350), commodities may be treated as a nonsymbolic, one-way, more specific medium from the former to the latter and labor services may be treated as a nonsymbolic, one-way, more specific medium from the latter to the former.

In any case, human (as well as nonhuman) social systems seem to rely on media that are specific as well as generalized, nonsymbolic as well as symbolic, one-way as well as two-way. Thus, Parsons' examination of the "generalized, symbolic media of interchange" bears upon a part of the broader and more complex question of how the several levels of action are integrated (or disintegrated), both within themselves and each with the other.

INTERESTS

Parsons' discussion of "media" bears on the maintenance of different levels, but Coleman's discussion of "interests" bears most directly on the equally important question of their origin (of course, given each author's definition of levels). The latter bearing is neither simple nor direct, however, and warrants examination in light of my claim that Coleman really wants to set purposive orientations aside in favor of "structural configurations."

It is true that Coleman begins here in an apparently social actionist fashion by posing "two kinds of orientation of one actor toward another." But then, in characteristic social structuralist fashion, he immediately explains both types of interests by objective structure, albeit at an intrapersonal organizational level: "Separation of selves [within each individual person] allows the acting self to have psychic investment not only in its own object self, but in the object selves of other persons." Furthermore, "persons may make psychic investments in [a social organization], just as they make psychic investments in another person."

Thus, Coleman would explain the origin (and perhaps also the maintenance) of social relations at the corporate level by positing an intrapersonal level that is structural rather than orientational, insofar as it consists of two behaving "selves"—one making investment and the other receiving investment. It is important to note that Coleman does not raise the question of how "investing" and "receiving" orientations might themselves originate and be maintained within the acting and object selves; for him the potentially infinite regress ends structurally, rather than orientationally.

Nevertheless, Coleman's theory does, in some sense, begin with interests, and that beginning is especially noteworthy in light of his present paper's addition of altruistic interest to egoistic interest. One can well imagine Coleman, or indeed almost any sociologist or social psychologist, becoming dissatisfied with the unrelieved self-seeking rationality of "economic man," largely because it does not encompass loyalty. This nearly ubiquitous orientational phenomenon, in its pure form appearing utterly selfless and irrational, seems often to overwhelm or displace the demands of rationally calculated egoism and can therefore confound theories based on it alone. For this reason, Coleman's addition of altruistic interest to egoistic interest as a beginning premise of his theory is understandable.

But it should not go unnoticed that in Coleman's theory altruism is quickly reduced to egoism, albeit at a different level. Thus, altruism performed by the whole person becomes egoism performed by that person's "acting self" which makes "psychic investment" in others; and lest we miss the self-seeking that is implied here, Coleman explicitly points it out: "such investments [are] based on expectations of psychic returns." Therefore, what began as altruism at one organizational level ends as egoism at another. Whatever one may think of the content of Coleman's argument, its form provides a clear example of the explanation of new purposive orientations by hierarchical emergence—a nonreductionist possibility apparently overlooked elsewhere in his theory.

Now let us set aside the structural supports and consequences of interests in Coleman's theory, and compare "interests" with "pattern variables," simply as two different classifications of purposive orientations. Perhaps the comparison will tell us something about Parsons' and Coleman's images of human beings as purposive, and social, actors. First, it should be noted that Coleman's egoistic-altruistic interest classification corresponds, roughly, only to the self-collectivity pattern variable (plus some apparent overlap with affectivity-neutrality); the cognitive, and part of the cathectic, dimensions represented by the other pattern variables do not seem to be present. But if we focus, therefore, on Parsons' and Coleman's treatments of the self-collectivity pattern variable and the egoistic-altruistic interest types, a parallel initially emerges between them, but a deeper opposition immediately divides them.

Parsons, at one point in his discussion of self-collectivity, includes self within collectivity by referring to the alternatives in question as specifying "the permissibility of [an actor's] pursuing any interests 'private' to himself as distinguished from those *shared with* the other members of the collectivity in which he plays a role" (1951:60; emphasis added). But at another point, he implies a mutual exclusivity between self and collectivity: "the actor who chooses [self orientation when collectivity orientation is normative] is *violating* his responsibilties, to the system as a unit and its participant members" (1951:97; emphasis added). Coleman parallels Parsons in his own equivocal treatment of egoism-altruism as, on the one hand, mutually exclusive (person i is not part of person j, and both have egoistic interests) and on the other hand, overlapping (persons i and j may have altruistic interests in each other).

I believe the equivocation thus shared by Parsons and Coleman reflects one of the most persistent, many-sided, and fundamental problems in sociology, namely, the relation between the individual and society. More specifically, the questions here are whether individual and society should be thought of as mutually antagonistic or not and which of them should be thought of as generative of the other. Let us therefore press beyond the equivocations to see how Coleman and Parsons, on the whole, answer these two questions.

Coleman's identification of personal freedom with the absence of society has already been quoted here. Parsons, on the other hand, argues that personal freedom is dependent on society: "individuality and creativity are, to a considerable extent, phenomena of the institutionalization of expectations" (1961a:38). Regarding the locus of causal dominance, as between individuals and society, Parsons continues on the side of society: "the patterning of the motivational system in terms of which [the individual] faces [the] situation . . . depends upon the social system, because his own personality structure has been shaped through the internalization of systems of social objects and the patterns of institutionalized culture" (1961a:38). Here, too, Coleman's position is opposite to Parsons', as is evident from his statement that "the values of events at the lower level give the interest of the corporate actor in actions at the next level," and his notion that a proper theory of action should begin with individual persons, rather than with social organizations.

In summary, the division between the authors seems clear: Parsons thinks of individual and society as non-antagonistic, while Coleman thinks of them as antagonistic; and Parsons believes that society mainly determines the individual, while Coleman believes the converse.

The Evaluation of Social Systems

Coleman says "My argument is simple and straightforward. A theory of action has as its base individual preferences. It then becomes possible to evaluate social arrangements, social structures or even whole social systems on the basis of their satisfaction of preferences." There are many secondary problems with this utilitarian calculus, including whether all preferences should be treated as equals—the lifelong goal the equal of a momentary whim, a taste for inflicting hurt the equal of one for giving help; whether all preferring individuals should be treated as equals at each observation, regardless of the extent to which their preferences have been satisfied or denied in the past; what range of alternatives should be presented when preferences are elicited and satisfactions measured; and so on.

But I am convinced that there is a primary problem with Coleman's argument, and that is the philosophical problem of whether human beings should be thought of as "wholly free" when unsocialized and outside social systems, and whether, therefore, we ought to use the image of such perfectly individuated individuals as our criterion of ideal humankind against which all real, socialized, and socially environed individuals are to be measured. Personally, I doubt this very much; but I do not mean to debate this question here. I mean only to point out that it is the pivotal question on which Coleman's claim to a normative social theory rests, and I mean to specify that question as a philosophical one—a matter of faith in the short run, and not fact (admitting, of course, that all fact is a matter of faith, in the long run).

Parsons also believes in the possibility of a scientifically based normative social theory, and he also believes that he has invented such a theory. In spite of his disclaimer (1971:3), Parsons strongly implies the evaluation that modern Western societies are superior to all others. This implication seems most clearly exposed by his choice of analog as when, in defending "a more general theory of the evolution of living systems," he claims that "one aspect of this continuity is the parallel between the emergence of man as a biological species, and the emergence of modern societies" (1971:2) and then argues that "modern societies . . . have a single Western origin [which has] extended beyond Europe only by colonization, or . . . by processes in which the model of the modern West has been indispensable" (1971:3, 2).

Whatever his evaluative decision, however, Parsons' evaluative criteria are radically different from Coleman's. Coleman says, essentially, let the greatest good (or more exactly the greatest satisfaction of preference—which may not be the same thing, as people may not know what's good for them; they often prefer things that do not bring them happiness and often do not prefer things that do bring them happiness) of the greatest number of individuals be the criterion. Coleman thus grounds societal evaluation in a single atomistic criterion: the subjective feelings of individual persons. Parsons, however, proposes only systemic criteria—including "differentiation," "adaptive upgrading," and so on (1966:21–24)—that refer to features of the society rather than of the individuals within it. It is important, then, to see that Parsons and Coleman have moved in very different directions with regard to the kinds of evaluative criteria they propose.

It is also important to see, however, that they have both been similarly enticed from initially empirical theories to normatively evaluative theories. (Parsons and Coleman, of course, are by no means alone in this; many others, of many different theoretic persuasions, have proposed the same transformation.) Thus, although he does not wish to press the argument too strongly, Coleman claims that "the possibility [of normative evaluations of society] is intrinsic to any theory which begins with individual preferences." Parsons is more difficult to quote as succinctly but he seems no less unequivocal, overall, on this topic. Thus, although Parsons assures us that he has "tried to make [his] basic criterion [of evolutionary classification and evaluation] congruent with that used in biological theory" (1966: 110), the proposed congruence rests on an initial and typically social actionistic conceptual substitution: "cultural innovations, especially definitions of what man's life ought to be . . . replace Darwinian variations in genetic constitution" (1967:494–95). Given that crucial substitution, it follows that in the evolutionary ranking of different societies, "the dividing criteria . . . center about critical developments in the code elements of the normative structures" (1966:26).

On the basis of their own statements, then, it seems fair to infer that both Coleman and Parsons claim some special normative potential for empirical theories that assign a key theoretic role to purposive orientations—whether these orientations be conceptualized as "individual preferences" or as "code elements of the normative structures." Obviously, if this claim were true, then the proponents of social actionist theory could rightfully sit in judgment over all human social behavior, not excluding the study of that behavior.

In summary, Coleman's and Parsons' papers seem to converge in certain respects and diverge in others, and so exemplify some of the principal conceptual, explanatory, terminological, philosophical, and in the broadest sense, political, problems that both unite and divide contemporary sociology.

8

Social Structure in Evolutionary Perspective

Gerhard E. Lenski

ONE OF THE more surprising developments in the social sciences in recent years has been the rebirth of interest in evolutionary theory. This rarely happens in the world of science: once abandoned, a theory is usually abandoned forever. But evolutionary theory may prove an exception, as its revival is already well underway in archaeology and anthropology, and developments in our own discipline have reached the point where a number of writers of other theoretical persuasions have recently felt compelled to warn against this ancient heresy (Nisbet, 1969; Peel, 1971; Utz, 1973).

The reason for this renewal of interest is not hard to find. Despite the abundance of theories in contemporary social science, none of the others takes seriously the need for *making sense of the basic patterns of history*.

Consider the alternatives. Structuralism and functionalism largely ignore the time dimension in their efforts to develop a synchronic mode of analysis. Human ecology has, until recently, limited its concern to very short-run trends, and when on occasion it has addressed itself to the broad historical record (Duncan, 1964; Hawley, 1971) it has been virtually indistinguishable from evolutionary theory. Certainly, many would nominate Marxian theory as an alternative to evolutionary theory. But as Engels (Mehring, 1935:555), Lenin

☐ I am greatly indebted to Jean Lenski for many valuable substantive and editorial suggestions made during the preparation of this paper.

(1932:70), and others (e.g., M. Harris, 1968: Chapter 8) remind us, Marx offers not so much an alternative to evolutionary theory as a special and distinctive brand of it.

The only serious challenge that I can see to evolutionary theory is provided by historical particularism with its denial that the historical record offers meaningful patterns which transcend the specific and the particular. No one has stated this basic position better than Robert Nisbet in his widely praised volume, *Social Change and History*. He argues there (1969:284) that ". . . philosophers of history and social evolutionists to the contrary, long-run directionality tends to be in the beholder's eye, not in the materials themselves."

For those who have not read widely in archaeology and history, this assertion, by a writer with the obvious erudition of Nisbet, carries great weight. Moreover, it justifies and legitimizes their own neglect of history. Yet I would argue that this denial of long-run directionality is not only mistaken, it threatens to cripple the development of sociological theory. For what it denies are some of the best clues we have concerning the nature of the forces that shape and mold social structures. As George Homans has observed (1971:377), if you want to know why institutions are what they are today, "look at the historical record of their development." The same can be said of social stucture.

Evolutionary Trends

What, then, are these long-run patterns of directionality that Nisbet and the historical particularists deny? Let me begin by listing just a few of the most important, while noting that others could easily be added (Lenski and Lenski, 1974:76–78).

First, and foremost, all the evidence of archaeology, history, and sociology points to the conclusion that over a span of many thousands of years, the human population has been increasing. More than that, the rate of increase has been accelerating. This is not to deny that there have been many local and regional reversals due to famine and plague. There may even have been short-run reversals on a global scale as when the Black Plague took such a heavy toll in the fourteenth century. But these localized and limited reversals do not refute the thesis of a long-run, directional trend for the world as a whole.

Second, there has been an equally durable trend involving the expansion of the human population into new territories and new environments. From origins somewhere in Africa millions of years ago, our ancestors spread throughout much of that continent and then into Asia and Europe. Still later—in the last fifty thousand years at most, according to present evidence—man migrated to Australia and the New World. Finally, in our own century, he has penetrated Antarctica, the last of the continents. But even this is not the whole story: with boats, submarines, diving gear, and oil rigs man has been expanding into marine environments, and, with planes, rocket ships, space probes, and satellites, he is also penetrating the atmosphere and outer space.

A third major trend is seen in the advance of technology—man's cultural tools and techniques for mobilizing information and energy in the pursuit of his goals. Technological innovation began in the remote prehistoric past, perhaps even before the hominid line itself became established. We know that certain other primates are not only tool-users but tool-makers as well, and it is possible that these are traits we and they inherited from some common ancestor. But whatever the facts may be in that regard, we know that slowly and gradually through that vast expanse of time we call the Paleolithic age, hominids were adding to their store of information about the environment and building up a tool kit which was comparable in sophistication, by the late Upper Paleolithic, to the level we associate with modern hunting and gathering peoples. With the discovery of the techniques of plant cultivation and animal domestication approximately ten thousand years ago, the pace of innovation accelerated considerably and has continued to accelerate down to our own day. There have been interruptions and local reversals, to be sure. But the long-run trend is clear: man's ability to mobilize information and energy for his own purposes has steadily escalated.

Growth in the production of goods and services constitutes a fourth major historical trend. The first clear evidence of this is found by archaeologists in Neolithic sites, where artifacts are much more numerous and man-made dwellings much more substantial than their Paleolithic counterparts. Later, with the rise of Bronze Age societies, the number and variety of man-made objects increases further and comes to include temples, pyramids, and other massive and costly structures of the kinds we associate with the civilizations of the ancient world. One hardly need comment on the growth of economic productivity in more recent times.

Linked to all these other trends, the historical record shows a striking increase in both the scale and complexity of social structures. For most of the prehistoric period, we have no direct evidence concerning the nature of social systems; but social theory and the findings of archaeology, ethology, ethnology, and ecology combine to support the view that throughout the Paleolithic Era, social systems were no larger and no more complex than those observed in modern hunting and gathering societies. That is to say, the populations of societies probably averaged less than fifty, and seldom more than one or two hundred, and economic, political, and religious specialization was minimal.

With the beginnings of horticulture, the situation began to change and societies began to grow significantly in both size and organizational complexity—trends that still continue. The growth in the scale of societal organization has reached the point in our own century where there are now eight societies with a population of a hundred million or more and one, the People's Republic of China, that numbers close to a billion.

At the community level there has been comparable long-run growth. Several communities today have populations of ten million or more. In the ancient world, a few great capitals of empire, like Rome and Constantinople, are believed to have attained populations of slightly over one million at the peak of their power, while during the Paleolithic Era a settlement with a thousand inhabitants was almost certainly a rarity.

As the scale of organization has increased, so has structural complexity. In every hunting and gathering society of which we have any knowledge, the division of labor has been limited to age and sex specialization, with occasional part-time roles for political and religious leaders. We have no reason to think that the situation was appreciably different in hunting and gathering bands during the Paleolithic. With the beginnings of horticulture and the subsequent emergence of urban centers, the adult male role began to be somewhat more specialized—though it is well to remember that even in the advanced agrarian societies of fairly recent times, eighty percent or more of adult males were still concentrated in the relatively undifferentiated role of peasant. With industrialization, specialization has increased enormously. In barely two centuries, much of the vast peasant mass of the Agrarian Era, both male and female, has been broken up and redistributed among thousands of new occupational specialties.

Long-run directionality is also evident in the growing complexity of systems of stratification. In hunting and gathering societies, social inequality seems always to have been minimal. The first evidence of notable inequality within societies appears in the Bronze Age, starting a trend which continues through at least the first stages of the Industrial Revolution. If we look at the distribution of power and wealth from a global standpoint, the trend not only continues, it is probably accelerating. Within advanced industrial societies, there is still a trend toward increasingly complex stratification systems, which manifests itself in what East European sociologists call the partial decomposition of status systems (Wesolowski, 1969:469–70) or what Americans have called the decline in class crystallization (Landecker, 1960).

Two Criticisms of Modern Sociology

One could go on adding to this list of long-run trends that contradict Robert Nisbet's assertion,[1] but perhaps those I have mentioned will suffice for present purposes. In view of them, however, how are we to respond to Nisbet and the historical particularists who assert that long-run trends are merely in the eye of the beholder and not in the materials themselves?

For myself, I see only one possible response: a categorical denial —and a friendly invitation to all who share that view to reexamine the evidence of archaeology, history, ethology, and ethnology, starting, perhaps, with the trends just noted. Long-run trends *are* a fact of human history and one of the most important ones at that—for

[1] Other long-run trends that might be mentioned include the growing destructiveness of warfare, man's increasing impact on the biophysical environment, the growth of literacy and the expanding speed and scope of communication, the enlargement of vocabularies, the growth of bureaucracies, the growth of trade and commerce both within and between societies, the resulting growth of economic interdependence, the growth of urbanism, and, last but not least, the accelerating rates of technological innovation and social change (Lenski and Lenski, 1974: 68–69, 130–32). Perhaps it should be added that no sensible evolutionist claims that all these trends will, or can, continue indefinitely into the future. On the contrary, some of them, such as population growth, have to stop if our species is to survive. Some critics seem to imagine that evolutionism is committed to the ridiculous view that long-term trends must be permanent and eternal, though it is not clear to me what the basis is for their belief. In any case this is not a view that is part of modern evolutionism as I understand it.

the social theorist as well as for the policy-maker and the ordinary citizen. Not only are they some of our best clues to the forces that shape and mold social structure, they also provide the key to the social revolution that is currently transforming human life so dramatically all around the globe. For there is every reason to believe that this revolution is not simply a product of the nineteenth and twentieth centuries, but rather an extension and an intensification of developments that have been underway for ten thousand years or more.

But if this is so, how is it that modern sociology has shown so little concern for these trends and for their implications? There are undoubtedly many reasons, but I would like to mention two. The first involves the "signal-to-noise problem," which the British astronomer, Sir Fred Hoyle, explains in this way:

> Physicists would describe most of what happens in everyday life as "noise" . . . [or] activity without information content. "Signal" consists of genuine information. A signal-to-noise problem in physics consists in digging out genuine information from activity without content.
> . . . The protagonists of studies in the humanities fail to appreciate the extent to which their problems are of the signal-to-noise kind. . . . Instead of separating the noise—throwing it away as the physicists do—they spend their energies chasing through every detail of the darned stuff. Students of history do this with ferocious concentration, spending year after year studying their "period" as they call it. Students of sociology might indeed be described as the ultimate students of noise, literally and figuratively. [1971: 119–20]

I think that Hoyle is too harsh with respect to sociology, and he oversimplifies somewhat, since what is noise on one level of analysis is sometimes signal on another (e.g., activities that are noise on the societal level may be signal on the social psychological). But he is correct in thinking that many social scientists, especially many historians and historically oriented sociologists, tend to focus on the exceptions to general patterns to the point of neglecting the patterns themselves. (This may well be a carryover from the prequantitative era in social science before the development of probabilistic models in theory.)

Another major reason for the neglect of long-run directionality is the reductionist tendency that has become such a prominent feature of our discipline in the twentieth century. We are not alone in this, as René Dubos, the distinguished biologist, reminds us. In his book *So Human an Animal,* Dubos argues (1968:28) that there has been a reductionist bias in all of science since at least the seventeenth century and that its philosophical heroes have been Democritus and Descartes, "both of whom taught that the way to knowledge is to separate substances and events into their ultimate components and reactions." He goes on to say,

> The reductionist scientist tends to become so involved intellectually and emotionally in the elementary fragments of the system, and in the analytical process itself, that he commonly loses interest in the phenomena or the organisms which had been his first concern. For example, the biologist who starts with a question formulated because of its relevance to human life is tempted, and indeed expected, to progress *seriatim* to the organ or function involved, then to the single cell, then to subcellular fragments, then to molecular groupings or reactions, then to the individual molecules and atoms. He would happily proceed, if he knew how to do it, until he reached the ultimate aspects of nature in which matter and energy become indistinguishable. [1968: 242]

Dubos maintains that this has been a profound mistake, and argues that:

> The most pressing problems of humanity . . . involve . . . situations in which systems must be studied as a whole in all the complexity of their interactions. This is particularly true of human life. When life is considered only in its specialized functions, the outcome is a world emptied of meaning. To be fully relevant to life, sciences must deal with the responses of the total organism to the total environment. [1968: 28]

This, it seems to me, is precisely what sociology has failed to do since it abandoned evolutionism more than half a century ago. In the hope of understanding societies better, we shifted the focus of our attention from societies themselves to their constituent elements —to institutions, communities, associations, roles, and individuals— and we became so fascinated with all of the substantive questions raised by these lesser entities and the methodological problems involved in their study that we often forgot the larger questions that gave rise to sociology in the first place.

To make matters worse, our reductionist zeal has led us to contract the scope of our work in other important ways: We have engaged in a kind of temporal-spatial reductionism, drastically shortening our time perspective, or even ignoring the time dimension altogether, while creating what Everett Hughes (1961) has called an "ethnocentric sociology" focused increasingly on American behavior and American experience. Thus, what began as the science of the development of human societies has been transformed into a science of contemporary American institutions and contemporary American social psychology, with little awareness by most of us of the change that has occurred.

Determinants of Social Structure

Once we recognize the emergent, developmental, and evolutionary quality of social structure, we are led to ask one of the most fruitful questions in sociology: What has been responsible for the trends? What has been responsible for the growing size of social systems over the last ten thousand years? What has been responsible for the long-term increase in their structural complexity, the growth in inequality, the growth of trade and urbanism, and all the other changes that have occurred?

Before I try to answer these questions, I need to clarify one point. The trends I am speaking of occur at the global level; they are trends in what Sahlins (1960) has called "general evolution." In many instances the trends involve transformations of global frequency distributions. The upper limits of these distributions have been raised dramatically, as have the measures of central tendency. But the lower limits have not changed appreciably in most cases—at least, not yet. Thus, more than nine thousand years after the beginnings of plant cultivation, there are still a few societies, like the recently discovered Tasadays in the Philippines, which are no larger and no more complex than societies of the Paleolithic Era. Critics of evolutionism sometimes point to the survival of such societies as though that constituted disproof of the trend itself when, in fact, they have misunderstood the nature of the trend in question.[2]

For the evolutionist, the starting point in an analysis of changes in social structure lies millions of years in the past when man's ancestors first ceased interbreeding with any other primates and thus

---

[2] It might also be noted that, with each passing decade, the number of societies at the minimal level of size and complexity is steadily declining, and thus it is quite likely that within another few decades the lower limit of the range will also begin to rise.

became a distinct species. Though we have no direct knowledge of these first hominids, we can draw a number of inferences about them from the study of modern primates, and contemporary anthropologists and achaeologists do so with increasing frequency (Clark, 1957: 172–73; Hole and Heizer, 1965:211–14 and Chap. 16; Pfeiffer, 1972). First of all, it is highly probable that from the very start, hominids were social animals (Pfeiffer, 1972:281ff.). In other words, the basic elements of social stucture are apparently something our species inherited, not something we invented. We know, for example, that all modern primates live in groups (Washburn and Hamburg, 1965: 612). More than that, we know that group life is a necessary condition for what is the primates' most important adaptive mechanism, namely, learning. As two leading primatologists put it recently,

> Why does the group exist? Why [do primates] not live alone, if not all year at least for much of it? There are many reasons but the principal one is *learning*. The group is the locus of knowledge and experience far exceeding that of the individual member. It is in the group that experience is pooled and the generations linked. [Washburn and Hamburg, 1965: 613]

Among modern primates, the basic features of social structure are determined by the interaction of the genetic heritage of a species with its biophysical environment. There is little reason, either theoretically or empirically, to suppose that conditions were different for our earliest hominid ancestors. Cultural influences on social structure seem to have come much later, as culture, unlike society, was almost certainly a hominid invention, and probably a rather late one at that.

A growing number of scholars now see the first major changes in hominid life and social structure coming as a consequence of the development of hunting skills and hunting technology, especially those associated with big-game hunting. These were almost certainly hominid inventions, since man is the only modern primate for whom meat is an important part of the diet (DeVore, 1965:43–48, 129, 262–63, 300–01, 477), and there is no evidence of big-game hunting in the archaeological record prior to the last half million years or so.

The shift to big-game hunting almost certainly brought a number of important social changes. First of all, it necessitated much greater cooperation among adult males, in both the production and the consumption of food. As one writer (Pfeiffer, 1972:158) has observed, all primates except man "are supremely self-centered when it comes to feeding; they forage strictly for themselves." In big-game hunting, by contrast, cooperation is imperative for success, and success, in turn, leads naturally to sharing, because no single individual can either consume all the meat before it rots or defend it against other carnivores and scavengers.

There is also good reason to suppose that the shift to big-game hunting strengthened the social bond in another way, by laying the foundation for the historic division of labor between the sexes. In modern hunting and gathering societies, hunting has been exclusively a male activity in most cases and predominantly a male activity in the rest; gathering vegetable materials, by contrast, has been predominantly women's work (Lenski and Lenski, 1974:139n). This new division of labor almost certainly made the sexes more interdependent, as the food obtained daily by the women could be counted on to offset the risk of a succession of unsuccessful hunts, while the men's efforts provided valuable protein and satisfied what soon became a dietary preference.

In short, big-game hunting seems to have strengthened the relatively weak social bonds among males and between males and females, thus supplementing the already strong primate bonds among females and between females and their offspring. In addition, many scholars now believe that the rise of big-game hunting played a critical role in the growth of the hominid brain and in the development of speech. If all this is true, there has never been a more critical development in human history from the standpoint of impact on social structure.

A second major revolution in social structure had its origins just ten thousand years ago, or slightly less, in that sequence of events which Gordon Childe (1936:chapter 5) dubbed "the Neolithic Revolution."[3] Once, again, the basis of the revolution was the development of a new subsistence technology—in this case, plant cultivation.

Without reviewing the circumstances of this critical new development—except to note that it was probably the work of women, since plants had become their concern—we can readily appreciate its

---

[3] Though some archaeologists today shy away from the word "revolution" on the grounds that the changes involved occurred slowly and over a long period of time, the term seems well justified in view of the enormity of the consequences that ensued.

revolutionary potential. For the first time ever, groups of humans could now escape the many constraints which the hunting and gathering mode of life usually imposed. For example, as a society came to rely more on horticulture, its members could settle down in one place for an extended period. This made the accumulation of possessions much more rewarding than it had been when everything one owned had to be carried from one campsite to another every few weeks or months. The new technology also made larger settlements possible. One of the oldest horticultural villages discovered contained over twenty stone houses and an estimated population of 150 (Braidwood, 1960:138–43), nearly four times the size of the average band of hunters and gatherers of modern times, and another early settlement spread out over an area of ten acres and may have had as many as two thousand inhabitants (Hammond, 1972:17). A third settlement from this same period provides some of the earliest evidence we have for full-time occupational specialization, a number of small workshops for artisans of several varieties (Mellaart, 1965:43–44). These are but a few of the scattered clues that indicate that important structural changes were occurring in response to the new technology.

By the beginning of recorded history, roughly five thousand years ago, the magnitude of the trend is clear. Substantial city-states were flourishing throughout the Fertile Crescent and, compared to the biggest settlements of the early Neolithic Era, were monstrously large and complex. One city covered two square miles (Hammond, 1972:38). This growth in size was matched by growth in structural differentiation. Cities became complex affairs, often divided into several fairly distinct districts: an inner city containing the temple and residence of a religious and political elite, suburbs with houses and gardens for commoners, and a commercial area for foreign as well as native merchants. From written records we learn of temples engaged in large-scale economic ventures requiring the coordination of substantial numbers of workers. A single enterprise might operate estates of 700 acres or more to support a staff of over a thousand priests, artisans, and administrators (Hammond, 1972:39).

Technological advance also played an important role in the formation of the coercive state and in the beginnings of imperialism. In China, for instance, we are told that within a few centuries of the invention of bronze, "the villages of the plain fell under the domination of walled cities on whose rulers the possession of bronze weapons, chariots, and slaves conferred a measure of superiority to which no Neolithic community could aspire, however populous and well-fed" (Watson, 1966:57).

As contemporary archaeologists survey these critical developments of the late prehistoric and early historic periods, there is a growing consensus that technological innovations were a necessary precondition for the revolution in social structure. Although many of the details of Gordon Childe's pioneering analyses are rejected today, the basic thrust of his analyses is not (Clark, 1970; Braidwood, 1968:246). Most archaeologists now agree that without the Neolithic Revolution in subsistence technology, the advanced societies of the ancient world could not have developed. As one French anthropologist (Maquet, 1972:22) put it recently, "A city of hunters is an impossibility."

We can, of course, go further and say that the rise of every civilization of the ancient world depended not merely on plant cultivation, but on hundreds of technological innovations—innovations and discoveries that enabled people to do things they could never do before. By Roman times, *Homo sapiens sapiens*—without experiencing any genetic change—was a very different animal from the animal he had been seven thousand years earlier. He could move faster, travel further, strike harder; kill at greater distances, move greater weights, cross larger bodies of water, and do a score of other things that previously had been impossible. In effect, the technology he acquired during the intervening years was the equivalent of a radical modification in man's genetic heritage. If we want an explanation of the dramatic changes in social structure that occurred between the end of the Old Stone Age and the era of Imperial Rome, we must look chiefly to the continuing revolution in technology that transformed man's behavioral potential and his capacity for action.

Further evidence of the strong link between advances in technology and change in social structure is provided by those societies which did not experience such change but kept their simpler social systems. Many anthropologists and sociologists, assuming it was by choice that these groups retained their simpler character, have hastened to declare values as the explanation. But the explanation is often far simpler: in most instances either these societies have been at too great a distance from the locus of innovation or there have been environmental barriers. Throughout history, obstacles, such as mountains, deserts, and large bodies of water, have prevented or greatly slowed the diffusion of technology. In other instances, the ecology of a particular area has prevented potential recipients from adopting new technologies: much of sub-Saharan Africa, for example, seems to have been unsuited to the plow under preindustrial conditions.[4] The geographical distribution of simpler societies in the modern world, with their concentration in deserts, rain forests, and arctic areas, is no mere accident of history, nor does it reflect some curious distribution of values.

Sometimes, to be sure, societies acquainted with more advanced technologies have rejected them for ideological reasons. But in doing so, they have usually reduced substantially their chances of survival. A hunting and gathering society, for example, finds it almost impossible to compete for land with a neighboring horticultural society. The horticulturalists' more permanent settlement and denser population upset the ecosystem on which hunters and gatherers depend. Game supplies and supplies of wild fruits and vegetables are seriously depleted, since the denser horticultural populations usually continue hunting and gathering to supplement their own food supply. In short, the ecological niche of the hunters and gatherers is destroyed, and they must migrate, be assimilated, or die.

Thus, as we look back on the development of social structure during the first 99.9 percent of hominid history, we see that its chief determinants were (1) man's genetic heritage (that is, the tools and behavioral tendencies with which he was endowed by the process of organic evolution), (2) the technologies he slowly fashioned to enhance this heritage, (3) the environmental barriers to human activity and technological advance, specifically environments that impeded the flow of information or precluded the adoption of more advanced subsistence technologies, and (4) the deadly competition between societies striving to maintain their territorial and resource bases. On the level of general evolution not much of the basic variance in social systems seems to require the invocation of cultural values. In fact, as one observes the slowly accelerating patterns of expanding scale and growing complexity of organization at the global level over this vast expanse of time, one cannot help but be reminded of other patterns in the biotic world—patterns which do not depend at all on the conscious will or intent of the creatures involved.

[4] The combination of poor soils and the presence of the tse-tse fly (which severely limited the areas in which cattle and horses could be raised) virtually ruled out the use of the plow before the development of modern commercial fertilizers and chemical insecticides (Davidson, 1966:8–9; Maquet, 1972:17).

This is not to deny that people have often been acutely conscious of alternative courses of action and been guided by ideological considerations in making their choices. But it is important to remember that those doing the choosing were the authors neither of the alternatives nor of the circumstances influencing their choices. The costs and the benefits of the various alternatives, for example, were determined for the most part by genetic, ecological, and technological factors beyond the control of the decision-makers. In effect, human decision-makers across the centuries have had to play with stacked decks and loaded dice. Under the circumstances, we should not be surprised to discover that societies widely separated not only in time and space but in ideology as well have so often made remarkably similar choices. Meanwhile, those groups which have chosen to oppose the dominant trend have greatly jeopardized their chances for survival, except where extreme geographical isolation or the occupancy of an unattractive ecological niche protected them from normal intersocietal competition.

Values and Social Structure

But what of the last fifteen hundred years? Even if one is willing to accept this ecological-evolutionary explanation of social structure for the first 99.9 percent of hominid experience, what about the most recent 0.1 percent? And what about the future? Can we so easily dismiss the role of human consciousness and human values in today's world?

These are not easy questions, and I cannot honestly claim there is any consensus among evolutionists regarding their answers. Students of modern social and economic development—who are, in effect, microevolutionists—have taken almost every conceivable position on the causes of social change, and macroevolutionists have not done much better. I cannot hope to review all the arguments here, much less comment on them critically. I will, however, call attention to several considerations that appear important and suggest the conclusions which they seem, to me, to indicate.

First, let me simply take note of a certain bias which we, as intellectuals, naturally bring to this task. Because ideas and ideologies are our stock in trade, we have a vested interest in the view that they are important. We need, therefore, to be on guard against the temptation to exaggerate their role (and our role) in history. The danger is especially great because our fellow scholars, on whom we normally rely for criticism when we spout nonsense, are likely to be as biased in this respect as we.

Second, I would point out that nature, of which man and his societies are an integral part, tends to operate in an orderly fashion. Basic causal patterns that have prevailed for thousands of years do not often suddenly become inoperative. Thus, it could be a serious error to assume that explanations which help us understand the first 99.9 percent of our species' history are irrelevant and inapplicable today. This is not to suggest that modification of relationships between factors does not occur in nature. Certainly this has happened and will continue to happen. In fact, there is good reason to believe that some important modifications are now underway in the relations between technology, ideology, and social structure. But I am inclined to believe that they are best understood when viewed as variations on certain ancient themes rather than as something totally new and unprecedented.

Third, and most important of all, in our attempts to assess the role of ideology today, we need to look much more closely at the massive social experiments undertaken in recent decades in response to the dictates of new ideologies and new value systems. In particular, we need to study the results of experiments in social reconstruction in Eastern Europe, Asia, and Cuba. There are a number of societies now that have been totally under the control of dedicated Marxist elites for a quarter century or more. We need to ask, to what extent have ideological imperatives in these societies displaced genetic, ecological, technological, and economic imperatives as the dominant forces shaping social structure?

Although there are sharp differences of opinion about many features of today's socialist societies, there is fairly widespread agreement on at least one point: None of them has found it nearly as easy to build a socialist utopia as many social theorists of the eighteenth and nineteenth centuries and the revolutionary fathers of modern socialist societies anticipated. It has proved far easier to seize control of governments than to create a truly socialist order.

Consider, if you will, the long list of un-Marxian social patterns that persist, even flourish, in most socialist societies: the male-dominated nuclear family with its "double burden" for gainfully employed married women (Kaiser, 1974); sexual stratification in the labor force (Lennon, 1971); differential access to higher education, with children of the professional and managerial classes favored over children of workers and peasants (Lane, 1971: Chapter 5); the division of labor; bureaucratic organization and administration; the state, itself, which refuses to wither; political repression (Medvedev and Medvedev, 1971; Solzhenitsyn, 1974); militarism; imperialism (ask the Chinese about the Soviet Union, or vice versa); crime, delinquency, alcoholism (Connor, 1972). Even the conditions of work for the worker, in whose name the revolution was fought, remain strikingly similar to conditions in nonsocialist societies. As Jan Szczepański (1970:125), Poland's leading sociologist, put it recently, ". . . the workers are still hired labor. The socialist revolution does not change the relation of the worker to the machine, nor does it change his position within the technological system of the factory." In Yugoslavia, efforts have been made to increase the power of workers in factories and elsewhere through workers' councils, but recent research indicated the results have been rather disappointing so far (Obradović, 1972).

If one looks at *trends* in social structure, the picture is much the same. Although there are certainly differences between socialist and capitalist societies, they are moving in similar directions in many important respects: both have declining death and birth rates, loss of productive functions by the family, decline of parental authority, shift from primary to secondary and tertiary industries, rise in GNP, shortening of the work week, improvement in standards of living, improved standards of health and education, rapid expansion of the professional and administrative classes, decline of unskilled labor and farm occupations, growing influence of the mass media, increased linking of populations by postal systems, telegraph, telephone, and modern modes of transportation, expansion of the functions of government, rapid growth of bureaucracies, increasing reliance on science and planning, on computers, and on data banks, the expansion of knowledge, and so on and on and on.

Whatever other conclusions one may draw from this list, one seems inescapable: socialist societies are subject to many of the same basic imperatives as capitalist societies. Genetic imperatives of human nature, environmental imperatives of various kinds, technological imperatives of production, economic imperatives of scarcity and the resulting necessity of relating costs to benefits, and the continuing imperative of societal competition—these limit the basic developmental possibilities for industrial societies, regardless of ideology, just as they did for simpler societies of the past. But that is not all.

These imperatives also influence a society as it makes its choices among the viable alternatives. Every option carries its own price tag, and the price tags are largely determined by those same imperatives. Even the most affluent society cannot consistently ignore the cost factor. When a society, for ideological reasons, opts for an expensive solution to one problem, it has that much less to spend on others. As Americans are discovering in trying to cope simultaneously with energy and environmental crises, it is impossible to adopt ideal solutions for every problem. In fact, it is usually impossible to adopt an ideal solution to even a single major problem.

Many leaders of socialist societies in the past half century have learned through bitter experience how powerful these constraints can be. Lenin's famous post-revolutionary slogan that "Communism equals Soviets plus electrification" (i.e., a state system plus technological advance) was one of the first expressions of this unpleasant truth. Stalin, Khrushchev, Brezhnev, Tito, Mao, and Castro have all made similar discoveries.[5] Successful socialist revolutions in the twentieth century have invariably been followed by a major reordering of historic socialist priorities, with the more conventional goals of economic growth, national security, and defense of the political status quo usually coming to take precedence over the more uniquely socialist goals. To say this is not to condemn the leaders of socialist societies for lack of fidelity or dedication. It is rather, I would argue, a commentary on the nature and potency of the basic determinants of social structure.

Summing Up

Let me try now to sum up the argument for the evolutionary, or ecological-evolutionary, approach to social structure. Essentially, I believe that it is the only approach which takes seriously the fact that there is a striking historical pattern or ordering to the basic variations observable in social structure. Robert Nisbet notwithstanding, there is a long-run directionality in the development of social structure that can help us achieve a better understanding of contemporary patterns and trends—especially those which are cen-

---

[5] One is reminded of Michels' unhappy observation (1959:391) that "The socialists might conquer, but not socialism. . . ." Though too pessimistic a conclusion, it contains an important insight for students of social structure.

tral to the dramatic social revolution of our own day. Ecological-evolutionary research and theory strive first to identify and describe the various patterns and trends as precisely as possible and then to find explanations by drawing on all the available evidence—not only from sociology but from other disciplines as well. The unit of analysis is the totality of human social structure, not any of the lesser units, not even an entire society or set of societies.

The explanation which most of the new generation of evolutionists offer is essentially a materialistic one. They maintain that the basic transformations of social structure result from the interaction of genetic, environmental, and technological factors, rather than from ideological factors or some inner dynamic in social structure itself. These latter undeniably explain some part of the variance —some of the differences, for example, between capitalist and socialist societies in the modern era or between Muslim and Christian societies in the agrarian.[6] But these variations are judged to be secondary compared with those generated by technological development, and often dependent on prior technological advance. It is well to remember that capitalism and socialism, even Christianity and Islam, have been factors in the evolutionary process for only a relatively short time, and a recent factor analysis indicates that even in this period, on the global level, their influence has been secondary to the impact of technology (Sawyer, 1967).

Yet evolutionary theory does not deny the importance of ideological considerations and influences. It recognizes in them some of man's best efforts to apply the light of reason and experience in constructing his social systems and in striving to shape and control his destiny. Even though the results have often been disappointing, the world would be a poorer place had these efforts not been made. But beyond this, evolutionary theory raises the possibility that through a combination of further technological advance, rigorous population limitation, and political consolidation at the global level, mankind could enter a new era in which the constraining effects of the ancient material imperatives would be drastically reduced and

[6] One cannot even attribute all of the variance between capitalist and socialist societies to ideological factors. For example, most experts agree that the ruthless suppression of political dissidence in the Soviet Union is at least partly a continuation of a pre-Revolutionary tradition. Similarly, the backwardness of Soviet agriculture, compared with American, is at least partly a function of environmental factors and the *preRevolutionary* gap between Soviet and American agricultural development. Thus, one must beware of exaggerating the influence of ideology even in situations where it is greatest.

the scope of ideology and planning substantially enlarged—a prospect that is simultaneously a cause for hope and a reason for concern.

Some critics of evolutionary theory regard its macrochronic, global perspective as a defect, as it seems to divert attention from the current problems of our own society. This would be a valid criticism, I suppose, if these problems were somehow unrelated to the larger temporal-spatial-social context with which evolutionary theory is concerned. But such is not the case. Most of our most pressing problems are related to the technologically generated social revolution in which every nation is now caught up. To fail to see this is to fail to comprehend the struggles and failures of so' many of the Third World nations, the fact of economic and political imperialism, war, "tribalism" (i.e., ethnic conflicts), the energy crisis, the environmental crisis, the population problem, poverty, the impending food crisis, the challenges to traditional forms of authority, changing relations between age and sex groups, new moral codes, and all the rest. Far from being irrelevant, evolutionism offers what I believe is an essential basis for considering contemporary social problems. Its mode of analysis, as I have suggested, is highly radical, in the sense that it addresses the root causes of problems rather than their surface manifestations.

I began this paper by saying that the recent revival of interest in evolutionary theory has come as something of a surprise and puzzle to many in our discipline. I might close by suggesting that in the not too distant future, the greater puzzle may well be why evolutionary theory was so long neglected.

9

Comment on Lenski's
Evolutionary Perspective

Robert S. Bierstedt

LET ME BEGIN my comments on Gerhard Lenski's paper by referring to an observation frequently made by Florian Znaniecki.
Znaniecki used to contend that the dismissal of Herbert Spencer in
the 1930s, if not abrupt, had nevertheless been unnecessarily complete—that the baby, in effect, had been thrown out with the bath
water. Forty years later, in the 1970s, we clearly see a reversal of
sentiment and one that would have pleased the old gentleman, as he
then was. The baby has been saved! The long brown lines of Spencer's works that occupied the shelves of the second-hand bookstores
on lower Fourth Avenue in the thirties have now disappeared; one
can only surmise that they have since been purchased, and possibly
even read. Spencer, who survived his initial fame, is enjoying a remarkable resurrection, one that may require the restoration of his
statue in the pantheon of sociological heroes. In England he has recently been extensively re-examined by Ronald Fletcher, by Stani-
slav Andreski, and by J. D. Y. Peel, the last of whom has written a
book on Spencer which carries the subtitle, inevitable perhaps, "The
Evolution of a Sociologist" (1971). The word "evolution" has become respectable again.

In this country Talcott Parsons, who quoted with approval Crane
Brinton's dismissal of Spencer[1] on the very first page of *The Struc-*

---

[1] Brinton's question "Who now reads Spencer?" appears in *English Political
Thought in the Nineteenth Century* (1933). His treatment is almost entirely

ture of Social Action (1937), has in his recent work become a Spencerian of sorts. Gerhard Lenski has almost single-handedly recreated the discipline of historical sociology—a discipline, one would have supposed, that died an unlamented death with the demise of Harry Elmer Barnes. It is indeed surprising, as Lenski observes at the outset of his paper, that a theory that was once abandoned, as was evolutionary theory, has attracted a renewed attention.

I should like, at the outset of my own remarks, to compliment Professor Lenski for finding a reason for this fascinating phenomenon. He says that, although we have an abundance of theories on the current sociological scene, none of the others takes seriously the task of tracing the patterns of human history. One would have thought that this was the task for which an autonomous science of sociology was designed, especially by Comte and Spencer. But it has now fallen into a sad neglect, a neglect to which Spencer's undeserved unpopularity has greatly contributed. It was not so in the nineteenth century. Comte, Spencer, Buckle, de Gobineau, Le Play, Démolins, Lecky, and Marx all had a theory of history. The modesty of the more analytical sociologists—Tönnies, Simmel, and Durkheim—turned sociology in upon itself when they began to study the threads of social interaction and to ignore the tapestry of historical events. Sociology thus suffered from the humility of some of its greatest practitioners. They resisted the seductions of Clio and turned instead to the characteristics of communities, the forms of social interaction, and the division of labor. And yet, Lenski is not entirely correct about the more recent scene. MacIver, for example, devoted the long last section of his book *Society* (1937) to social evolution. Sorokin overwhelmed us with four volumes on social dynamics, Hobhouse and Ginsberg wrestled mightily with evolutionary themes, I have already mentioned Parsons, and only five years ago Robert Nisbet gave us this thoughtful work on *Social Change and History* (1969).

In any event, it is Nisbet's denial of directionality that distresses Lenski. He therefore offers ten arguments of intended refutation: (1) the growth of population; (2) expansion of population into new territories; (3) advances in technology; (4) increasing capacity to manipulate the environment; (5) increasing complexity of social structures; (6) steady growth in the size of urban settlements; (7)

---

negative and concludes with the remark that Spencer "was a salesman of ideas and we no longer like his goods."

increase in the degree of social inequality; (8) expansion in the volume of trade; (9) increased literacy; and (10) "a rising rate of technological innovation and social change."

This is a versatile series of facts but one whose recital raises a few questions. Several of them are simple corollaries of the first, the increase in population. Moreover, this increase itself did not assume significant proportions for some 100,000 years, until roughly the middle of the seventeenth century, when the curve began a steep ascent. More seriously for Lenski's point, this steep ascent assures an inevitable reversal of direction a few centuries hence because the earth is not large enough to sustain the current rate of growth. Several of Lenski's other trends are simple corollaries of the third, the advancement of technology. One—increasing capacity to manipulate the environment—conceals a problem; that is, we may have learned to insulate ourselves from some of the harsher features of our environment but not to control or manipulate it in any significant way. The current drought in the American Midwest, the encroachment of the Sahara upon previously fertile lands in Africa, and the very real possibility of thermal pollution for much of the planet must give us pause. The increase in social inequality is surely debatable and, in the absence of units of measurement, it is impossible to assign precision to something called "a rising rate of social change." In substance, therefore, we have only two or three factors here—most notably the demographic and the technological—and the count of ten is an artifact of a defective taxonomy.

Let us not quibble about the number, however, and let us concede to Lenski that there are such things as trends in human history. Let us concede in addition that some of these trends may have a single and, so far, an unreversed direction. But trends that remain unreversed in 1974 are not necessarily irreversible, and on this possibility we have to maintain a certain agnosticism. We do so especially because readers of Spencer's *First Principles* do not often notice that it contains not only a theory of evolution but also a theory of "equilibration" and a theory of dissolution. The theory of dissolution is explained by an historian of philosophy in words that I could not improve upon and which I quote, with omissions, as follows:

> Every motion, being motion under resistance, must sooner or later come to an end; every rhythmic oscillation suffers some loss of rate and amplitude. The planets will ride through a lesser orbit than once they rode; the sun will shine less warmly as the centuries

pass away; the friction of the tides will retard the rotation of the earth. This globe, which throbs and murmurs with a million motions, and luxuriates into a million forms of riotously breeding life, will some day move more leisurely in its orbit; the blood will run cooler and more slowly in our desiccated veins; we shall not hurry any more; like dying races, we shall think of heaven in terms of rest and not of life; we shall dream of Nirvana. Gradually, and then rapidly, equilibration will become dissolution, the unhappy epilogue of evolution. Societies will disintegrate, masses will migrate, cities will fade into the dark hinterland of peasant life; no government will be strong enough to hold the loosened parts together; social order will cease to be even remembered. The earth will be a chaotic theatre of decay, a gloomy drama of energy in irreversible degradation; and it will itself be resolved into the dust and nebula from which it came. The cycle of evolution and dissolution will be complete. [Durant, 1926:400–01]

I quote these poetic and melancholy words to suggest that the rising line of the cosmos may be only the first half of a cycle that will reach its climax and then encounter an ineluctable decline. If an ancient like Spencer is not to be trusted, I invite your attention to the recent and pessimistic book of Robert L. Heilbroner, entitled *An Inquiry into the Human Prospect* (1974), and to my own recent paper in the Morris Ginsberg memorial volume (Bierstedt, 1974), in which I suggest that belief in progress is more an attitude than an idea and that it is only a temperamental response to history. For that matter, most of us, I suspect, could easily agree with Voltaire that history is an endless succession of needless cruelties.

I would also question Lenski's contention, on another subject, that contemporary sociologists have shown little interest in demographic and technological trends. What he means, or doubtless has to mean, is that their interpretations are not the same as his. His use of Hoyle's primitive distinction between noises and signals lacks a degree of relevance because, as he himself seems to notice, one man's noise is another man's signal. René Dubos' denigration of Democritus and Descartes similarly lacks relevance in Lenski's context, though not, of course, in others. One can appreciate the virtues of holism without subscribing to an evolutionary theory. Of course we have to attend to societies themselves, not only to their constituent parts, and Lenski's emphasis here has many merits; but there are several ways of indulging in this inquiry, of which the evolutionary way is only one. Spengler, Toynbee, or Sorokin, for example, may be nearer the mark than Spencer. History may be a

Jacob's ladder, as evolutionary theory would suggest, but then again it may be an Ixion's wheel.[2]

On another point I am in agreement with Lenski. I would, as he does, reject the parochial notion that sociology ought to focus its inquiries upon the American society. Sociology is not ethnography, and Everett Hughes is right in warning us against an ethnocentric bias. With that part of Lenski's paper in which he traces the evolution of the human species we need have no current concern. It is an orthodox story; and he tells it well. Whether the term "revolution" is an appropriate one for the vast social changes he describes is entirely a semantic question and one that presents no substantive issue. On the role of ideas and ideologies in these changes, Lenski is inconclusive, first constricting that role and then enlarging it. An adequate commentary on this issue would require a separate paper.

In spite of the questions I have raised, I want to conclude with applause. Lenski's efforts in this paper and in his book *Human Societies* written with Jean Lenski (1974) to direct our attention to the importance of evolutionary theory and, in consequence, to the pulse of history are altogether commendable.[3]

[2] Frank Manuel (1965) reminds us that we have a choice between these two images of history.

[3] The commentary above was addressed to the version of Lenski's paper read at Montreal. In the published version he has changed the number of indicators of directionality (now six in the text and nine more in a footnote), deleted "steady increase in the degree of social inequality," conceded (in the same footnote) that population growth will have to cease, and denied that evolutionary theory requires commitment to the view that "long-term trends must be permanent and eternal."

10

Structure and History

Tom Bottomore

IN THE MID-1960s I happened to be reading a book by Dwight Macdonald, somewhat curiously entitled *Memoirs of a Revolutionist*, and I was struck particularly by a passage in which he recollected his youthful political activities in the following terms (1957:4):

> I remember once walking in the street and suddenly really *seeing* the big heavy buildings in their obstinate actuality and realizing I simply couldn't imagine all this recalcitrant matter transformed by socialism. How would the street *look* when the workers took it over, how would, how could revolution transfigure the miles and miles of stubborn stone?

This perhaps expresses the feeling of many radicals, especially in periods of reaction, when they confront the massive apparatus of regulation and repression embodied in an existing form of society. At the same time it portrays in a dramatic way one important aspect of the opposition between structure and history—and between structural and historical modes of studying social life—namely, the contrast that can be drawn between society conceived as a fixed, stable, and persisting structure and society conceived as a process in which there is continual breakdown and renewal, development and decline, the disappearance of old forms and the creation of new ones.

But of course this image conveys a very simplified and partly misleading notion. Though men have talked about "eternal empires," a "thousand-year Reich," or even "stable democracies," it seems to be the case that social structures are far from possessing the rocklike solidity and indestructability that some writers have attributed to them. Just at the time when I was reading Macdonald's book we were in the midst of a great wave of radical movements which, for a few years at least, made more apparent the fragility of social structures, and in two instances—the mini-revolution in France and the humanist-socialist movement in Czechoslovakia—seemed to be on the verge of accomplishing profound changes in society. And in a broader perspective the whole of the twentieth century thus far can be seen as a particularly agitated historical period, in which wars, revolutions, and counter-revolutions have created and destroyed, and are still creating and destroying, many different types of social structure.

Yet we should not go to the other extreme, and regard social life as a ceaseless, formless flux of events. As sociologists we want to say that every distinct society has a particular relational structure, that it exhibits a certain order, a specific interconnectedness of the diverse elements, or spheres, of social life; and most of us would want to claim further that beyond or behind the unique structures of particular societies there are more general structural "types"—that there are "tribal," "feudal," "capitalist," "socialist," "industrial," and perhaps even "post-industrial" forms of society. The real problem is to formulate a conception of social structure which does justice to these elements of regularity and order in social life, while not neglecting the flow of historical action by individuals and social groups which sustains, recreates, revises, or disrupts this order.

A useful starting point for such a formulation is to be found in the work, now somewhat neglected, that was done by the French sociologist Georges Gurvitch.[1] According to his view social structure is a "permanent process," a "perpetual movement of destructuration and restructuration." This notion has the advantage that it gets us away from the idea of an abstract impersonal social structure which is fixed and given once for all, and makes a place for that aspect of social life which has been strongly emphasized in recent phenomenological sociology, namely, the production and reproduction of society by real human beings living and thinking in a particular milieu. Gurvitch recognized this feature explicitly when he observed, in the course of his analysis, that "social structures are at the same time the producers and the products of cultural activities (*des oeuvres culturelles*).

---

[1] See especially the discussion in Part II, Chapter IV, of his *Traité de Sociologie* (1962).

But this conception of social srtucture as the outcome, at any given time and place, of processes of destructuration and restructuration still leaves open a number of questions which need to be explored further. First, we can ask: What is the source of these processes themselves? Here Gurvitch offered indications of an answer by distinguishing social structure as only *one aspect* of a "total social phenomenon" which also comprises other levels and forms of human sociability. This idea is summed up in the comprehensive definition of social structure which he provided at the end of his discussion, and which I will quote at some length since it is not available in English:

> Every social structure is a precarious equilibrium (which has to be constantly recreated by ever-renewed effort) between a multiplicity of hierarchies incorporated in a total social phenomenon . . . of which it provides only an approximate representation. It is an equilibrium between the specific hierarchies of the various levels of social life, of the manifestations of sociability, of social regulation, of different social times, of mental orientations, of the modes of division of labour and accumulation, and in some circumstances of functional groups, and of social classes and their organizations. This equilibrium is reinforced and consolidated by the models, signs, symbols, habitual social roles, values and ideas —in short, by the works of civilization—which are proper to each social structure. . . . [Gurvitch 1962: 214]

This account allows for the influence of a variety of factors in the processes of destructuration and restructuration, and it may be useful at this point to consider some examples in order to illustrate this kind of historical movement. One obvious source of variation in the social structure is the continual circulation of the membership of a society. Older members die, and new members are born into it. Other changes in its composition may occur as a result of migration, conquest, and other circumstances. It is difficult to conceive that such circulation leaves the social structure entirely untouched, for it seems doubtful, even in the light of our ordinary experience, that incoming members are ever socialized so thoroughly that they precisely re-enact the social life of their predecessors. A more plausible view is that which Karl Mannheim (1956) suggested in his essay on generations, when he wrote that belonging to the same generation or age group endows the individuals concerned "with a common location in the social and historical process," limits them "to a specific range of potential experience, predisposing them for a certain characteristic mode of thought and experience, and a characteristic type of historically relevant action." Mannheim thought that cultural creation, in particular, depended to a large extent upon this flow of new individuals who make a fresh contact with the accumulated heritage, which "always means a changed relationship of distance from the object and a novel approach in assimilating, using, and developing the proffered material." In this case then, by the elaboration of new ideas and values, younger generations clearly play a part in the destructuring and restructuring of society; but they may also do so in other, related ways, by interpreting roles differently and thus eventually bringing about a new organization of roles, by forming new groups which engage in different types of action, and so on. These consequences of the succession of generations have not been very fully studied as yet,[2] but their importance is evident.

Another historical process which may profoundly affect social structure is the growth (or for that matter, though it is a less familiar phenomenon, the decline) of knowledge. This is associated to some extent, as I have indicated, with the succession of generations, but it can also be treated as a partly independent process. Its consequences may be seen in the emergence of new social groups with new values and interests, in the refashioning of some institutions (for example, educational institutions), and in the decay of others (as is suggested by the decline of religion in relation to the progress of science). A good deal of recent sociology has been much concerned with the effects of knowledge upon social structure; on one side, for instance, Daniel Bell has argued that the growing importance of theoretical knowledge is bringing into existence a new form of society which he calls "post-industrial," while from an entirely different perspective Habermas and Wellmer, elaborating one of the distinctive ideas of the Frankfurt School, assert that the pre-eminence in present-day culture of scientific and technological thought (or "instrumental reason") is the principal factor which maintains a system of domination and obstructs human liberation. But this recognition of the independent significance of knowledge is to be found, of course, in much earlier sociological writing; it is tantalizingly present, for example, in parts of Marx's discussion in the *Grundrisse*,

[2] Although they may be referred to in particular cases; for example, in *The Structure of Scientific Revolutions*, Kuhn (1962) notes that a paradigm change in a particular field of science may depend upon the disappearance of an older generation of scientists who are totally committed to the established paradigm.

where the transition from a capitalist to a socialist society is occasionally, and rather vaguely, related to what Marx describes as the progress of the general intellect.

I would like to turn, finally, to a third example of a historical process that has important consequences for the social structure; namely, the development of the division of labour, and more broadly, of social differentiation. This process, which is associated with the growth of knowledge and with the increasing size and density of a society, including the growth of urban centres, produces a variety of effects. On one side, as Pirenne (1914) noted in his study of the social history of capitalism, it brings into existence new social groups which at different stages take a leading role in the economy, develop economic activity in new directions, and initiate modifications of the social structure. In a Marxist view of this process the various groups are seen as sections of a class which eventually establishes its dominance over the whole society and creates its own distinctive structure. On the other side, increasing social differentiation may be regarded as producing a much greater cultural diversity, a greater range of intersecting social circles, as Simmel (1950:409–24) suggested in his account of the metropolis and mental life, or it may be seen, in a related way (by Durkheim, for instance), as fostering a much greater, and perhaps excessive, individualism. In either case, the process of differentiation as a cultural phenomenon is likely to have an impact upon the social structure, modifying the ideas and values which sustain it, engendering new mental orientations, provoking redefinitions of established roles, and creating new interests.

These examples will have shown, I hope, that the idea of social structure as a changing reality produced by processes of destructuration and restructuration, which themselves may arise from nonstructural sources in the totality of social life, can be fruitful in the analysis of actual social situations or courses of events. Nevertheless, some major theoretical problems remain. The process of destruction and recreation of social srtucture, as Gurvitch depicted it, is a continuous one; and this conception takes little account, and provides no analysis, of those breaks in historical continuity, in periods of social revolution, when there is a more comprehensive, fundamental, and abrupt transition from one form of society to another. Clearly we need to distinguish here between partial and total change, between a process of gradual modification and adjustment and a process of rapid transformation. How are we to make this distinction, and in what way can we relate one process to the other? First, it needs to be said that the distinction is not absolutely clear-cut. A major historical movement to a new social structure and form of society is not something that occurs overnight; and in this sense it is perhaps more reasonable to speak of an "age of revolution" rather than a revolution and to recognize that the processes of gradual and rapid change may be closely interwoven and often difficult to disentangle. But this line of argument should not be carried so far as to obliterate the distinction altogether; most of us would want to recognize, in our different ways, the existence of distinct types of society—feudal/capitalist/socialist or nonindustrial/industrial—and of determinate historical periods in which the transition from one to another took place.

Accepting such a position, what can we then say about the causes of, or reasons for, such major upheavals in social life, in relation to the process of building up and breaking down a social srtucture that goes on all the time? One obvious answer would be to say that the accumulation of small and gradual modifications eventually reaches a critical point at which a fundamental change in the social order becomes unavoidable—and here we might think of the growth of towns, the geographical discoveries and the expansion of trade, the development of artisan and commercial groups within the European feudal societies, which brought into existence an alternative form of society (as Marx would say, in the womb of the old society); or again, we could think of the extension of factory production and the growth of the labour movement in nineteenth century capitalist society, which gave rise to a new confrontation between capitalism and socialism as alternative societies. In both these cases the changes in the composition and distribution of the population, in the division of labour, in social roles, and so on were accompanied by cultural changes, the development of the natural sciences and their applications, the formulation of new social doctrines, and revisions of legal, moral, religious and artistic conceptions; and we could, therefore, regard these historical processes as resulting from what J. S. Mill called the "intermixture of laws" or, as I would express it, from the intersection of separate and distinct quasi-causal chains and the accumulation of their effects during certain periods in the history of a society, which produce a dominant tendency toward a major change in the social structure.

But the examples I have given also permit another account of such major social changes. It may be argued that there are certain elements in the totality of social life which have a crucial importance in determining the general form of a society at any time and the occurrence of a transition from one form to another. Marxism obviously makes a claim of this kind, by attributing the main characteristics of a specific type of society to the dominance of a particular class and explaining the major historical transitions by the rise of new classes and their successful struggles to establish themselves as ruling classes. Equally obviously, in spite of its frequently discussed weaknesses and difficulties, more especially in the interpretation of the development of modern capitalism, the Marxist theory has the immense merit of defining with some precision major historical forms of society and of providing, at least in principle, a genuinely explanatory account of the transitions between them. The general Marxist framework of explanation, in terms of the relations between classes and their connections on one side with the system of material production and on the other side with cultural production, can be used in various ways; and it does not in my view commit us to a single philosophy of history or to a rigid conception of the total historical process. One interesting variant of the Marxist approach is to be found, for instance, in Barrington Moore's *Social Origins of Dictatorship and Democracy* (1966), which gives a central importance to the analysis of class relations but is set within a theoretical scheme which identifies the historical transition that is being explored as "modernization," as the passage from pre-industrial to industrial types of society, in democratic and nondemocratic forms, not as the sequence from feudalism via capitalism to socialism.

A second set of problems concerns the extent to which a major transition from one form of society to another might be explained as the consequence of stresses or "contradictions" within a particular social structure itself. Here again the Marxist theory has provided the principal model, although it has proved difficult to give it a general application or to demonstrate in a precise way the necessary effects of the postulated contradictions. On the first of these points I will only remark briefly that while there are frequent references in the Marxist literature to the "contradictions of capitalism," there are few references to the "contradictions of feudalism" (or of other types of society), and the whole notion of "structural contradiction," in its most general form, does not seem to have been very fully worked out.

So far as capitalist society is concerned it has generally been recognized that Marx referred to two main contradictions: that between the capitalist class and the working class and that between the productive forces (i.e. the development of the output of goods or use-values, influenced by technological progress and by the division and coordination of labour) and the relations of production (i.e., the market economy and exchange). The first of these should not perhaps be regarded as a structural contradiction at all since it involves rather the opposition and conflict between actual individuals and social groups (and obviously has analogues in other forms of society), though it is evidently related to structural characteristics of ownership, political authority, and so on.

On the other hand, the second contradiction *is structural* and might be conceived as producing, through its own development, a major change in the form of society. This is the line of argument advanced, for example, by Maurice Godelier (1967) in an essay on "System, Structure and Contradiction in *Capital*," who suggests, first, that Marx saw this contradiction as manifesting itself in the form of periodic economic crises and, second, that it makes necessary the appearance of a socialist economic system:

> . . . the *structure* of socialist relations of production *corresponds* functionally with the conditions of rapid development of the new, gigantic, more and more socialized productive forces created by capitalism. . . . This correspondence is totally *independent* of any *a priori* idea of happiness, of "true liberty," of the essence of man, etc. Marx demonstrates the necessity and superiority of a new mode of production. . . . This value-judgment is not a judgment of "people," it does not demonstrate any progress in "morality," any victory of "ethical principles" in socialist society as against capitalist society. It is a judgment of the "properties" of a structure. . . .

But this argument involves considering, in the first place, Marx's theory of crisis, which is far from being unambiguously expounded or interpreted. It is not at all clear that Marx thought the periodic crises, even worsening crises, would actually bring about the "breakdown" of capitalism; on the contrary he seems to have regarded crises as enabling capitalism to resume, temporarily, its development of the productive forces. The theory of "capitalist breakdown" and the inevitability of socialism has been a subject of intense controversy within Marxism since the end of the nineteenth century, and it has become increasingly difficult to accept as plausible the more deterministic, economistic versions of the theory, such as Godelier adopts.

In any case, it seems to me more accurate, in a comprehensive reading of Marx's analysis of the historical transition from capitalism to socialism, to assign a very much greater importance to the development of classes and class conflict. An interpretation such as Godelier's, in terms of a process determined wholly by structural contradictions without any intervention of human consciousness, distorts radically the sense of Marx's thought on the possibility of socialism, in which the growth of class consciousness and of working class organizations—that is to say, a succession of conscious, historic actions—has a crucial place. We might say, therefore, that in Marx's theory structural contradictions establish only the preconditions, or potentiality, for large-scale social change and that this will be realized only insofar as other, nonstructural processes occur, in the development and organization of new social groups, the formulation of new interests and values, and a general transformation of culture and consciousness.

Thus, there is embodied in this theory a recognition of the distinction between structural elements and historical forces which corresponds closely with the view that I have been putting forward here. Indeed, I have devoted my attention chiefly to the Marxist theory because it is the main source of such a view and presents in the most systematic manner the range of problems and possible ways of analyzing them which arise from the interrelations between social structures and historical movements which together constitute the total social phenomenon. I am not claiming, however, that Marxism provides the only possible model. Certainly, there is a dearth of alternatives, and we often find ourselves confronted by revisions of Marx which do not offer a different and equally comprehensive paradigm, or else by models and approaches which emphasize only one aspect and deal exclusively either with structural relations and the logic of structures or with the seamless and shapeless web of everyday social life. But it remains possible that a structural analysis different from that of Marx could be made, and that it could be related in different ways to historical movements which themselves would be differently evaluated. Only it has still to be done.

So far in this paper I have discussed social structure in what is doubtless a very familiar and traditional way, without reference (except obliquely in talking about Godelier) to the recently fashionable "structuralist" doctrines which have spread from structural linguistics into the field of anthropology, mainly through the work of Lévi-Strauss, and have even taken possession of a small portion of Marxist territory. One reason for not devoting too much attention to this approach is that it has not yet had any considerable impact upon, or made a significant contribution to, sociological thought and inquiry. Nevertheless, it does raise some general questions which deserve to be mentioned briefly.

The first of these is really a minor issue, though it has been inflated by some writers. The new structuralists sometimes claim that the object of their investigation is something "hidden," a "deep structure" which has to be discovered by inference and rational analysis and which is to be distinguished from the "surface structure" or directly observable social relations with which, it is suggested, the earlier theorists of social structure were largely concerned. But this is a great exaggeration. Every serious scholar or scientist is concerned with much more than the immediately visible appearance of things and looks for some inner principle, or system, to which the fleeting empirical phenomena can be related, or in terms of which they can be explained; he constructs models and hypotheses representing this hidden structure. In sociology, from the outset, attempts have been made to construct theoretical models of the different types of society, in which the particular features of a given society are related as "messages" to a "code" which may be conceived as "feudalism," "capitalism," "industrialism," "bureaucratic rationality," and so on. The examples are numerous and inescapable, from Saint-Simon's analysis of the "industrial regime" to Marx's analysis of capitalist production, Max Weber's ideal types, and the theoretical models of Durkheim and Pareto. What the new structuralists have done is simply to write more explicitly and fully (sometimes obsessively) about the construction of models, largely under the influence of a general movement towards a more developed and sophisticated philosophy of the social sciences.

But the idea of a "deep structure" may also be interpreted in another sense, as referring to a basic or universal structure, and this raises more substantial issues. In the work of Lévi-Strauss the intention is to reveal the fundamental properties of all human societies and to relate these to fundamental characteristics of the human mind, thus establishing psychological universals which would presumably constitute the ground for all sociological explanations. This attempt poses a number of problems. In the first place, it has been objected (Leach, 1970:19–20, 97–98) that in the two spheres of social life to which Lévi-Strauss has applied his method—kinship and myth—there are serious discrepancies between his interpretation and the ethnographic evidence. This kind of objection cannot be met by simply dismissing "mere empiricism," for the distinction between code and message requires at least that the messages are consistent in some way with the code and that the code produces specific, identifiable kinds of message.

A second objection is that this method of structural analysis has not been applied seriously to any societies beyond the tribal level, and in particular to modern societies; that it is difficult at present to see how it could be successfully applied to phenomena other than those of kinship and myth; and hence that its claim to reveal universal characteristics of human societies rests as yet upon very slight foundations. Finally, it can be objected that even if the method succeeded eventually in demonstrating the existence of some universal properties of human societies, this would still not answer the greater part of the questions which are of interest to the sociologist; for there is manifestly a great diversity of forms of society and historical changes from one form to another, and it is these phenomena above all that the sociological theorist attempts to explain.

It is clear, in any case, that a Marxist thinker cannot be a "pure" structuralist in the manner of Lévi-Strauss, for the Marxist theory has as its starting point the idea of historically distinct social structures; and the most obvious feature of its method is that it aims to locate all social phenomena in a specific historical context. Marx, it is true, recognized that there might be "abstract characteristics common to all forms of society," including characteristics of the system of production, but he attached much greater importance to the specific historical forms that these characteristics assumed and to the actual sequence of such forms. A Marxist structuralism, then, would have a more limited character; it would be concerned with the basic structure of each particular type of society, not with universal structural properties. And it would be qualified, as I have already indicated, by making actual historical events and processes depend not simply upon the unfolding, unconscious logic of a structure but also upon the conscious value preferences, choices, and decisions of men, both individually and collectively, in the given historical situations that confront them.

The principal contribution of recent structuralist doctrines has been, I think, to reassert the importance of structural analysis and of the development of structural models in the social sciences. Its influence upon sociology, as I have already suggested, has not yet been very marked, but it may well lead us in the future to pay greater attention to the definition and classification of types of society and to the elucidation of the processes of change from one type to another, as well as helping to introduce a greater rigour into such analyses; although we could well have learned these lessons elsewhere. The impact upon Marxism seems to have been rather stronger, especially in the criticism of that Hegelian form of Marxism which relies heavily upon philosophical insights into the historical process and presents its conclusions in sweeping interpretations that largely ignore both structural relationships and the detail of historical events. Here the influence of structuralism may be to encourage Marxist social scientists to analyze in a more precise and thorough way the general structure of capitalist societies, and also of socialist or collectivist forms of society, in the late twentieth century; and to investigate more closely than they have yet done some of those partial structures—for example, the class structure or the political system—which exist within the global structure of a given society.

But if the influence of recent structuralism may be salutary in certain respects, its more extreme versions, especially those in which it is presented as a doctrine about reality rather than a method, do not seem likely to advance sociology along fruitful paths. The idea of a "deep structure" may be developed into a conception of a "basic," "fundamental," or "ultimate" structure, which would be quite misleading in its implication that there is some timeless, inalterable, constraining arrangement of social relations, perhaps psychologically or biologically grounded, which renders all historical inventiveness, experiment, innovation, or retrogression irrelevant to the understanding of social life. In the first place, this view suggests a very sweeping claim to have discovered one, and only one, fundamental structure; and it ignores the point made by Piaget (1970) that advances in scientific understanding have often been made by negating a particular structural model, conceiving alternative models, and going beyond the original model. In any structural analysis we should remain aware of the possibility of other models, recognize the partly arbitrary character of each particular model (along the lines indicated by Max Weber's discussion of the "ideal-type") and experiment with different models. Second, the more extreme structuralist view fails to consider one important feature, namely, the creation and destruction of structures, that I discussed earlier. Piaget also makes this point, though only from one aspect, when he refers to the need to take into account "genetic construction" in the analysis of biological, psychological, and social phenomena. The models that we build can scarcely be adequate if this genetic or historical aspect is excluded.

But is it, then, simply a matter of saying that a structuralist method needs to be complemented by other methods—by historical inquiry, by the study of functions, and so on? Up to a point, this may be acceptable. There is a contrast between structural analysis and historical analysis, in their methods and in their formulation of problems; and they may well complement each other, without becoming merged in some more comprehensive approach. Nevertheless, I am reluctant to agree with those who argue, in the intellectual confusion of the present time, that each and every approach has some value in its own sphere and that we should simply accept their diverse results as parts of the vast unwieldy sum of sociological knowledge. Something more than this is needed; at the least, a more systematic conception of the relation between different methods and, if possible, a better integrated array of methods.

Marx's theory of society I regard as having been a sociological crystallization out of the philosophy of history, in which the analysis of social structure and the interpretation of broad historical movements went hand in hand (as the chapters of *Capital* themselves illustrate so strikingly). We cannot begin again today from Hegel's philosophy of history, any more than we can accept as a basis for our studies all of Marx's propositions about the character of modern societies and the main trends of their development; but I am inclined to think—and many of the new directions in sociological thought tend to support this view—that the working out of an acceptable general theory in sociology may depend more than anything else upon the formulation of a new theory of history. And this might well be an updated, more flexible version of the "economic interpretation of history."

11

Social Structure and Social Change

Seymour Martin Lipset

SOCIOLOGICAL ANALYSIS, particularly in its functionalist form, has been frequently criticized by extramural as well as intramural critics for its emphasis on explaining (and hence supposedly justifying) the stability of social systems, while neglecting the forces making for breakdowns and change. The focus by functionalists on "values" as distinct from "interests" seems to the critics to result in an underestimation of the inherent forces for social conflict among those having different interests.

The very concept of social structure, which is basic to all forms of sociological analysis, also appears to confirm the image of sociological preoccupation with statics in that the term as used by many sociologists refers to stable interrelations among parts of a system, e.g., the relation between a husband and wife or between workers and employers. As Max Weber emphasized, such relationships always involve "at least a minimum of mutual orientation" of the actors involved.

> The "meaning" relevant in this context is always a case of the meaning imputed . . . in a given concrete case, on the average, or in a theoretically formulated pure type. Even in cases of such forms of social organization as a state, church, association, or marriage, the social relationship consists exclusively in the fact that there has existed, exists, or will exist a probability of action in some definite way appropriate to this meaning. . . . A "state," for example, ceases to exist in a sociologically relevant sense whenever there is no longer a probability that certain kinds of meaningfully oriented social action will take place. [Weber, 1968a: 27]

Basically, when we say that groups or systems have an organization or structure we refer to the standardized normative patterns, rights, rules of behavior, and the like. Consequently, at the core of sociological analysis is a concern with norms, with expected patterns of behavior held in the minds of individuals. The sociologist, therefore, is concerned with all that sustains or undermines norms, including deviance, innovation, and rebellion.

This chapter starts with an effort to clarify some misconceptions about the structural-functionalist analysis of social change and suggests a considerable overlap in its approach with that of Marxism. It then deals with the way functionalists have dealt with value-induced tensions, interest-conflict, and coercion in the analysis of stratification as a source of instability and change. Finally, Weber's and Mannheim's concepts of different forms of "rationality" are used to help account for the expression of political conflict in contemporary society.

Functionalist Analysis of Social Change

There can be little doubt that, as contrasted with Marxist analysis, with its predominant interest in change and conflict, functionalist sociology has devoted much more of its theoretical energies to explaining social order—the ways in which society is held together. Yet any paradigm for social analysis that ignores change, revolutions, and breakdowns would be unrealistic, just as is a framework that sees society predominantly in terms of Hobbesian conflict. Sociology has had to deal with both stable patterns and instability. The three main theoretical approaches to social stratification—Marxian, Weberian, and Durkheimian (functionalist)—have sought to account for the existence and persistence of inequality, while assuming that a form of "alienation" is inherent in all stratification systems. To put it in other words, each theory implies that systems of hierarchical inequality contain both stabilizing and destabilizing mechanisms (Lipset, 1970: 157–201). Similarly, it may be noted that studies which focus on conflict have contributed to the analysis of cohesion, as Lewis Coser (1956) has demonstrated. Alvin and Helen Gouldner (1963: 596) have noted the importance of the "line of analysis stemming largely from the pioneering work of . . . Georg Simmel . . . as amplified and developed by Robert Dubin, Lewis Coser, Max

Gluckman, and others" which stresses the integrative consequences of conflict.

Marxist analysis shares with functionalism the assumption that social systems "constantly tend to an equilibrium . . . [which, however,] is exercised, only in the shape of a reaction against the constant upsetting of this equilibrium" (Marx, 1959: 355–56; Bukharin, 1925:72–79). Talcott Parsons also has emphasized the "precarious" nature of the equilibrium and notes "that breakdown of equilibrium is scientifically as important a phenomenon as its preservation . . ." (Parsons, 1961:338).

Pierre Van den Berghe (1963:705), in fact, is led to see the basis for a rapprochement between functionalism and Marxism because "both theories are fundamentally based on an equilibrium model. . . ." There can be little doubt that Robert Friedrichs (1970:262) is correct when he stresses that "Contrary to the impression of most American sociologists, Marx's stance . . . is at a number of points startlingly congruent with system theory as we have come to know it in Western sociology." A number of Marxist scholars have emphasized the same point. Thus Pradeep Bandyopadhyay (1971:19), writing in the oldest Marxist scholarly magazine in the English language, *Science and Society,* observes that "Marxian sociology is often just as concerned [as functionalism] with the analysis of system, structure and equilibrium." Writing from inside the Communist world, Steiner and Schkaratan (1970:3) note that with all its deficiencies from a Marxist point of view, Parsons' "functional system theory is preferable to most of the other mentioned [Western sociological] concepts because it tries to understand the social structure as a social organism."

The Polish sociologist Sztompka (1974:169–70, 177–78) also concludes "that there is a *fundamental affinity* between Marxism and functionalism," as both are variants of the same "systemic-functional methodological approach."

Perhaps the most succinct discussion of Marxism as a variant of structural-functional theories with "good claims to be the first of them" has been presented by E. J. Hobsbawm (1973a:273), the leading Marxist historian in the English-speaking world. Although written in the context of elaborating the differences between Marxism and other forms of functional analysis, Hobsbawm's comments are worth quoting at length since they may serve as a point of comparison with more "academic" approaches.

[Marxism] implies the analysis of the structure and functioning of . . . [social] systems as entities maintaining themselves, in their relations both with the outside environment—non-human and human—and in their internal relationships. Marxism is far from the only structural-functionalist theory of society, though it has good claims to be the first of them, but it differs from most others in two respects. First, it insists on a hierarchy of social phenomena (e.g. "basis" and "superstructure") and second, on the existence within any society of internal tensions ("contradictions") which counteract the tendency of the system to maintain itself as a going concern. (It need hardly be said that the "basis" consists not of technology or economics, but "the totality of these relations of production," i.e. social organization in its broadest sense as applied to a given level of the material forces of production.) . . .

The importance of these peculiarities of Marxism is in the field of history, for it is they which allow it to explain—unlike other structural-functional models of society—why and how societies change and transform themselves; in other words, the facts of social evolution. . . . Human societies must, if they are to persist, be capable of managing themselves successfully, and therefore all existing ones must be functionally adequate; if not they would have become extinct. . . . The point here is not that it is illegitimate to develop separate analysis models for the static and the dynamic, such as Marx's schemas of simple and extended reproduction, but that historical enquiry makes it desirable for these different models to be connected. . . .

The point about . . . internal contradictions is, that they cannot be defined simply as "disfunctional" except on the assumption that stability and permanence are the norm, and change the exception. . . . It is rather that, as is now recognized much more widely than before among social anthropologists, a structural model envisaging only the maintenance of a system is inadequate. It is the simultaneous existence of stabilizing and disruptive elements which such a model must reflect. And it is this which the Marxist model—though not the vulgar-Marxist versions of it—has been based on.

Such a dual (dialectical) model is difficult to set up and use, for in practice the temptation is great to operate it, according to taste or occasion, either as a model of stable functionalism or as one of revolutionary change; whereas the interesting thing about it is, that it is both. It is equally important that internal tensions may sometimes be reabsorbed into a self-stabilizing model by feeding them back as functional stabilizers, and that sometimes they cannot. Class conflict can be regulated through a sort of safety-valve, as in so many riots of urban plebeians in preindustrial cities, or institutionalized as "rituals of rebellion" (to use Max Gluckman's illuminating phrase) or in other ways; but sometimes it cannot. The state will normally legitimize the social order by controlling class conflict within a stable framework of institutions and values, ostensibly standing above and outside them (the remote king as "fountain of justice"), and in doing so perpetuate a society which would otherwise be riven asunder by its internal tensions. This is indeed the classical Marxist theory of its origin and function, as expounded in *Origin of the Family*. Yet there are situations when it loses this function. . . .

Difficult though it may be, social scientists of various kinds . . . have begun to approach the construction of models of equilibria based on tension or conflict, and in so doing draw nearer to Marxism. . . . [Hobsbawm, 1973a:273–74, 276, 277, 279–80, 281]

Most sociologists understand that propensity for change is as much an inherent component of human society as are the stabilizing factors (Moore, 1960; Van den Berghe, 1963; Williams, 1966). Talcott Parsons has pointed out that "there is a certain falsity in the dilemma between 'static' and 'dynamic' emphases. If theory is *good* theory, whichever type of problem it tackles most directly, there is no reason whatever to believe that it will not be equally applicable to the problems of change and to those of process within a stabilized system" (1951:535). More recently, he has emphasized that "The reason for insistence on the importance of keeping the concepts of structure and process and of stability and change analytically distinct is not a predilection in favor of one or the other item in each pair, but in favor of orderly procedure in scientific analysis" (Parsons, 1964:84). Eisenstadt (1964:235) has summarized the position of functionalist sociologists as insisting that change is inherent in all social systems "because of basic problems to which there is no overall continuous solution. These problems include uncertainties of socialization, perennial scarcity of resources relative to individual aspirations, and contrasting types of social organization or principles of social organization (e.g., *Gemeinschaft* vs. *Gesellschaft*) within the society."

If we look at the main approach of functionalist sociology in dealing with social change, it turns out to be the dialectic notion of contradiction. As Robert Merton (1957:122) has pointed out the "key concept bridging the gap between statics and dynamics in functional theory is that of strain, tension, contradiction, or discrepancy between the component elements of social and cultural structure." David Lockwood (1964:250) also notes that "the idea of structural contradictions is central to the functionalist view of change." Gideon Sjoberg (1967:339, 341–42) calls attention to the "presence of 'contradictory functional requirements'—inferred from contradictory structural arrangements" and insists that "a dialectical theory of change, to be meaningful, must be set within a structural-functional framework." Sjoberg notes that Parsons' pattern variable analyses implicitly assume "inherent contradictions within systems." Parsons (1951:522) himself explicitly discusses the "serious strains and inconsistencies in the value-implementation of any complex social system." As Lewis Feuer (1962:191) has noted, "Parsonian 'inconsistencies' have some resemblance to Marxian 'contradictions.' " Gouldner (1959:249) also points up similarities between Marxian and functional analysis, in the way each has applied the "principle of functional reciprocity" to account for change, as a breakdown in "reciprocal functional interchanges" among structures results in contradictions and reduces their ability to persist.[1] "Hence," correctly notes Robert Nisbet (1969:236), "the incessant search by the functionalist for the specific type of strain and stress that tend naturally to inhere in a given social system."

Surprising as it may seem to those who would emphasize the theoretical differences among schools of sociology, functionalist analysis shares with Marxist thought Hegel's insight that all social systems inherently contain contradictions, the resolution of which press for social change.[2] As Demerath (1967: 515) has stressed, the gap between functionalist and Marxist analysis of change "is not as wide as is customarily assumed. . . ." The British radical sociologist, Dick Atkinson (1971: 174), also emphasizes that "even in the field of social change Parsons, Marx, and those whom their interpretations influence . . . show crucial similarities" (Atkinson, 1971: 124). He points out that the main variation in the structural analyses of the two men flows from differing initial assumptions concerning human nature. "Marx felt it was basically cooperative, rational, self-controlling. Parsons, following Hobbes and Durkheim, felt it was in competition with itself and implied conflict in social relationships

---

[1] "The principle of reciprocity enters Marx's theoretical analysis not in peripheral but in central ways; it is most importantly implicated in his concept of 'exploitation'; . . . If one puts aside Marx's moral condemnations of exploitation and considers only its sociological substance, it is clear that it refers to a breakdown in reciprocal functionality" (Gouldner, 1959:267).

[2] "The notion of intrinsic contradictions within the social order has been the main-stay of Marxist types of explanations . . ." (Coser, 1967:141).

generally. . . . Parsons and Marx were consequently faced with a similar problem. For Marx, the question became: how is conflict possible when man is rational and cooperative? For Parsons, the question became: how is order possible when man is basically destructive and competitive?" (Atkinson, 1971:109)

A similar point has been made by the French-Canadian sociologist Guy Rocher, who stresses that Parsons has devoted so much of his writing to an analysis of the sources of social stability because of his "perpetual astonishment at the existence of *order,*" an orientation which resulted in his wrongly gaining a "reputation as a social conservative interested only in maintaining the *status quo.* . . . [His critics] *forget that for Parsons, order appears less as a fact than as a problem.* . . . What is most surprising is not that there are conflicts and struggles, but that in spite of the sources of breakdown, some order persists. . . . [For Parsons] order cannot be taken for granted, but must be explained" (Rocher, 1972: 51–52).

Atkinson (1971:109), who focuses on the logical similarity in Marx's and Parsons' analyses of conflict and order, concludes that "It should not be a source of surprise that each man arrived at similar solutions. . . ." He emphasizes that both rejected the Kantian and liberal concept of "free and rational choice." Each stressed the ways in which the objective tensions associated with the "actor's structural position (for Parsons the 'status' position, for Marx his class position. . . .)" may produce normative conflict. The essential difference between them is that the "norms" which for Parsons are "placed between the actor and the goal internalized within the actor are predominantly placed by Marx in the external situation itself . . ." (*Ibid.:*112). But Marx was forced "to begin to offer an explicitly normative explanation at the theoretical level when action is not based on full awareness or when rationality is seen as constraint." In seeking to explain "false consciousness," Marx poses a "rigid and overtly normative structure between the actor and his false, irrational values as a means of explaining those 'false' values and rational actions" (*Ibid.:*112). Atkinson concludes that Parsons reaches "exactly the same methodological position which Marx arrives at with the crucial aid of 'false-consciousness.' For Parsons, empirical deviance from the theoretically expected is to be explained in terms of a theoretical concept of 'deviance,' " seen as a consequence of exposure to conflicting sets of normative "expectations such that complete fulfillment of both is realistically impossible." (*Ibid.:*120; Parsons, 1951:280). On the most universal level, as W. E. Moore

(1963:20) has emphasized, for the functionalist such pressures for change lie "in a universal feature of human societies which in its most general form may be stated as the lack of close correspondence between the 'ideal' and the 'actual'. . . ."

It should be noted that while Parsons emphasizes the impact of normative contradictions which help produce "a set of alienative motivational orientations," the source of the breakdown in support for the dominant ideologies lies in structural changes which upset a given equilibrium. Thus to "account for the existence of widespread alienative motivation is scarcely a problem in any society which has been undergoing a very rapid process of industrialization" (Parsons, 1951:523). And in discussing the dynamics of social change in *The Social System*, Parsons begins with an analysis of the "repercussions of the changes introduced by scientific and technological advance," first with respect to their effect on the creation of new roles and obsolescence of old ones, and second with concomitant changes in the character of instrumental organizations. Both changes produce large-scale alienation, as well as defensive behavior by those with "a strong vested interest in their ways of doing things." Such changes in turn may be linked to shifts in cultural and ideological expressions (Parsons, 1951:505–20).

In tandem with a Marxist approach, Parsons notes that to analyze the way in which such technological changes "will affect the total society over a long period . . . , the *only* way to proceed outside of sheer 'intuition' is to attempt to trace meticulously the repercussions of the changes through the various parts of the system, and back again to the locus of the original changes." Any given society responds by adjustments designed to maintain "a relatively precarious state of moving equilibrium." But this equilibrium

> . . . can break down in either of two main directions, both of which if they occur should be interpreted as consequences of the fact that strain in certain parts of the system has mounted to points which cannot be coped with short of major alterations of the moving equilibrium state. One of these centers on the mounting resistance of the "vested interests" elements to further change, so that the essential process itself is finally choked off and the society stabilized on a traditionalistic basis. This, fundamentally, seems to be what happened in the society of later Mediterranean antiquity partly at least under the influence of Christianity. The other direction is that of mounting strain in "progressive" sectors so that a radically alienated revolutionary movement develops.

Parsons (1951:505–20) notes that both processes "are continually occurring in sub-sectors of our society." As Devereux (1961:33–34) emphasizes, Parsons' concern with equilibrium reflects "the view that society represents a veritable powder keg of conflicting forces. . . . That any sort of equilibrium is achieved at all, as it evidently is in most societies, most of the time, thus represents for Parsons something both of miracle and challenge."

Amitai Etzioni has effectively summarized the normative functionalist analysis of change:

> A societal structure is, thus, to be viewed . . . as a temporary form reflecting the past actions of conforming and deviating member-units and internal and external elites, and as a base line for future interaction among these actors within the environmental limits. Societal structures are expected to be continually restructured or transformed; it is an exception rather than the rule when the relations among the units, supra-units, and elites are so balanced as to cause a forward and backward "swinging" of a pattern as if it were the focal point of a stable equilibrium. This concept of structure assumes that *the extent and intensity of deviance will be greater, the less the patterns of the distributive structure and the political organization parallel the patterns prescribed by the symbolic-normative system.* Moreover, even when this parallelism is maximal, a built-in strain is to be expected; differences between the symbolic-normative and asset facets of society are never completely resolved because the symbolic-normative systems tend to be relatively more integrated than the asset bases. This is the case because societal assets must provide for a multitude of partially incompatible functions, and because non-symbolic elements are more scarce than symbols. Additional societal strains are generated by differences in the distributive patterns of the various kinds of assets which create stratification imbalances. [Etzioni, 1968: 329; italics supplied]

The convergence on structural contradiction as a main source of destabilization and social change does not, of course, explain the breakdown of specific systems or catalytic events which seemingly gives rise to drastic or revolutionary changes. Most social analysts from Marx to Parsons have pointed to the fact that social systems are able to endure chronic serious contradictions or sources of strain without breaking down or making major adjustments to alleviate the tension. The identification of structural contradictions no more permits an analyst to predict the direction and ultimate outcome of the changes which may occur than does the existence of large-scale poverty, racism, or other form of exploitation indicate that a mass protest movement will occur. Tension-ridden social systems may collapse and retrogress, as occurred with the Roman Empire; they may provide the motivation for support for successful revolutionary movements; they may readjust their internal relations to reduce the strain without experiencing fundamental systemic change; or they may simply continue to go on without any significant adjustments because of given power relationships or absence of bases for alternative structural relationships. Marx, for example, emphasized that "no social order ever perishes before all the productive forces for which there is room in it have developed . . ." (Marx, 1936a:356–57). And Trotsky argued, in seeking to explain the reemergence of a sharply stratified society in the Soviet Union, that Marx had anticipated that efforts to create socialism, except under conditions of extremely high productivity in which all could enjoy material wealth and total freedom from disagreeable work, would break down. He quoted Marx to the effect that "A development of the productive forces is the absolutely necessary practical premise [of Communism], because without it want is generalized, and with want the struggle for necessities begins again, and that means that all the old crap must revive" (Trotsky, 1937:56).

Specific major structural changes and successful social movements usually occur as a result of the cumulation of a variety of developments or events, the occurrence of which may in some cases even be fortuitous (MacIver, 1942: 251–65; Myrdal, 1944: 1065–70; Etzioni, 1968: 387–427). Parsons has emphasized the need to distinguish "sources of change which are external to the society from those which are internal" (Rocher, 1972:98). In many cases, the decisive catalytic thrust which made possible or required system change was provided by external forces or events. The barbarian invasions of the Roman Empire which undermined that society occurred, according to the quantitative studies of Frederick Teggart, as a response to climatic changes in central Asia which gave rise to migrations and invasion of Europe (Teggart: 1939).

The most comprehensive effort to codify the important determinants of collective efforts at social change has been formulated by Neil Smelser (1962). These include: "(1) Structural conduciveness . . . ; (2) Structural strain . . . ; (3) Growth and spread of generalized belief . . . ; (4) Precipitating factors . . . ; (5) Mobilization

of participants for action, . . . ; (6) The operation of social control
. . ." (Smelser, 1962:15–18). Although Smelser is a functionalist
theorist and a student and disciple of Talcott Parsons, it should be
noted that all six of the factors he classified may be found scattered
in the writings of Marx and Lenin in their discussions of the conditions for the emergence of revolutionary movements.

The methodological convergence in the analyses of social change
in various theoretical approaches is not new. Eisenstadt (1973b:7)
emphasizes that the "founding fathers," such as Durkheim and
Weber, shared with Marx and his followers an insistence that social
systems are characterized by "contradictions." "[B]oth Durkheim
and Weber saw many contradictions inherent in the very nature of
the human condition in society in general, and saw them articulated
with increasing sharpness in the developments of the modern order
in particular." He argues that the "bourgeois" fathers were far less
"optimistic" than Marx and other chiliastic revolutionary thinkers
about the possibility of ever ending the processes of basic social
change, i.e., tensions and contradictions, for they "stressed the
ubiquity and continuity of tensions between the creative and re-
strictive aspects of modern life, of potential contradictions between
liberty and rationality, between these on the one hand and justice
and solidarity on the other."[3]

In pointing out the similarities in varying sociological approaches
to change, social structure, and inequality, it is not my intention to
argue that the theoretical (or political) differences are minimal, or to
deny that varying theoretical emphases result in quite disparate
analyses of comparable phenomena. As I put it in an earlier discussion of stratification theories:

> The interest of students of social change in why men rebel, why
> they want change, has led to an emphasis within the tradition of
> class analysis on the way in which inequality frustrates men and
> leads them to reject the *status quo*. Functional analysts, on the
> other hand, are much more concerned with how the social system
> gets men to conform, to seek and remain in various positions in
> society, including ones that are poorly rewarded or require oner-
> ous work. The former, in other words, often ask how systems of

[3] Marx and Engels, on the other hand, believed in the possibility of the emergence of a social system without contradictions. Engels predicted that "there
would be an end to all ideology," and politically relevant conflict (Engels,
1957: 263). As Lewis Feuer pointed out: "The obsolescence of ethical ideology
is a corollary of historical materialism as applied to the superstructure of a
socialist society" (Feuer, 1942: 269).

stratification are undermined; the latter seek to know how and why they are held together.

. . . [These] two polar traditions of social thought . . . do not, of course, occur in pure form in real life. Marx, the foremost student of class and social change and the advocate, par excellence, of instability and revolution, was also aware of the functional aspects of social stratification. Many of his writings attempt to show how ideologies, value and patterns of behavior—all at different class levels—serve to maintain the stability of the social order. In fact, Marxian analysis is replete with functional propositions.

The functionalists, on the other hand, are of course aware that change and conflict occur and that men not only accept but also reject the given stratification system. Thus . . . the most influential stimulator of functional thought in sociology, Emile Durkheim, sought to show the way in which strains in value emphases within the same social system lead individuals and groups to reject the dominant value system and to deviate from expected forms of behavior.[4] [Lipset, 1970:161–62]

As a final note on the congruence among the varying approaches to social change between normative functionalism and structural Marxism, it is important to recognize that functionalists from Durkheim to Parsons have shared with Marxism a commitment to an evolutionary approach (Van den Berghe, 1963; Parsons, 1966; Nisbet, 1970: 193–96). At the heart of the analysis of the former has been an emphasis on structural differentiation as the source of the change. For Durkheim "the focus of structural differentiation is economic organization." As Robert Bellah (1964:90) has summarized Durkheim's analysis, "as size and dynamic density increase, competition between unspecialized units engaged in the same activities in-

---

[4] See also Coser's (1967:138) statement: "Marx's stress on the function of social interests in the historical process can serve as a counter argument to those who claim a functional orientation precludes concern with power and social change." Gouldner (1959:269–70) also has emphasized that Marx and Engels, as well as latter-day Marxists such as Bukharin, "were deeply concerned about system analysis." Conversely, Durkheim stressed that the "exploitation . . . rendered possible by power discrepancies . . . conduces to a sense of injustice which has socially unstabilizing consequences" and to end these he advocated the abolition of the "institution of inheritance . . . ." (Gouldner, 1973a:386).

Charles Loomis (1967:876) effectively pointed up some of the similarities in approach when he presented a number of graduate students in sociology with a number of quotations from Marx dealing with system and function and asked them to choose from a list of names the author of the quotations. Almost all of them selected Parsons, not Marx.

creases. Structural differentiation is then seen as an adaptive response to this increased competition. . . ."[5]

Parsons, of course, though also stressing structural differentiation, does not share the emphasis of Durkheim and Marx on the primary role of any one factor such as the economic in social change, but as Gouldner (1959: 265–66) has argued, the

> . . . divergence between [the] analytic models . . . is not so radical as is often assumed. . . . [I]t may be that the distinction between social theories has not so much been between system and factor theories, but rather between overt and covert factor theories, or between implicit and explicit system theories. . . . It may be . . . that earlier functionalists neglected the problem of weighting system parts, because they lacked the mathematical tools requisite for a rigorous resolution of the problem. Today, however, mathematical and statistical developments may be on the verge of making this possible. . . .

To illustrate the way in which an emphasis on the normative concept of social structure has resulted in an understanding of the way in which normative "contradictions" facilitate social change, I would like to discuss two examples, first, social stratification and second, different systems of rationality, *Wertrationalität* and *Zweckrationalität*. The first of these topics deals briefly with the factor which has been traditionally emphasized by all major schools of sociological thought to interpret conflict and protest in industrial society, while the second treats in more detail recent efforts to account for the use of new sources of tension and rebellion in "postindustrial" society.

Social Stratification

The assumptions about value consensus with respect to stratification imply that hierarchical systems are inherently contradictory, that their very existence produces the conditions for deviance and rebellion, for both moderate and revolutionary social change. The conviction that a stratified social structure is inherently unstable may, of course, be found in the great precursor of modern French functionalist thought from whom Durkheim drew many of his in-

[5] For a general discussion of Durkheim's theory of "structural differentiation," see also Schnore (1958: 620–34). Rüschemeyer (1974) has recently stressed the links between Marx's and Durkheim's analyses of differentiation.

sights, Alexis de Tocqueville. Though insisting on the necessity of inequality and of hereditary privilege, as conditions for liberty and social leadership, Tocqueville also concluded that endemic to stratification was rejection of inequality by the underprivileged. "There is, in fact, a manly and lawful passion for equality that incites men to wish all to be powerful and honored . . . which impels the weak to attempt to lower the powerful to their own level and reduces men to prefer equality in slavery to inequality with freedom." Tocqueville, 1954I:56; Nisbet, 1966: 183–95; Benson, 1973:751-53). Tocqueville (1954II:266) went on to generalize: "Remove the secondary causes that have produced the great convulsions of the world and you will almost always find the principle of inequality at the bottom."[6]

Tocqueville's emphasis on the omnipresence of both inequality and rejection of hierarchy points up the sources of the inherent "contradictions" in the values of complex social systems. Thus, all social systems lay down assorted ends or goals, as part of the cultural structure, and a set of socially structured means or prescribed behaviors that may be legitimately used to attain them, which are often rooted in institutions (Merton, 1957:162–64; Parsons *et al.,* 1953:67–78; Durkheim, 1951:246–57).[7]

Most functionalists assume that differentiated rewards are assigned to various positions to encourage people to seek to achieve the diverse positions necessary in a complex society (Davis and Moore, 1945:242–49). Given this assumption, any system of stratification requires a general set of ideological justifications, which explain and propagate the system of inequality, to induce men to accept as legitimate the fact of their own inequality. But it is logically doubtful, as Tocqueville argued, that the socially inferior can ever totally accept the propriety of their position. The generally accepted sociological assumption that individuals seek to maximize the esteem in which they are held implies that those who are in low-valued positions experience such disesteem as punishment. Consequently, there is an inherent tension (contradiction) between the need to maximize esteem and the requirements of a stratified system.

Different societies, of course, have varied in the severity of such tensions. Durkheim assumed that they were less in preindustrial

---

[6] See also Zeitlin (1971: 40–42).

[7] "[C]ultural structure may be defined as that organized set of normative values governing behavior which is common to members of a designated society or group" (Merton, 1957: 162–64).

societies with overt ascriptive positions. These systems prescribed varying sets of goals for different strata, so that those belonging to ascribed lower strata could obtain a sense of self-respect within their own ascriptive group. In many cultures, transvaluational religious beliefs which identify poverty with virtue and reward in the hereafter appear to have relieved some of these tensions. Societies, however, which justify inequality on meritocratic grounds and which encourage people to seek to "get ahead" serve to exacerbate the contradiction between the values of hierarchy and self-esteem.

Durkheim's account of what Merton (1957:123) has called the "seeming contradictions between cultural goals and socially restricted access to these goals" is a key aspect of the theory of social change and stratification that is inherent in functionalism. Since no complex society can achieve a complete balance between its emphases on ends and means, stratification systems always generate pressure on individuals and strata to deviate systematically from the cultural prescriptions of the society.

The relations between approved goals and prescribed means, as analyzed by Merton and others, create a variety of strains fostering change. Merton's analysis of these social and individual tensions emphasizes that such tensions may produce rebellion, which may be viewed as an adaptive response called for when the existing social system is seen as an obstacle to the satisfaction of needs and wants. In means-ends terms, rebellion involves the establishment of a new set of goals which are attractive to those who feel themselves "outcasts" in the existing system. Although rebellion is not a generalized response and is often limited to relatively powerless groups, it may also take a political form in an effort to overthrow the existing society and replace it with one that stresses other values.

Emphasis on these and allied sources of rebellion advances the study of alienation and prospective lower-class rebellion beyond concern with objective social inferiority and economic exploitation. The study of values in this context helps to explain the phenomenon that relatively affluent strata whose position is improving objectively often provide the mass base for widespread rebellion (Durkheim, 1951:254). A well-to-do group whose aspiration levels have been raised sharply as a result of rapid urbanization, greater education, access to international media, recent involvement in industry, and exposure to the blandishments of unions and leftist political parties may experience the phenomenon of unlimited "rising expectations" and hence feel dissatisfied and prove receptive to a new myth which locates "the source of large-scale frustrations in the social structure and . . . portray[s] an alternative structure" that would be more satisfying (Merton, 1957:156).[8]

As noted, functionalist sociology stresses the way in which stratification fulfills certain needs of complex social systems and so becomes one of the principal stabilizing mechanisms of complex societies. Like the Marxist and Weberian forms of analysis, however, it points to ways in which the demands of a stratification system press men to act against their own interests and alienate them from autonomous choice. Moreover, the focus in functionalism on means-ends relationships reveals the conflict-generating potential of stratification systems, in which goals are inherently scarce resources. Hence, functional analysis, like Marxism, locates sources of consensus and cleavage in the hierarchical structures of society.

In stressing the relevance of the Durkheim-Merton emphasis on the congruity or discongruity of the relationship between means and ends in producing conformity or "aberrant behavior" it is not my intention to suggest that the ultimate stability or instability of a society is primarily a function of the degree of satisfaction or frustration engendered. Reinhard Bendix and I (1953:13) noted the fallacy of such assumptions a number of years ago in our introduction to the first edition of *Class, Status and Power:*

> [T]he stability or instability of a society cannot be judged by the degree of satisfaction or frustration which it engenders. The fact that European feudalism or the Indian caste system have persisted for centuries does not prove that a majority of the people living in these societies were adjusted to their position within them. In feudal Europe there were many peasants who ran away to join so-called robber bands, and who revolted against the local manorial lords. The prolonged existence of feudalism may not have been due primarily to the stability of this social structure, to the degree of satisfaction with which each individual enjoyed his privileges and bore his burdens, but rather to the fact that the iso-

---

[8] Or as Parsons (1951:513–14) put it: "Frustration, we must remember, is always *relative* to expectations. It is this circumstance which serves to explain why movements for radical change have so often centered on relatively privileged groups who by common sense standards are 'well off.' " Marx also advanced a theory of "relative deprivation" in various of his writings, noting, for example, that increases in wages of workers may be followed by greater discontent on their part. "The material position of the laborer has improved, but at the cost of his social position. The social gulf that separates him from the capitalist has widened," since capital normally accumulates more rapidly than wages rise (Marx, 1936b: 273) .

lated peasant-rebels had no means of organizing a successful revolution. A society is characterized not only by the facts of social
stratification, but also by a system of power-relations between conflicting social groups. Hence the fact that a dominant social group
possesses most of the power in a society may be a more important
reason for the apparent stability of that society than the fact that
people accept privileges and burdens which are theirs by virtue of
their social and economic position.

Of course, "power" refers to more than control over the instrumentalities of coercion. It refers to all the means by which an
individual or a group of individuals can exert a controlling influence over others. Perhaps one of the most effective means of exercising power has been the doctrine that the poor are worthy and
will be rewarded in the next world. At times this doctrine probably helped to stabilize the society by making it psychologically
easier to be content with a low social position. At such times it
would have been plausible to conclude that the society was "in
equilibrium" and that each individual was more or less content
to play his "social role." But the same doctrine has also been used
to challenge the established order by claiming that the poor were
more virtuous and deserving than the rich, that poverty made
legitimate the protest of the poor against the prevailing order.
The fact that the same doctrine could be made to serve such conflicting purposes illustrates that the study of stratification cannot
be safely premised on any theory which rests on the assumption
either of stability or of change.

Our emphasis on the role of power or coercion is congruent with
that of exponents of normative functionalism. Thus, as Gouldner
notes, Durkheim argued that the system of stratification "offends the
moral expectations of people in contemporary cultures, because it
constrains to an unequal exchange of goods and services. The exploitation thus rendered possible by notable power disparities
among the contracting parties conduces to a sense of injustice which
has socially unstabilizing consequences. Thus, almost surprisingly,
both Durkheim and Marx converge on a concept of 'exploitation' as
a contributant to current social instabilities" (Gouldner, 1973a:386).

Less surprising, since he drew on both Durkheim and Marx, Talcott Parsons' analysis also converges with theirs. In his earliest major
work, *The Structure of Social Action,* Parsons (1937:658) criticized
"the great majority of liberal economists," arguing that "it must be
sharply emphasized that considerations of the logical simplicity of a

system of economic theory that excludes coercion should not be allowed to obscure the enormous empirical importance of coercion in actual economic life." He noted that "Weber is not subject to this criticism. He had a deep, almost tragic, consciousness of the importance of coercion in human affairs." A decade later, in discussing "Social Classes and Class Conflict," Parsons not only stressed the "arrogance" of the successful and the "resentment" of the "losers" in the stratification system, but reiterated, first, that a system of hierarchical "organization means that there must be an important part played by discipline and authority," second, that there is "a general tendency for the strategically placed, the powerful, to exploit the weaker or less favorably placed," and third, that there "will tend to be a differentiation of attitude systems, of ideologies, and of definitions of the situation to a greater or less degree around the structure of the occupational system and of other components of the instrumental complex, such as the relation to markets and profits. . . . A leading modern example is the opposing ideologies of business and labor groups in modern industrial society" (Parsons, 1954: 330–31).[9] And more recently, in discussing "political power" on an abstract level, Parsons (1969:353) emphasized that an understanding of both the consensual and the coercive aspects are essential to an analysis of the role of power. He treats power not only as involving legitimation, but notes that the capacity of the system "to secure performance of binding obligations . . ." implies that "in case of recalcitrance there is a presumption of enforcement by negative situational sanctions . . ." (*Ibid.:* 361).

> Legitimation is, therefore, in power systems, the factor that is parallel to confidence in mutual acceptability and stability of the monetary unit in monetary systems.
>
> . . . [Q]uestioning the legitimacy of the possession and use of power leads to resort to progressively more "secure" means of gaining compliance. These must be progressively more effective "intrinsically." . . . Furthermore, insofar as they are intrinsically effective, legitimacy becomes a progressively less important factor

[9] In commenting on this analysis, the radical British sociologist Dick Atkinson (1971:24) notes Parsons' emphasis on the inevitability of interest conflicts inherent in role differentiation in complex society as part of his "continuing concern for aspects of conflict." The French leftist sociologist, Alain Touraine, (1971:76) has also written approvingly of this discussion of Parsons and stresses that he has been "wrongly accused of being only interested in consensus and social equilibrium. . . ."

of their effectiveness—at the end of this series lies resort, first to various types of coercion, eventually to the use of force as the most intrinsically effective of all means of coercion.[10] [Parsons, 1969: 362]

Value Rationality

The functionalist analysis of the tensions inherent in systems of stratification assumes a fundamental "contradiction" posed by the scarcity of means available for the attainment of generally accepted goals, a dilemma present in many areas of life. In a different context, Max Weber (1968a:24–26; 1947:115–18; 1968b:6–7) and Karl Mannheim (1950:51–60) posited the existence of a basic social tension between the emphasis on one or the other, found in the conflicting implications for action of the two forms of rationality, *Wertrationalität,* or "substantive rationality," involving conscious judgments about goals or ultimate values and *Zweckrationalität,* or "functional rationality," referring to means "to attain the given goal." Societies, in other words, require ultimate values which are believed in, independently of prospects for actual achievement. But they also require people to be instrumentally rational, that is, to choose effective means for attaining given ends.

The tension between the two sorts of rationality is built into the whole structure of social action. A society cannot maintain its pursuit of rational means-ends relationships, except in the context of a set of absolute values which anchor and direct the search for means. Yet a passionate commitment to absolute ends must break down. Weber traced the secularization of Protestantism, the rise of *Zweckrationalität* in the West, to its tremendous commitment to certain absolute values. Trying, as Calvinism did, to see every action as a means to some higher end required tremendous zeal which had to recede (Swidler, 1973:38–41). But the routinization of charismatic *Wertrationalität* ultimately leaves a gap in the motivational system which legitimates functionally rational action and encourages the emergence of new forms of charismatic rationality.

---

[10] Jessup (1972:42) notes that Parsons (1961a:30–79) "seems to recognize that values and stratification are maintained primarily by a dominant class in arguing that differentiation and adaptive upgrading make it increasingly difficult to maintain a class system in which one class is excluded from full membership in the societal community by another, superior class."

As Anthony Giddens (1971:184) indicates, Weber's analysis of the basic contradictions of capitalist society rests on a similar logic. Modern capitalism emphasizes the "values of efficiency or productivity" which, however, "contravene some of the most distinctive values of western civilization, such as those which emphasize the importance of individual creativity and autonomy of action. . . . In this sense, western society can be said to be founded upon an intrinsic antimony between formal [functional] and substantive rationality which, according to Weber's analysis of modern capitalism, cannot be resolved."

Talcott Parsons (1937:643, 653), building on Weber's analysis, noted the inherent conflict between those committed to a "plurality of legitimate directions of value achievement," hence seeing action as determined by "interest," and those who orient "action to a single specific value, e.g., salvation, which is absolute in the sense that all other potential values become significant only as means and conditions, possible aids or hindrances, to the attainment of this central value." Derivative from the former, *Zweckrationalität* is an emphasis on the "ethics of responsibility," the recognition that the means used shape the ends which are achieved. Conversely, an emphasis on *Wertrationalität* is more likely to result in a commitment to the "ethics of absolute ends" (Weber, 1946b:117–22). The two orientations in their pure form, as Weber (1946b:120) indicated, are inherent in the structural situations of different groups whose outlooks are "fundamentally differing and irreconcilably opposed" to each other.

These varying *Weltanschauungen* have been used since the time of the ancient Greeks to account for conflict between the generations concerning the pace of directed social change. Thus Aristotle noted that youth are more disposed to emphasize what would later be called *Wertrationalität* and the "ethic of absolute ends," while older age cohorts are disposed to *Zweckrationalität* and "the ethic of responsibility." As he (1941:1404) put it 2500 years ago: "[Youth] have exalted notions, because they have not yet been humbled by life or learnt its necessary limitations; moreover their hopeful disposition makes them think themselves equal to great things—and that means having exalted notions. They would always rather do noble deeds than useful ones; their lives are regulated more by moral feeling than by reasoning. . . ."

These distinctions have continued to be cited by contemporary analysts of politics to explain the differential age base of "extreme" and "moderate" political forces, i.e., the fact that movements of the extreme right and left draw heavily from the young. As I noted in an earlier publication:

> It is the essence of extremism in politics to eliminate restraint, to conceptualize the struggle as one between absolute good versus absolute evil, thereby justifying the use of any tactics. . . . And the greater propensity of youth for the "ethic of absolute ends" as distinct from the "ethic of responsibility" . . . is another way of saying that youth politics are more likely to reflect impulse than restraint. It also is another way of indicating that youth are more prone to favor change, reform, radicalism of all varieties, than older people. Youth-based movements, therefore, whether of the left or right, should have major elements in common. [Lipset, 1972c:120]

The assumption that youth, particularly those defined in a marginal status as students or adolescents, between childhood and adulthood, will be disposed toward *Wertrationalität* has seemingly been confirmed by their disproportionate participation in revolutionary movements, from Luther's religious rebellion through the events leading up to the American Revolution, the Revolution of 1848, the assorted French and Russian revolutionary movements of the nineteenth century, others in various colonial and less developed nations, and in the fascist movements of the 1920s and 1930s. These clearly indicate that much of what we see today in the expressive styles of radical student activists is not new but is rooted in the processes Aristotle described (Lipset, 1967:3–53; Lipset and Altbach, 1969:v–vii; Lipset, 1972c:23–30, 127).

Various developments in the contemporary world may be analyzed in terms of shifting commitments to the two forms of rationality. Writing at the end of the 1920s, Karl Mannheim (1949:222–36) anticipated that existent political and intellectual trends would result in a decline within industrial society of the ideological and utopian impulses (*Wertrationalität*), as total doctrines (*Weltanschauungen*) were reduced to partial pragmatic ones (*Zweckrationalität*). In part such changes resulted from the fact that as a movement associated with utopian doctrines gains governmental or state power, "the more it gives up its original utopian impulses and with it its broad perspective . . ." (Ibid: 225).[11] But he (231) also noted that

---

[11] Max Weber (1946b:104–11), drawing on the work of the Russian scholar Moisei Ostrogorski, had much earlier noted that a blurring of ideological differences is inherent in the situation of political parties operating under

the impulses of the lower "strata whose aspirations are not yet ful-
filled, and who are striving towards communism and socialism"
would decline if society is able "to reach a somewhat superior form
of industrialism, which will be sufficiently elastic and which will give
the lower strata a degree of relative well-being. . . . (From this
point of view it makes no difference whether this superior form of
social organization of industrialism, through the arrival at a position
of power on the part of the lower strata, will eventuate in a capitalism which is sufficiently elastic to insure their relative well-being,
or whether this capitalism will first be transformed into communism.)" Such developments in the political arena, Mannheim argued,
were necessarily paralleled in various forms of intellectual life:

> This process of the complete destruction of all spiritual elements,
> the utopian as well as the ideological, has its parallel in the most
> recent trends of modern life, and in their corresponding ten-
> dencies in the realm of art. Must we not regard the disappearance
> of humanitarianism from art, the emergence of a "matter of fact-
> ness" (*Sachlichkeit*) in sexual life, art, and architecture, and the
> expression of the natural impulses in sports—must all these not be
> interpreted as symptomatic of the increasing regression of the
> ideological and utopian elements from the mentality of the strata
> which are coming to dominate the present situation? Must not the
> gradual reduction of politics to economics towards which there is
> at least a discernible tendency, the conscious rejection of the past
> and of the notion of historical time, the conscious brushing aside
> of every "cultural ideal," be interpreted as a disappearance of
> every form of utopianism from the political arena as well? [*Ibid.*:
> 230]

The tendencies Mannheim noted in 1929 seemed to become
realities in the two decades following World War II when the belief
in diverse forms of charismatic *Wertrationalität* in the religious,
economic, and political orders broke down in part because the various ideologies and utopias became routinized operational realities.
Protestantism and Catholicism, fascism, capitalism, communism, and
social democracy all lost their power to inspire men to work hard, to
live morally, or to change the world. Their ideological legitimization

----

conditions of universal suffrage. In a letter to Robert Michels in 1906 discussing socialism, Weber (Roth, 1963:252) predicted that although the party
still had "something like a *Weltanschauung*," the fact that it accepted the
logic of a political democracy would lead to a decline in its ideological commitments in favor of a more pragmatic orientation.

was expressed increasingly in secular *Zweckrationalität* terms, i.e., as efficient operating social orders or representatives of interest groups. Noting these developments, a number of social analysts of varying persuasions—T. H. Marshall (1950), Raymond Aron (1955), Edward Shils (1955), Otto Kirchheimer (1957), Herbert Marcuse (1964:xii–xiii), Daniel Bell (1960), Kenneth Keniston (1960), Judith Shklar (1957), Stein Rokkan (1958), Lewis Feuer (1955:126–30), David Riesman (1959:20), myself (Lipset, 1960:403–17), and others—wrote, implicitly or explicitly, of the decline or end of ideology, essentially reiterating Mannheim's analysis of the inherent shift from total to partial ideological appeals. The different forces and societies defended themselves in more moderate *Zweckrationalität* terms. Most of these analysts noted that intense ideological commitments, charismatic *Wertrationalität*, remained potent in the Third World, whose poverty as compared to the wealth of other nations forced awareness of massive problems of radical reorganization, while some writers also emphasized that intellectuals and youth in the more developed world were disposed to find new forms of commitment to the charismatic ethic of absolute ends and to reject the emphasis on *Zweckrationalität*. In a limited sense, some of the commentators anticipated the conflicts that emerged in the late 1960s, when these groups gave ideological expression to a rejection of the *Zweckrationalität* of industrial society.[12]

The renewed tensions between the two forms of rationality have been described by Eisenstadt and Bell as a source of "intergenerational conflicts and intellectual antinomianism" in the context of specific developments in modern society. As Eisenstadt (1973b:250–51) notes, these

> . . . are rooted in the contradiction between the "liberating" or creative potential given in the extension of substantive rationality as against the potential for constriction and compulsion inherent in the organizational extension of functional rationality, which can be most clearly seen in the growing tendencies to bureaucratization inherent in modern societies. This contradiction—which has sometimes been seen as parallel to that between the liberating power of charisma as against the more constrictive tendencies of the process of its routinization—is not abated by the

---

[12] Edward Shils (1955:57), for example, predicted that total ideologies "will creep in through . . . a rebellious younger generation" in the article in which he first sought to analyze the "end of ideology." For a discussion of related anticipations by other writers see Lipset (1972b:17–22).

fact that very often it is the very extension of substantive rationality (as evident, for example in the broadening of the political community, or in the extension of scientific knowledge) that creates the conditions for the intensification of the more constrictive tendencies inherent in extension of functional rationality in almost all spheres of human endeavor and of social life.

The spread of contemporary youth rebellion is in part a consequence of the contradiction between the widespread diffusion of the goal of freedom as an absolute value and the emergence of "a new type of social alienation focused not only around the feeling of being lost in a maze of large-scale, anonymous organizations and frameworks, but also around the possibility of the loss of the meaning of participation in these political and national centers." In other words, substantive and functional rationality in modern society have produced ultimate goals for a good society and means to sustain the social order which are sharply divergent. The basic contradiction between a superordinate emphasis on a free, egalitarian, and participant society as ideal and the constraints derivative from the bureaucratic hierarchical organization as means is inherent in the economic growth of modern industrial society. This tension makes for intense frustration, particularly among the educated young, who most accept the charismatic *Wertrationalität* of the social order. And Eisenstadt (1973b:249) has argued that it is no accident that the university has become the symbol of the strain, charged with hypocrisy. "The choice of the university as the object of . . . attack rather emphasizes the denial that the existing order can realize these basic premises of modernity: to establish and maintain an order that could do justice to the claims to creativity and participation in the broader social order. . . ." Hence the generational attack is directed against the basic values of modernism concentrated in academe, an antinomian rejection of science and reason.

The tension between *Wertrationalität* and *Zweckrationalität*, between substantive and functional rationality, is in many ways at the heart of Daniel Bell's analysis of the basic contradictions of postindustrial society. As he sees it, antinomian attitudes have repeatedly appeared among the culture creators reflecting their desire to reduce or abolish restraints "to attain some form of ecstasy." As such, they are in sharp opposition to the means orientation of the workaday world, "the economy, technology, and occupational system . . . [which] is rooted in functional rationality and efficiency . . . . shaped by the principle of calculation, the rationalization of work and of time, and a linear sense of progress" (Bell, 1973:477–78). The "adversary culture" of the intellectuals, their opposition to the basic values and institutions of the owners and controllers of industry and politics in capitalist and post-capitalist societies, is inherent in the nature of their work, the emphasis on creativity, originality, and "break-throughs" (Lipset and Dobson, 1972). It is interesting to note that Max Weber, writing soon after World War I, anticipated the desire of many intellectuals to find some form of ecstasy in a period characterized "by rationalization and intellectualization and, above all, by the 'disenchantment of the world.'" Faced with "disenchantment," with the absence of charismatic *Wertrationalität,* some will shift their value emphasis "into the transcendental realm of mystic life or into the brotherliness of direct and personal human relations." They may try "intellectually to construe new religions without a new and genuine prophecy," which can only result in "miserable monstrosities. And academic prophecy, finally, will create only fanatical sects but never a genuine community." For Weber, the most ethical reaction for the intellectual "who cannot bear the fate of the times" is to return to traditional religion. "In my eyes, such religious return stands higher than the academic prophecy, which does not realize that in the lecture-rooms of the university no other virtue holds but plain intellectual integrity" (Weber, 1946b: 155).

A few years later, Karl Mannheim (1949:230–31), in the same essay in which he anticipated the decline of ideology and utopia, noted the difficulty of living in "congruence with the realities of . . . a world, utterly without any transcendent element, either in the form of a utopia or an ideology." He foretold the rise of an emphasis on "'genuineness' and 'frankness' in place of the old ideals." And like Weber before him, Mannheim (1949:232–33), predicted that it would be "the socially unattached intellectuals . . . even more than now in increasing proportions recruited from all social strata rather than merely from the more privileged ones . . ." who, unable to accommodate to a situation without ideological conflict, will seek "to reach out beyond that tensionless situation."

The decline in *Wertrationalität* in the economy and polity has become an increasing source of strain and instability in modern society, as the numbers, prestige, and influence of those involved in intellectually related institutions increase sharply, as the system becomes increasingly dependent on facilities and trained manpower able to operate complex technology and to innovate in research and development. Although, as Bell (1973:479; Trilling, 1965:xii–xiii) notes, the countercultural life-styles stemming from the antinomian tendencies fostered by the intellectuals and students are absorbed within the market economy of western society, "the cultural chic of 'modernism' . . . retains its subversive thrust however much it is absorbed by the system."

The extent to which these cultural contradictions become the source of social change in advanced industrial or post-industrial society may be seen in the inversion of past class relationships with respect to propensity to protest. Traditional class theory, congruent with Marxist analysis, suggests that opposition to the status quo comes primarily from the ranks of the underprivileged, because they are oppressed. This generalization has held up in most societies. Insofar as the predominant political issue has been the existing distribution of privileges, the redistributionist or egalitarian movements have been supported by the poorer strata and by those subject to discrimination because of ascriptive traits.

This relationship, however, does not hold up within the intellectual community, nor with respect to movements and tendencies that reflect antinomian values, seeking to break down restraint and to reject functional rationality. A variety of surveys of opinion and behavior among those engaged in intellectually related work find that the more socially critical, those more rejective of the status quo, are more likely to come from the more successful, those who are regarded by their peers as the most creative. Within the academy, those most involved in research activities, who publish more, who are in the more prestigious universities, are more disposed to a critical *Weltanschauung*. Those more engaged in transmitting culture, i.e., teaching, as distinct from creating, tend to be more conservative, even though they are found disproportionately at the less distinguished institutions, receive less pay, and experience more onerous working conditions. Those academics involved in disciplines concerned with "basic" research or the creative arts are much more disposed to favor the "adversary culture" than professors dealing with the more applied professional fields (Lipset, 1972a; Lipset and Dobson, 1972; Ladd and Lipset, 1975). A survey of the opinions of 110 American intellectuals, judged as eminent by their peers, reports that they are somewhat to the left of the elite academics, who in turn are the most socially critical within the university world (Kadushin, 1974). Similar findings have been published with respect to the media. The more prestigious the newspaper or broadcast medium, the more liberal its editors, culture critics, or reporters (Johnstone, et al., 1972–73; United Church of Christ, 1970). A survey of over 500 leaders of American life in business, labor, government, politics, voluntary associations, government (civil service), and the mass media conducted in 1971–72 found that the latter—publishers, editors, TV executives, and columnists—were more liberal in their views than all other groups on foreign policy and social issues. Solid majorities of the "media leaders" supported the youth rebellion and lacked confidence in the leaders of major institutions and the operation of the political system (Barton, 1973). These studies confirm Bell's generalization that the "new class, which dominates the media and the culture, thinks of itself less as radical than 'liberal,' yet its values centered on 'personal freedom,' are profoundly anti-bourgeois" (Bell, 1973:479–80).

The preference of the intellectual elite for antinomian socially critical and countercultural values is related to the differences in social outlook among university students. As a myriad of empirical surveys have demonstrated, anti-system politics and countercultural life styles have appealed disproportionately to the more affluent students in the more academically selective institutions and in the liberal arts, particularly the social sciences and humanities, as distinct from less well-to-do students in the more vocationally oriented schools and subjects (Lipset, 1972c:80–113).

There is some evidence to suggest that the values stemming from the intellectual and university community, transmitted through the elite media, are also affecting the orientations of many employed in bureaucratic executive levels of government and industry, where more are working "in professional than in line executive capacities" (L. Harris, 1973:45). Public opinion analyst Louis Harris (1973: 45–47) reports that interview surveys of such elite groups indicate "that the professionals felt much more beholden to their outside discipline—whether it be systems engineering, teaching, scientific research, or other professional ties—than to the particular company or institution they worked for." On a variety of issues bearing on changing moral attitudes, black equality, and the Vietnam war, "the burgeoning professional group, now a majority of those in the $15,000 and up group" were much more likely to support change than the line executives, or those with incomes under $5,000 a year, the most conservative of all on these issues. The "new professionals, who had as a group incomes higher than the line executives, were the most dedicated to changing the system."

A similar basis for the divisions within the European elite has been noted by the British Marxist, E. J. Hobsbawm (1973b:258–59). The intellectually oriented professionals

> . . . are more numerous, since both the growth of scientific technology and the expansion of the tertiary sector of the economy (including administration and communications) require them in much larger numbers than before. They are technically proletarianized, in as much as the bulk of them are no longer "free professionals" or private entrepreneurs but salaried employees. . . . They are recognizable by specific attitudes. . . ; e.g., reading the *Guardian* rather than the *Daily Telegraph,* and being relatively impervious to the sales appeals of status symbols as against *Which*-type [Consumers Union] criteria. Politically the bulk of this stratum . . . is probably today left of centre in western countries. . . .

In discussing France, Hobsbawm points out that the 1968 general strike was militantly backed by "the research-and-development types, the laboratory and design departments and the communicators . . . whereas the administrators, executives, sales departments, etc. remained on the side of management."

More generally, similar findings have been reported for entire populations. The political scientist Ronald Inglehart, using survey data from a number of North Atlantic countries, has differentiated between materialist and post-materialist values, which in many ways correspond to functional and substantive rationality, and turn out to correlate with political orientations, though not with the traditional class correlates of party choice. Materialist values emphasize "economic and physical security" (*Zweckrationalität*), while "Post-Materialist values emphasize individual self-expression and achieving a more participant, less hierarchical society" (*Wertrationalität*). And though adherents to the latter are the most change-oriented in contemporary society, "Materialists tend to be recruited from lower income groups, which traditionally have supported the Left—while the Post-Materialists come mainly from middle class families . . ." (Inglehart, 1973: 2, 8; Inglehart, 1971).[13]

Inglehart's research has been repeated in Japan by Joji Watanuki (1975), with somewhat similar results. "Post-industrial" values are weaker there than in various European countries, possibly reflecting the fact that Japan has only recently fully entered the stage of a developed industrial society. But, as in Europe and the United

---

[13] Statistical data from American opinion surveys demonstrating the same point may be found in Harris, 1973:36–41.

States, these values found their strongest support in Japan among "the younger and the more educated."

In Germany, as a detailed analysis by Erwin Scheuch (1974) shows, blue-collar workers oriented toward materialistic gains have become much more positive in their attitudes toward the socio-political system from the late 1960's on. Conversely, however, the better educated, those in high white-collar occupations, reveal a steady decline in trust in the system. A sizeable percentage of the latter have moved to the left in their voting preferences. The rise of a significant New Left type left-wing within the Social Democratic party during this period is based on the entrance of well educated young people and women, largely from affluent backgrounds, into the party.

Not surprising, as Erik Allardt (1975) demonstrates, Scandinavia exhibits the same pattern. In Denmark, Norway, and Sweden, the Social Democrats continue to secure their electoral support largely from the working-class, with little "upper-class" backing. Parties to their left, mainly reflecting New Left tendencies, derive a considerable part of their growing vote from the "upper" and "new middle" classes. In Denmark, for example, "it appears that 14 percent of the Danish upper class voted for some of the parties left of the Social Democrats while only 2 percent voted for the Social Democrats (Allardt, 1975: 47–48).

Inglehart suggests that the basis of political cleavage in the emerging post-industrial society will differ from that of industrial society. The latter has emphasized economic or interest conflict, linked in Weberian terms to *Zweckrationalität,* while the new type emphasizes the more intangible values of participation and freedom from restraint and reveals "a relative *aversion* to traditional bureaucratic institutions" (Inglehart, 1973:12). As one would expect, they are to be found most commonly among young well-educated relatively affluent people.

The variations between materialist and post-materialist orientations are difficult to sort out in contemporary politics because they are linked to two different forms of "leftist" orientations, which still may be found within the same movements. The traditional left of industrial society has "sought change in the direction of economic equality above all—even, if necessary, by means of increased governmental interference with the liberty of the individual. . . . The Industrial Left has generally accepted a considerable degree of organizational discipline and hierarchy as necessary for effective political change and economic progress." The post-industrial left, reflecting the emerging values of a new type of society, found more prevalently among intellectuals, those employed in the knowledge-related and opinion-forming occupations, and the better-educated young, "is distinguished by an emphasis on the self-development of the individual —even, if necessary at the cost of further economic expansion. . . . [T]he Post-Industrial Left tends to give a relatively low priority to economic growth. . . . Suspicious of the State, they are far more sympathetic to both individualism *and* communalism than to the norms of rational bureaucracy. For the individual is, in part, that which he is born" (Inglehart, 1973:69–70).

Inglehart (1973:72) finds that in countries in which parties with a New Left coloration have contested national elections, individuals classified as post-materialists on the basis of their attitudes, are much more likely to back New Left than traditional left parties, findings which are congruent with the research on student activism. Thus though Inglehart is apparently unaware of the linkages between his own concepts and those of Weber, Mannheim, Parsons, and Eisenstadt (he derives much of his approach from Bell), his comparative analysis of attitudes and electoral behavior sustain their assumptions that the basic tensions between the values of *Wertrationalität* and *Zweckrationalität* constitute a major social contradiction which fosters social change.

The post-industrial leftists are the real revolutionaries of modern society precisely because they have rejected functional rationality and adhere to the "ethic of ultimate ends." As Weber noted well over half a century ago in prescient words which describe developments within the contemporary New Left: "In the world of realities, as a rule, we encounter the ever-renewed experience that the adherent of an ethic of ultimate ends suddenly turns into a chiliastic prophet. Those, for example, who have preached 'love against violence' now call for the use of force for the *last* violent deed, which would lead to a state of affairs in which *all* violence is annihilated" (Weber, 1946b: 122).

These value conflicts are rooted in the twin developments of modern society noted earlier, the steady growth of bureaucracy with its accompanying emphasis on hierarchy and restraints and the increase in the demand for participation, free choice, equality, and creativity inherent in greater numbers exposed to higher levels of education, the situation of the studentry, the freedom from economic necessity. As Eisenstadt (1973b:250) puts it

> . . . the most important constrictions on such freedom and creativity—and hence also the most important sources of change, instability and alienation in societies in general and in modern societies in particular—are rooted in the contradiction between the structural implications of the types of rationality. . . . [T]hese constrictions are rooted in the contradiction between the "liberating" or creative potential given in the extension of substantive rationality as against the potential for constriction and compulsion inherent in modern societies. This contradiction . . . has sometimes been seen as parallel to that between the liberating power of charisma as against the more constrictive tendencies of the process of its routinization. . . .

Lest this line of analysis be dismissed as another effort to deny or to challenge a materialistic or structural analysis of change by normative functionalists, let me close my discussion of the contradictions implied by the need for the two forms of rationality by noting with the radical sociologist Richard Flacks the congruence between this body of analysis "by 'bourgeois' social analysts" and assorted "radical intellectuals. . . [who] perceive that this situation might have revolutionary implications—that the emergence of a post-industrial system represents the final realization of capitalism and hence its demise." Summing up the analyses of a number of neo-Marxist analysts, including his own trenchant one, Flacks (1972:86-90) notes that the opposition to a post-industrial capitalist society comes to a considerable extent from *"those whose social position is already post-industrial*—who have been able to aspire to be able to make a life outside of the goods producing sector—i.e., in the production and distribution of knowledge, culture and human services, or as free persons—and those whose needs in a material sense have been satiated by the existing system." And this movement projects a new *Wertrationalität*,

> . . . a vision of a society in which the *primary vocational activities* would be focused around the production and distribution of knowledge and art, around the provision of a vast array of human services, and around collective efforts to create maximally beneficial communal and natural environments. . . . It is a *culture* which values cooperation and love over competition and dominance, self-expression over self-denial, equality over materially-based status differentiation. It is a quest for a *political*

order in which the nation-state is replaced by self-governing communities.[14]

In short, what Flacks anticipates is the dominance of *Wertrationalität* over *Zweckrationalität*, the triumph of antinomian values; and he and other New Leftists locate the support for these trends in the same liberated privileged elements of post-industrial society as the "bourgeois" social analysts. Where most of the neo-Marxists differ, however, is in their insistence that at the heart of the revolution of post-industrial society is a "new working-class," who support change because they are subject to economic and bureaucratic constraints, a hypothesis which seeks " 'to save' the Marxist concept of social change" (Bell, 1973:39-40). In fact, however, as Flacks, who knows the relevant empirical data, has also noted, the heart of the "adversary culture" comes from the most successful and socially privileged elements among the "new class." The differences in the analyses of social change in post-industrial society between the "bourgeois" and the "neo-Marxist" analysts are minimal.

Conclusion

Sociology in recent years seemingly has witnessed a breakdown in consensus about what the discipline is all about, particularly as to appropriate theoretical and methodological approaches. Norman Birnbaum (1971:230) suggests that "at the moment, . . . sociology presents the appearance of chaos, an intellectual tower of Babel." The Dutch sociologist C. J. Lammers (1974) has noted in less dramatic language that a multiplicity of paradigms has become the "natural state" of the field.

This situation is quite different from the one which existed a decade ago when agreement appeared to exist concerning the basic approaches and methodologies of the discipline. Writing as recently as 1967, Donald MacRae (1968:vii-viii) in introducing a book on *Modern Social Theory* (Cohen, 1968) noted that its author, Percy Cohen, had demonstrated that "a unity" in sociological analysis "which is not merely manufactured but genuine is possible and, indeed, is largely achieved," and it may lead to "a comparatively long period of quiet, logical refinement and cleaning-up operations . . . ,

[14] See also Touraine, 1971; Sklar, 1969; Gorz, 1969; and Rowntree and Rowntree, 1968.

[T]his book is fortunate in its timing, both because of that unification of theory to which it contributes, and because of the lull that must for some time be expected and in which the newest generation of sociologists can and will be educated."[15] C. Wright Mills (1959) stood out almost alone among the prominent figures in the field as a critic of the dominant orientations. Writings concerned with what has come to be called the "sociology of sociology" were almost non-existent.

The change which occurred during the late sixties was, of course, closely related to the revival of left-wing activist concerns within intellectualdom generally, but particularly within the academy. It resulted in heightened levels of politically related conflicts, especially within the social sciences. A comparative study of the political life of American academic discipline associations by Ira Wessler found that the social sciences have been by far the most engaged. All of them passed political resolutions dealing with the Vietnam war and other social issues during the late 1960s. Political caucuses were organized in each. By contrast, almost no political resolutions were passed by the various natural science associations between 1965 and 1971, and radical caucuses were largely absent from them, with the single exception of the physicists. The humanists were somewhat more politically involved than the scientists, largely within the American Philosophical Association, the Modern Languages Association, and the American Historical Association (Wessler, 1973:214-47). Wessler (1973:412) contends that the strong commitment of social scientists to political activism follows from the influence of three basic and widely noted factors: "[that] their subject matter is basically connected with values . . . , [that] social scientists constantly participate in value laden situations and . . . [that] social scientists are essentially activated to contribute to human welfare." To these may be added the related factor derivative from analyses of the Carnegie Commission's surveys of faculty and student opinion, that the subject matter of the social sciences attracts individuals committed to socially critical views both as undergraduates and graduate students and that the differences among the disciplines evidenced by the behavior of the professional societies are already evident in the attitudes of students and young faculty (Ladd and Lipset, 1975).

---

[15] It should be noted that MacRae deplored this possibility and voiced the "hope" that it would not occur because of the weaknesses in the unified theory.

But if the social sciences as a group are more disposed to liberal-left views than other segments of academe, the available data, drawn from surveys of students and faculty, indicate that sociology is the most left of all. Hence, it is not surprising that, during a period of intense politicization, the sociological community has been most exposed to political differences of opinion. As Ladd and I suggested, "perhaps the reason that there is so much literature in sociology attacking other sociologists for their alleged 'conservatism' is that the left is more heavily represented in this field than in any other, and that within a 'left' discipline (as within a radical political party) the question of who is the 'most revolutionary' becomes salient" (Lipset and Ladd, 1972:95).

But if the stronger left disposition largely accounts for the "Babel" in the field, for the fact that sociologists recently have emphasized the implications of differences among them, rather than seeking to find bases for theoretical agreement, as in most other fields, studies of the opinions of sociologists do not bear out the assumption of some critics that theoretical divergencies are related to sharp variations in orientations toward social change or even social reform. Thus depth interviews with "30 outstanding sociologists" at seven major American universities, conducted in 1963–64 by a Yugoslav Marxist sociologist, Mihailo Popovich (1966:135), reported that when asked "which problems are among the most important in contemporary sociology," more (10) mentioned "social change" than any other issues, while "social problems of economic development" was in second place (5). When asked about the relationship of Marxism to other sociological approaches, the majority indicated that there is a considerable overlap in approach and concerns. As Popovich commented, "it is a significant fact that almost all of the interviewed sociologists think that there are some 'common points' between Marxist theory and non-Marxist sociological theories. These common points concern not only certain categories or principles, but also some problems. As is pointed out above, problems of social change and economic development are mentioned as *the* important issues of modern sociology." The findings of this set of interviews with leading sociologists in 1963–64, before the wave of intense activism of the 1960s began, were reiterated in the largest single survey of sociological opinion based on over 3,000 questionnaire responses conducted in 1964 by Alvin Gouldner and his then doctoral student, J. T. Sprehe (Gouldner and Sprehe, 1965). This study found that as a group sociologists are disposed to the left and favor major social changes. As of 1964, race relations was perceived as the most pressing issue of concern by sociologists, followed by un-employment, mental health, and urban problems. Three-fifths thought that "Many modern institutions are deeply unstable and tensionful." Over three-quarters of those sampled indicated that "Basic Change in Structure and Values" of American society was necessary to solve its major problems. Since, as Gouldner has indi-cated, the great majority (82.4 percent) also favored functional anal-ysis, this meant that they did not see any incompatibility between that theoretical orientation and the need for "basic change." In line with Popovich's interviews, and other surveys, the Gouldner-Sprehe data indicated that the more prestigeful the sociologist, the more he published, and the more involved he was in extramurally financed research activities, the more likely was he to support a more change-oriented view, to identify with sociology's playing a role in "solv-ing society's problems," and to reject a value-free approach (Sprehe, 1967).

Further evidence that support for a functional approach to socio-logical analysis is compatible with a commitment to radical social change may be found in a survey of Japanese sociologists. This study indicated that most sociologists voted for the left-wing Marxist Social-ist party, with the Communists receiving the next highest support. Only one in 10 voted for the "bourgeois" Liberal Democrats, the majority party in the country, while less than 10 percent chose the pro-Western Democratic Socialists. Yet these predominantly radical Japanese scholars, when asked to name non-Japanese sociologists worthy of considerable attention, listed Talcott Parsons more fre-quently than anyone else (24 percent), with Robert Merton in second place (19 percent). Endorsements of Parsons and Merton and for Marxist parties were inversely related with age. The younger the Japa-nese sociologist, the more likely he was to mention Parsons and Mer-ton and to vote for the Marxist left (Suzuki, 1970:368, 383).

Analysis of the way in which different schools of sociology approach the study of social structure and social change, as well as surveys of the professional opinions and sociopolitical values of soci-ologists, suggests a considerable basis for convergence or, if one prefers a dialectical term, synthesis, among divergent orientations rather than dissensus within the field. In a recent evaluation of the discipline, S. N. Eisenstadt (1937a:260–61) has noted the "growing convergence and potentially constructive mutual impingement of the different approaches in contemporary sociology . . . on several levels." These include both "conceptual convergence" with respect to a "similar range of concepts such as roles, resources, rewards," and various other terms, and in

> . . . the basic assumptions of each approach—the existence of division of labor and systematic organization; of groups and so-cieties; the pursuance by individuals of various goals—both 'private' and institutionalized in social interaction; the importance of symbolic models of orientation in the patterning of such be-havior and organization, the importance of the meaningful defi-nition of the situation by those participating in it; the existence of some eco-systemic organizations—seem to have been accepted as evolutionary universals of any human society, by almost all these approaches.

His conclusions are reinforced by the recent work of the Polish theorist, Piotr Sztompka (1974:177), who notes that in Eastern Europe, "The concepts of system, structure, function, relationship, interaction, organization, etc., acquired a central place in Marxist sociology."

Although Alvin Gouldner (1970a) has strongly criticized aca-demic sociology's emphasis on "continuity, cumulation, codification, convergence," as reflecting "the joyless prescriptions of a structural-izing methodology" (265, 17-18), he has also suggested that "not despite, but because of" its approach, it has "focused attention on some of the new sources and sites of social change in the modern social world."

> For example, and to be provocatively invidious about it, it was not the Marxists but Talcott Parsons and other functionalists who early spotted the importance of the emerging "youth cul-ture," and at least lifted it out as an object for attention. It was the academic sociologists, not the Marxists, in the United States who helped many to get their first concrete picture of how Blacks and other subjugated groups live, and who contributed to such practical political developments as the Supreme Court's desegre-gation decision. It is the ethnography of conventional academic sociologists that has also given us the best picture of the emerging psychedelic and drug cultures, which are hardening the separation and conflict of generations. (Gouldner, 1970b: 21)

The limitations of an ideological emphasis on the sources of different paradigmatic orientations in sociology may also be illus-trated by noting the methodological and conceptual similarities between the Parsonian structural approach—included its efforts to find universal rules, the functional prerequisites of human society—and those of a number of contemporary western radical social theorists. In discussing critical theory in Germany, Rolf Klima (1972:80) points out its current leading spokesman, Jurgen Habermas, "has been trying all along to give Parsonian functionalism a hermeneutic-dialectic reinterpretation." George Lichtheim (1969:33-38) and Harold Bershady (1973:133) note "that Louis Althusser, the French Marxist, defines certain of the theoretical tasks of structural Marxism in similar ways" to Parsons, a fact which also leads him and his followers to be criticized for their "a-historicism." And Bershady emphasizes that "if Marxism is not merely historicism. . . . Parsons' epistomological enterprise is not nearly so anti-Marxist as has been made out." Noam Chomsky has argued the case for an ahistorical structuralism, for looking for the structural limitations of the forms of human organization, in even stronger terms than Althusser, Parsons, or Lévy-Strauss (Bershady, 1973:14–19). In the *New Left Review,* Chomsky (1969:32) recommended that social science follow the model he has developed for linguistics of looking for the universal aspects of social structure, those that underlie and limit the nature of all social systems—feudalism, capitalism, and socialism.

[A]s a linguist I am interested in the fact that English and Japanese are rather minor modifications of a basic pattern. . . . Now it is possible to carry out this study as a linguist because we can move up to a level of abstraction from which we can survey a vast class of possible systems and ask how the existing human linguistic systems fit into this class. And I think we will discover that they fit into a very narrow part of it. A serious study of morals or of social systems would attempt the same thing. It would ask itself what kinds of social system are conceivable. Then it would ask itself what kinds have actually been realized in history and it would ask how these came into existence, given the range of possibilities that exist at some moment of economic and cultural development. Then, having reached that point, the next question is whether the range of social systems that human beings have constructed is broad or narrow, what is its scope, what are its potentialities, are there kinds of social systems human beings could not possibly construct and so on. We have not really begun this kind of investigation. Hence it is only a guess when I say that the range of possible social systems may turn out to be very narrow. Of course, there is an enormous human significance in living in one social system rather than another. . . . But that is a different question from asking which kinds of social organizations are possible for human beings and which kinds are not.

Clearly the larger goal which Chomsky sets for the social sciences is almost identical with that which Parsons has attempted. As Bershady (1973:16) stresses "the analogy between Parsons' and Chomsky's endeavors should help elicit the fact that the endeavor itself need not be associated necessarily with any specific 'sentiments' or 'metaphysical' assumptions," or it may be added a lack of interest in the sources of social change and conflict.

These conclusions point up the criticisms of Polish sociologist Stefan Nowak (1974), who, in challenging "recent discussions about the 'conservative assumptions' of functionalism" notes that "the critics of functionalism failed to perceive that it has such conservative implications—for conservatives only." And Nowak goes on (italics supplied) to "defend . . . the *general problem area of functionalism,* which stresses the importance of looking for the social functions of different cultural patterns and institutions, and leaves (or should leave) open the problem of acceptance of the functions and of various kinds of social equilibrium. The conclusions to be drawn as to the appropriate *social actions* must be based on the confrontation of these empirically assessed functions with different human values."

In suggesting that a genuine basis for synthesis and intellectual cooperation exists among sociologists with varying theoretical orientations, it is not my intention to imply that sociology is approaching a state of agreement about a theoretical paradigm, or that criticism of the approach or research of any given school or sociologist is bad for the discipline. The contrary is true with respect to both points. Efforts to understand the basis for theoretical and empirical disagreements are necessary for the progress of any field of inquiry. But it does little good to conduct such critical analyses in the spirit of ideological controversy, one which assumes that to "reveal" the underlying political assumptions says anything about the validity or usefulness of a given work: Sociology is a discipline concerned with stability and change. Hopefully this symposium on social structure will demonstrate both how much we have in common as members of that field and how much different analytic approaches contribute to our understanding of social processes. What one man sees, another misses. What any of us reveals, no one of us can ignore.

12

Structure and Conflict

Lewis A. Coser

I WAS MOST PLEASED with Peter Blau's decision to make social structure the central theme of a collection of papers. At a time when so many of our colleagues have succumbed to what I have called elsewhere "a veritable orgy of subjectivism," it is most fitting, I think, to re-emphasize that the analysis of objective social structures, rather than exclusive concern with variegated constructions of reality, is the cornerstone of the sociological enterprise. If we are not to give in to a social psychologism that would disregard an outside reality which sets bounds to the strivings and desires of individual actors and retreat into prepotent concerns with individual cognitions, perceptions, and subjective impressions, we have to return to the heritage of Marx, Simmel, and Durkheim, which is teaching us that individual striving is not sufficient to free us from the grip of societal constraints. And if we do not wish to limit ourselves to queries about how the ethnos thinks, but desire instead to provide instrumentalities for changing society with the help of our interpretation, lasting concern with the stubborn facticity of structural arrangements will have to continue to be in the very center of our inquiries.

Nevertheless, I would like to show that structural analysis, like love, crucial though it is, is not enough. Exclusive concern with structural factors could lead, intentionally or unwittingly, to a neglect of social process. Structural factors, I would like to show at the hand of a few concrete examples, do not operate directly upon social behavior but are mediated through processes of social interaction among which social conflict is a major, though by no means the only one.

Let me start out with a very simple illustration. It is certainly most important, when analyzing sociologically a suit in civil law, to pay attention to the structurally determined oppositions of values or interests that lie at the roots of the contention and determine the expectations of the contender. Yet the outcome of the suit will be crucially influenced by the interactive process of the trial, framed though it certainly is by the formal structure of the law and the patterned relationships of its practitioners. When persons variously placed in the social structure encounter one another in a court of law which is to adjudicate their claims, they engage in a set of direct or mediated interactions that lead to outcomes that could not be predicted solely in terms of structural positions, even though certain outcomes are much more probable than others. The living process of interaction, bounded and channeled by various structural factors, gives rise to emergent qualities and events.

Social movements offer somewhat more complex illustrations: The civil rights and Black power movements, and the women's liberation movement, have in recent years had a crucial impact upon our social scene; they provide useful illustrations of my analytical point.

It stands to reason that in explaining the Black movement one cannot dispense with a close investigation of its background in structured historical conditions. The mechanization of Southern cotton production and the attendant migration of large masses of Black men and women from a rural to an urban environment, the wartime scarcity of labor which allowed Blacks access to industrial employment heretofore closed to them, these and other developments that the Parsonian analyst would lump together under the rubric "structural differentiation" are undoubtedly among the main forces that affected growth of the civil rights and Black power movements of the sixties. However, had Martin Luther King, Jr., and other later leaders not taken advantage of structural conditions that provided them with potential militants and publics, a critical mass to furnish them the troops to mount their assault on previous wont and use in the field of race relations, most of the advances they achieved on behalf of their constituency would most probably not have occurred.

The moves and countermoves of the defenders of the *status quo* on the racial front and of the resolute advocates of fundamental change were conducted in terms of the structural positions they respectively occupied. They made use of opportunities provided by their positions in an effort to maximize their power and to make their values prevail while at the same time exploiting the structurally given vulnerabilities of their adversaries. Yet the specific conflict strategies adopted, such as the use of nonviolent tactics, the selective and carefully modulated use of methods of civil disobedience, the effort to enlist public opinion while at the same time goading it forward, the attempt to combine appeals to the established legal and political authorities with occasional confrontations of these same authorities, these and many other strategic and tactical moves ensured successes that would not otherwise have been forthcoming— at least not at that time. The travail of structural differentiation is slow; had King and his co-workers failed to take the lead, it is doubtful indeed that the state of affairs on the racial front would resemble in any way the current condition, unsatisfactory though it still is.

Although the white values and norms in regard to Blacks had been changing in the decades prior to the sixties, if often at a somewhat glacial speed, the racial gains of the Blacks in recent years could hardly have been achieved without the civil rights movements, without sitdowns, mass civil disobedience, and similar manifestations which brought the plight of the Blacks to the forefront of white awareness. The last ten or fifteen years have seen large-scale changes in the social consciousness, the construction of reality, of both whites and Blacks, but these depended not only on underlying structural shifts in the relations between the races, but also on specific conflict strategies and specific mobilization of Black militancy that helped transform mere potentialities into concrete results. Their strategies and militancy effected a change in the very structure that was being attacked.

The analysis of the women's liberation movement should pursue parallel lines. Undoubtedly that movement would not have been possible without the impact of large-scale industrial employment of women in wartime and the postwar shifts in employment patterns that made womanpower a major part of the total employed labor force. Nor is it likely that the movement would have assumed its present proportions without a secular decline of the birthrate, partly due to the revolutionary fact that for the first time in human history women now have the ability to control fertility and reproduction. Nor should it be overlooked that major structural changes in the technology of household management and in production of goods for the home have freed millions of women, and not only middle-class women at that, from the drudgery of household maintenance which has been their fate from times immemorial.

What is more, these changes took place within the peculiar structure of the American political system, which is based on pluralistic loyalties and allegiances and deemphasizes rigid ideological alignments, which stresses the creative contributions of voluntary associations and is suspicious of political decisions that do not grow out of participatory activities of the citizenry, and which relies on a political culture that puts heavy emphasis on the political responsibility and sensitivity to the constituency on the part of political decision-makers. These factors, and there are surely many others, provided the opportunity for collective actions.

Yet, without the skilled conflict strategies of women leaders who have led their troops to invade the political arena hitherto largely barred to them, to use legal facilities hitherto unavailable, to mount pressures not only on the bar of public opinion but in the office and the factory and even, yea, in the privacy of individual homes, I would doubt that the important changes in the relations between men and women that have occurred in recent years would in fact have taken place. There were indeed both manifest and latent structural factors that facilitated such changes, but these factors alone would not have brought these changes about.

It is the combination of background factors, the social and political structure, and the emergence of skilled political actors taking creative advantage of these factors in the process of conducting the conflict which explains to an important extent the success of movements such as the women's liberation movement. Where all three are not present, such movements are likely to fail.[1] Many of the same general structural conditions existed in other societies, but the political structure proved to be less favorable in those polities where, for example, stress on participatory politics and voluntary association were less securely legitimized. This, in turn, made for the fact that strong leadership failed to emerge and to enlist mass support. The inability of women in these societies to band together in

[1] Seymour Martin Lipset's (1950) well-known study of the Cooperative Commonwealth Federation of Saskatchewan shows in instructive detail why essentially similar structural conditions among wheat farmers in Saskatchewan and in neighboring North Dakota led to dissimilar political responses. Divergent political cultures in Canada and the United States, as well as divergent types of leadership and strategies, led to the emergence of an autonomous socialist movement in one case and of a radical agrarian faction of the Republican Party, the Non-Partisan League, in the other.

a coordinated political and social movement to change their unequal social positions accounts in large part for the fact that the decided gains that have been achieved in this country were not duplicated elsewhere to the same extent. Women in other countries did not have the same structurally provided opportunities, and hence they largely failed to evolve creative responses to the challenge of new conditions.

Another example, this time far removed from immediate and contemporary concerns, is provided by a brilliant new interpretation of the Salem witchcraft trials by the social historians Paul Boyer and Stephen Nissenbaum (1973). They argue most persuasively that structural factors lay at the roots of the epidemic. They speak of the resistance of back-country farmers to the pressures of encroaching commercial capitalism, the breaking away of outlying areas from the control of parent towns, and the slow transformation of Puritan saints into land-hungry Yankees. Such changes, however, were at work all over New England and yet led to the witchcraft epidemic in Salem alone. Belief in the evil designs of the devil and the mobilization of such belief in the service of local ideologues cannot be accounted for solely by reference to structural tensions among Puritans about to become unsaintly acquisitive individualists. To be sure, the ecology of Salem Village and Salem Town provided some of the tinder that was set afire during a witchcraft epidemic which nearly tore the community apart. Yet the fact that these happenings occurred in Salem rather than in Andover or Plymouth must be accounted for by close analytical reference to the ideological alignments and the conflicts of interests that set in motion specific conflictual processes and created patterns of leadership peculiar to Salem, moving men and women at that time and in that place to confront each other in deadly accusations and fratricidal disputes.

Structural factors, such as those discussed by Bayer and Nissenbaum, do not operate directly on social behavior. Such behavior was informed by the impact of specific sets of values and specific interests. These led to the emergence of strategies, of moves and countermoves, engaged in by motivated actors as they attempt to have their cause prevail in interaction upon the public arena on which they confront each other.

The sociology of conflict must search for the structurally rooted interests and values that lead men to engage in conflicts with each other, if it is not to dissolve into psychological disquisitions about innate aggressiveness, original sin, or plain human cussedness. But, in addition, one must ask what led specific actors in specific roles to oppose each other with specific techniques of struggle under specific circumstances. In attempting to account for concrete conflict situations due attention needs to be paid both to structural and processual factors.

A peculiar type of crude structural determinism has in recent years been in the forefront of much discussion: the evolutionary approach to the theory of modernization and the related attempts of some scholars to predict the future of industrial societies in a limited repertoire of structural terms.

The prevailing orthodoxy in the study of modernization in the postwar period as it was expounded, among many others, by Talcott Parsons and his disciples, conceived of modernization and industrialization as a relatively uniform, worldwide process. It is a neo-evolutionary scheme stressing the ineluctability of the increasing differentiation of social forms and institutions on the road toward more perfect modes of adaptation. The common assumption among these scholars is that modern structures will undermine traditional ones all over the world and that societies will become increasingly alike in social institutions, cultural orientations, and patterns of human interaction as particularistic criteria will be replaced by universalistic standards, as *Gemeinschaft* will give way to *Gesellschaft*. After "taking off" from the slough of tradition, all societies will progressively converge on a particular "modern" type which, incidentally, usually bears a close resemblance to the contemporary United States.

But it has become increasingly clear in the last few years that such exclusive focus on structural factors ignores the processes that modernization sets in motion in specific and concrete societies. As Eisenstadt, himself previously committed to a perspective of structural evolutionism, has recently stated, the notion of structural differentiation is incapable of providing a sufficient means for distinguishing between types of societies on an evolutionary scale. Levels of structural differentiation may indicate the nature of the new forces that are generated within a society, but, as Eisenstadt (1973b: 306) puts it, "in such situations of change there develops not just one possibility of the restructuring of forces and activities . . . but rather a great variety of possibilities." Structural changes certainly allow for the mobilization of heretofore unavailable resources in both the economic and the political realm, but who will gain access to these resources, who will use them, will largely depend on the outcome of contentions and confrontations between classes, ethnic groups, or centralizing and decentralizing tendencies, to name but a few.

The mere destruction of traditional forms does not necessarily assure the development of a viable modern society but may simply result in anomic breakdowns when neither of the contending forces is able to have its way in the quest for dominance. Development, far from necessarily leading to increased popular participation, may lay the groundwork for the emergence of new types of despotisms. Militaristic backwoodsmen may command their cowed countrymen from seats in the glittering skyscrapers of modernity.

It has turned out that societies do not develop in a stately progression of orderly structural stages toward modernity; they exhibit instead startling incongruities and discontinuities in the course of their development. An initial centralization of societal resources may be followed by the seeping away of resources to peripheral centers of power, debureaucratization might follow in the wake of bureaucratization. The forces of modernization may indeed, as in contemporary Portugal, lead to the toppling of authoritarian regimes, but they may also lead, as in contemporary Brazil, to the iron rule of military oligarchies. The attempt to put the course of development into an evolutionary straitjacket based on a theory of the succession of structural stages, has foundered on the shoals of historical specificity and on the inability of structural evolutionary theory to deal with the variability of the processes through which societal forces, old and new alike, struggle for dominance in the social and political arena.

Nisbet puts the matter well when he writes in his *Social Change and History* (1969):

> Professor Parsons suggests that the theory of social evolution is in substantially the same position . . . as the theory of biological evolution where "morphology," including comparative anatomy, is the "backbone" of evolutionary theory. But this leaves a good deal out. Morphology and comparative anatomy may set the stages for evolutionary theory in biology, but the real "backbone" of the theory is a highly specific process of change—natural selection.

Needless to say that no sociological theorist has come anywhere near providing the counterpart to natural selection in social developments, but it seems most likely that such a counterpart might one day emerge from close analytical attention to the struggles and contentions between various social formations, be they classes, races, communities, or what have you. Structures and their differentiation set the stage and provide opportunities, but only specific interactive processes determine the outcome.

Finally, I should like to make some parallel comments about the work of Daniel Bell (1973), the most prominent among the growing group of scholars who have set out to forecast the future of modern societies in terms of a limited number of structural factors. In *The Coming of Post-Industrial Society,* Bell argues that the old structure of corporate capitalism in America is rapidly decaying and is about to be replaced by a new "knowledge-based society" in which the professional and technical strata will have preeminence and in which "intellectual technology" and theoretical knowledge will have pride of place. As American society moves from a goods-producing to a service economy, expertise and knowledge will serve as a prepotent source of societal power. Scientists and engineers, Bell argues, will impress their distinctive stamp on post-industrial society, much as Schumpeterian entrepreneurs constituted the central dynamic element in classical capitalism. But why should this be so? Here Bell seems to argue from the twin grounds of indispensability and numbers. He shows that white-collar workers are now considerably more numerous than blue-collar workers; that the professional, technical, and kindred workers, a relatively small category under classical capitalism, now constitute over 12 percent of the labor force, and will continue to grow. They are "the heart of post-industrial society" because they are indispensable to its functioning.

I find both arguments less than convincing. Blue-collar workers in manufacturing surely constituted the single largest category of all workers in industrial society, and they were evidently indispensable to its operation, yet Bell would be the first to recognize that they were at no time the master class. If indispensability were really a source of societal power, sanitation workers or baby sitters would be a formidable social and political force. They are clearly not. Indispensability results in societal power only when it is accompanied by a self-conscious will to act in common for shared supraoccupational objectives. Such self-consciousness, in turn, is likely to emerge only under specific conditions. Around the middle of the nineteenth century, when Marx discussed the French peasantry which then was, of course, a large majority of the French population, he asserted that the conditions of their existence were such that they could not form common bonds and a common consciousness, that they were like "potatoes in a sack" rather than a solidary collectivity which could put its stamp on society. Here Marx developed a sophisticated structural argument as to the social position of the peasantry and pointed to a major reason why the peasants possessed few resources to make their weight felt in the process of power contentions of French society.

Bell's simplified structuralism, however, lacks Marx's sophistication and his sure sense of the sources of social power. He fails to stress social interactions and social relationships and rests his case on purely morphological data. He furnishes no evidence that knowledge has replaced property as the main source of power. He only shows that modern society increasingly depends on the activities of scientists, educators, engineers, social workers, technologists, and researchers and simply assumes that they are therefore our new masters. He does not seem seriously to entertain the notion that the employers and funding agencies, both public and private, who employ them or contract for their work, may in fact direct their activities much more than they themselves are directed by them. One need not hold the vulgar notion that he who pays the piper always calls the tune to remain skeptical of the idea that the knowledge "estates" are gaining ascendancy because we all depend on them as resources.

Bell's otherwise most interesting treatise founders on his futile attempt to ground forecasts of things to come in a structural analysis that ignores the processes through which power is wielded by various contenders in the social conflicts of the future. His is an attempt to forecast the future with power and political process left out. And that, I submit, is a self-defeating undertaking.

In concluding let me reiterate that I consider the study of social structures to lie at the very center of the sociological enterprise. What I have attempted in this paper was meant not to denigrate that study but to stress its insufficiency when it is not accompanied by a concomitant concern with those social processes that arise against the background of given structural arrangements. Just as Marx's magnificent vision finally foundered on his inability to foresee the concrete social processes that led to the integration of the working class into modern welfare-state societies rather than to the overthrow of capitalism by workers who had nothing to lose but their chains, so any exclusively structural interpretation, be it of modernization or of post-industrial society, is bound to fail for want of a grasp on the concrete social processes and social conflicts that shape the future out of the materials provided by the structures of the present and the past.[2]

---

[2] I have incorporated in this text a few passages from two earlier reviews, "Ideas about Modernization," *Science,* Vol. 183: 742, and "The Politics of the Future," *Partisan Review,* Spring 1974: 128ff.

13

Parameters of Social Structure

Peter M. Blau

THE CONCEPT of social structure is used widely in sociology, often broadly, and with a variety of meanings. It may refer to social differentiation, relations of production, forms of association, value integration, functional interdependence, statuses and roles, institutions, or combinations of these and other factors. A generic difference is whether social structure is conceived explicitly as being composed of different elements and their interrelations or abstractly as a theoretical construct or model. Radcliffe-Brown (1940) and Lévi-Strauss (1952) represent these contrasting conceptions of social structure. The first view holds that social structure is a system of *social* relations among differentiated parts of a society or group, which describes observable empirical conditions and is merely the basis for a theory yet to be constructed to explain these conditions. The second view holds that social structure is a system of *logical* relationships among general principles, which is not designed as a conceptual framework to reflect empirical conditions but as a theoretical interpretation of social life.[1] If one adopts the first view, as I do, that social structure refers to the differentiated interrelated parts in a collectivity, not to theories about them, the fundamental question is how these parts and their connections are conceived.

☐ Originally published in *American Sociological Review* 39 (1974) : 615–35. Reprinted by permission.

[1] In Lévi-Strauss's (1952:322) words: "The term social structure has nothing to do with empirical reality but with models built after it." For a discussion of the two contrasting views of social structure, see Nadel (1957:149–51) , Boudon (1971a) , and Lévi-Strauss (1952:336–42) himself.

My concept of social structure starts with simple and concrete definitions of the component parts and their relations. The parts are groups or classes of people, such as men and women, ethnic groups, or socioeconomic strata; more precisely, they are the positions of people in different groups and strata. The connections among as well as within the parts are the social relations of people that find expression in their social interaction and communication. This is a less abstract concept of social structure than one in terms of institutions and their integration, for example, inasmuch as it focuses on groups into which people can actually be divided and on observable manifestations of their social relations. Although this view of social structure is not abstract in one sense, it is in another. Its concepts pertain to differences among people and their relations, not to higher-order abstractions, but it abstracts analytical elements from social life to trace their interrelations and does not construct ideal types to gain an intuitive understanding of total configurations.[2] Of course, people differ in many respects—in age, religion, occupation, and power, to name a few—and the analysis of social structure moves from lower to higher levels of theoretical abstraction as it seeks to explain the combinations of forms of differentiation and their implications. In short, by social structure I refer to population distributions among social positions along various lines— positions that affect people's role relations and social interaction. This intricate definition requires explication, and I will use the term structural parameter to clarify it.

Forms of Differentiation

A social structure is delineated by its parameters. A structural parameter is any criterion implicit in the social distinctions people make in their social interaction. Age, sex, race, and socioeconomic status illustrate parameters, assuming that such differences actually affect people's role relations. The social positions that govern the social relations among their incumbents define the social structure. The simplest description of social structure is on the basis of one parameter. Thus, we speak of the age structure of a population, the

[2] In the first sense, this conception differs from Parsons' more abstract ones; in the second, it conforms to his (1937:34–36, 603–24, 748–53) stress on abstracting analytical elements and contrasts with Weber's theoretical approach and Blumer's.

kinship structure of a tribe, the authority structure of an organization, the power structure of a community, and the class structure of a society. These are not types of social structure but analytical elements of it distinguishing social positions in one dimension only. The different positions generated by a single parameter are necessarily occupied by different persons—an individual is either a man or a woman, old or young, rich or poor—but the case differs for positions generated by several parameters, because the same person simultaneously occupies positions on different parameters—he or she belongs to an ethnic group and lives in a community and has an occupation. Social structures are reflected in diverse forms of differentiation,[3] which must be kept analytically distinct. The complex configuration of elements that compose the social structure cannot be understood, in my opinion, unless analytical dissection precedes attempts at synthesis.

To speak of social structure is to speak of differentiation among people, as social structure is defined by the distinctions people make, explicitly or implicitly, in their role relations. An undifferentiated social structure is a contradiction in terms.

The thesis of my paper is that the study of the various forms of differentiation among people, their interrelations, the conditions producing them, and their implications is the distinctive task of sociology. No other discipline undertakes this important task, and sociologists too have neglected it, despite the theoretical emphasis on differentiation as a core sociological concept ever since Spencer. We have been much concerned with the characteristics and behavior of persons, yet little with the forms and degrees of differentiation among them, which constitute the specific structural problems. The subjects of structural inquiry are, for instance, ethnic heterogeneity, not ethnic background; political differentiation, not political opinions; the division of labor, not occupational performance; income inequality, not poverty. My objective is to suggest a framework for such structural analysis.

NOMINAL AND GRADUATED PARAMETERS

Two basic types of parameter can be distinguished. The first is a nominal parameter, which divides a population into subgroups with explicit boundaries. There is no inherent rank order among

[3] As Nadel (1957:97) puts it, "it seems impossible to speak of social structure in the singular."

these groups,[4] though empirically group membership may be associated with differences in hierarchical status. Sex, religion, racial identification, occupation, and neighborhood exemplify nominal parameters. The second type is a graduated parameter, which differentiates people in terms of a status rank order. In principle, the status gradation is continuous, which means that the parameter itself does not draw boundaries between strata; but the empirical distribution may reveal discontinuities that reflect hierarchical boundaries. Education, age, income, prestige, and power are examples of graduated parameters.

The assumption is that the differences in group affiliation and status created by structural parameters[5] affect role relations and the social interaction in which these relations find expression. Existing evidence often suffices to satisfy this assumption. Thus, research has shown that social intercourse is less frequent between blacks and whites than within each group, that the role relations between supervisors and subordinates differ from those among subordinates, and that differences in socioeconomic status inhibit friendships. If such evidence does not already exist, the assumption must be tested. In the case of nominal parameters, sociable intercourse is expected to be more prevalent within groups than between persons from different groups.[6] In the case of graduated parameters, sociable intercourse is expected to be inversely related to the status distance between persons. Unless these expectations are met, the investigator must abandon his initial assumption that a factor is a structural parameter. The salience of various parameters is revealed by the strength of their associations with sociable intercourse.[7] Therefore, the proposed analysis of structural differentiation in terms of parameters takes into account processes of social interaction.

[4] The term *group* is used throughout for classes of people whose members collectively interact more with one another than with outsiders but all of whom are not necessarily in direct contact, as the members of primary groups are. For a discussion of the concept of group, see Merton (1968:338–42).

[5] To state that parameters create differentiation is speaking elliptically, of course. Parameters are concepts for observing the lines of differentiation among people created in their social interaction. For convenience of expression, such shorthand phrases as "the differentiation produced by a parameter" are used throughout the paper.

[6] To be precise, ingroup rates are expected to differ from outgroup rates, and the former are nearly always higher than the latter. An exception is sex with respect to sexual intercourse and marriage, though not with respect to sociable relations, which are more frequent among men and among women than between the two sexes.

[7] Further refinements are possible by distinguishing parameters on the basis of their significance for the content of social interaction. Whether a graduated

A fundamental distinction in the generic form of differentiation is that between heterogeneity, which does not involve hierarchical differences, and status inequality, which does. Nominal parameters produce horizontal differentiation or heterogeneity, and graduated parameters produce vertical differentiation or inequality. A given nominal parameter's degree of heterogeneity depends on the number of subgroups into which a population is divided and on the distribution of people among them. The larger the number of ethnic groups in a community, the greater is its ethnic heterogeneity. But if nine tenths of a community belong to the same ethnic group and merely one tenth to a few others, there is less ethnic heterogeneity than if the population is more evenly divided among several ethnic groups. Both factors—number of groups and distribution among them—are taken into account by the index of heterogeneity proposed by Gibbs and Martin (1962), which measures the chances that two randomly selected individuals belong to different groups. This index enables one to compare heterogeneity of various kinds and in various places and to analyze the conditions associated with different forms and degrees of heterogeneity.

The inequalities resulting from graduated parameters also vary in degree. Equality is an absolute term. One cannot say "more equal," except sardonically, to imply lack of equality. But there can be a greater or lesser departure from equality. The meaning of much inequality is equivocal, however. I am referring neither to the problem of how to combine various dimensions of status nor to the problem that some of these dimensions, like power, are difficult to measure. A more basic question is how to conceptualize degree of inequality in the simplest case when a single and precise indicator of status differences is under consideration. Wealth is a good illustration, because the meaning of individual differences in wealth is unambiguous. Nevertheless, inequality in wealth can be conceived of in two contrasting ways, both of which seem plausible. On the one hand, if nearly all people are equally poor and only a few have more wealth than the rest, one would say that there is less inequality than if great diversity in wealth exists among the population. On the other hand, if the total wealth is widely distributed, one would

---

parameter reflects a monotonic rank order of status, for instance, can be ascertained by investigating whether expressions of deference and compliance conform to the status gradations of the parameter for the entire range of positions. Such a test would undoubtedly show that age is not a unilinear status dimension, because the oldest people are unlikely to command most deference and compliance. Negative salience—aggression against an outgroup—may also be examined.

also say that there is less inequality than if most of it is concentrated in the hands of a few. These two views of extent of inequality conflict, though both contrast with complete equality. For when few own most of the wealth, all the rest are roughly equal; and the greater the diversity in wealth among people, the less tends to be the share of the total concentrated in few hands.

Two forms of status inequality should therefore be distinguished. The first pertains to the concentration of wealth, power, or other status attributes in a small elite and the consequent status distance between the elite and the majority. The second refers to the diversity in status among people and implies many fine status gradations.[8] Most empirical measures of inequality, such as the Gini coefficient, primarily indicate elite concentration; and it is necessary to devise distinctive measures of status diversity.[9] Large and differentiated middle strata reflect great status diversity. Whereas elite superiority and status diversity vary within limits independently of each other, and hence occur in various combinations, their extremes are opposite. The paradox of inequality is that much concentration of power or some other status advantage is more compatible with widespread equality than with status diversity, in accordance with Simmel's insight that despots fortify their position by leveling status distinctions among their subjects and "equalizing hierarchical difference" (1950:198).

QUASI-CASTES

The relationships of a nominal parameter with graduated parameters indicate the status differences among groups, for example, the differences in education, income, and prestige among religious groups. Substantial correlations of nominal with graduated parameters make it possible to construct new parameters, which may be

[8] Not all status attributes are, like wealth, a stock of scarce resources distributed among a population. But even for those that are not, like education or prestige, it is meaningful to distinguish between great diversity and elite concentration of status, for instance, between a population with great diversity in years of schooling and one with a university-educated elite and largely illiterate masses.

[9] Examples of measures of diversity are the interquartile range and other measures of dispersion that are, unlike the variance and the standard deviation, not strongly affected by extreme values. Indications of elite concentration for status attributes that do not permit computing the Gini index (or the top stratum's share of the total) would be the proportion of the population having high status, such as the proportion with graduate degrees or the proportion with managerial authority over more than one hundred employees.

called ordinal parameters and which divide people into groups with distinct boundaries that are ordered in a hierarchy of ranks.[10] Thus, Duncan (1961) has created an index of occupational status by ranking occupational groups on the basis of their differences in education and income. In the polar case, a nominal parameter is perfectly correlated with at least one graduated parameter, because a hierarchical ranking of groups has become institutionalized, so that groups differ not merely in average status but in the status of all their members without overlap. Castes illustrate such an institutionalized hierarchy of ranked groups. So does the administrative structure of organizations, which divides employees into official ranks that differ in authority and perquisites.

There are no castes in modern society. Yet one of its major institutions—formal organizations—resembles a caste structure in some respects, though not in all, of course, since administrative rank is not an ascribed position. Moreover, there are quasi-castes in modern society. If a nominal parameter indicative of ascribed positions is strongly associated with graduated parameters, it reveals hierarchically ranked groups that exhibit little overlap in status. Such groups may aptly be described as quasi-castes, provided that there are also restrictions on intimate relations between members of different groups. Racial differences in the United States are strongly associated with differences in prestige, education, income, wealth, and power; and they inhibit intermarriage and intimate social contacts generally. American blacks and whites are quasi-castes. Sex differences too are associated with differences in various aspects of status, but men and women are united through marriage in intimate family relations. Women and men cannot be designated as quasi-castes, therefore, though sex differences are not without caste ingredients.

If caste is dissected into its analytical elements rather than viewed as a global type, it becomes evident that caste ingredients can be found in many groups. Three basic attributes of caste are ascription, a hierarchy having no status overlap, and severe restrictions on social intercourse. The three do not have to occur together, however; and they do not have to be conceptualized as dichotomies that

[10] The distinction of the three types of parameters is related to but not identical with that of nominal, ordinal, and interval scales of measurement. A main difference is that in terms of measurement, ordinal scales are an intermediate type between nominal and interval scales, whereas conceptually ordinal parameters are the derived type because they combine the two criteria for defining nominal and graduated parameters, respectively.

cannot vary in degree. Thus, instead of thinking of ascription in the usual way as an attribute that is either present or absent, we may treat it as the extreme value of a continuous variable, specifically, of rates of intergroup mobility. Ascription means that there is no mobility from the social positions people occupy at birth. If the mobility rates among social positions are very low, these positions hardly differ from ascribed ones and may be said to contain much of one caste ingredient. Similarly, the hierarchical character of castes with no status overlap represents the terminal point of the continuous variable indicating how little status overlap exists and how great the hierarchical differences are between groups, which is reflected in the correlations between a nominal parameter and graduated parameters, with perfect correlations revealing the extreme of caste. Finally, restrictions on social intercourse are manifest in the actual rates of intermarriage and intergroup sociability, with very low rates indicating both a most salient parameter and a third kind of caste element.

By decomposing the ideal type of caste into its analytical elements, we can discover which groups display which caste ingredients to what extent. But the concept of quasi-caste should not be trivialized by applying it to nearly every group. All group differences are accompanied by some restriction on intergroup contacts, and most are also accompanied by some differences in average status and some restriction on intergroup mobility. Groups should be designated as quasi-castes only when a nominal parameter exhibits substantial positive correlations with graduated parameters, disclosing great status differences, and substantial negative correlations with both rates of intergroup contacts and rates of intergroup mobility, which show that restrictions on social intercourse between groups are severe and that social positions are virtually ascribed. Race is the polar case in our society, but there are other groups that resemble quasi-castes, like the Appalachian whites or Main Line Philadelphians. As this discussion illlustrates, structural analysis tends to involve inquiries into the interrelations of parameters and their relationships with processes of social interaction and social mobility.

STRUCTURAL ANALYSIS

Parameters are the framework for the macrosociological analysis of social structure in empirical and theoretical terms. But are not

parameters simply variables disguised by a fancy label? Although
they are indeed variables characterizing individuals, they are used
in structural analysis in distinctive ways. The variation in individual
characteristics among people is the new variable that describes a
feature of the social structure—the degree of variation or the shape
of the distribution. Thus, concern is not with the occupations of individuals but with the extent of variation in their occupational
positions, which is indicative of the division of labor; not with the
income of individuals but with the distribution of incomes in a
society, which reflects income inequality. Empirically, structural
parameters find expression in various measures of dispersion. Conceptually, specific forms of differentiation must be distinguished, and
so must their combinations that generate still other forms of differentiation.

The theoretical aim is to explain the forms and degrees of social
differentiation and their implications for social integration and social change. Hence, it is to explain variations in the structural features of societies, not variations in the behavior of individuals, in
contrast to Homans (1961). Moreover, it is to explain the differentiation among people in societies, not the global characteristics of societies (Lazarsfeld and Menzel, 1964:428–29), such as their cultural
tradition, social institutions, or dominant values, in contrast to
Parsons (1951; Parsons and Smelser, 1956). This conception of social
structure does not try to encompass everything important in social
life but focuses on the differentiation among people. The prevailing
values and the existing technology, though surely important social
conditions, are not part of the social structure in the narrow sense
in which the term is used. Value orientations are taken into account
indirectly insofar as they are reflected either in social differentiation—as exemplified by religious and political differences—or in the
salience of parameters for social intercourse—as exemplified by the
influence of cultural values on whether religious background or
occupational success most affects choices of associates. Many social conditions may influence, and in turn be influenced by, the structural
features under intensive investigation, such as society's technology
and its affluence, and prevailing cultural values are considered to be
simply another one of these conditions.[11]

Three problem areas in structural analysis may be explored. The
first is the connection between structural differentiation and pro-

[11] I consider this structural approach to be in the tradition of Simmel, Durkheim,
and Marx.

cesses of social integration. Here concern is with the implications of differentiation for the processes of social interaction and communication in which social relations find expression and through which individuals become integrated in groups and the various groups are integrated in the larger social structure. The second problem is to refine the distinctions among forms of differentiation, analyze the conditions on which the specific forms depend, and investigate the relationships of one form of differentiation with others. For example, what are the distinct forms of the division of labor, which conditions govern the form it takes, and how is the division of labor related to status inequalities? A third question is how the actual combinations of the analytically distinguished forms of differentiation affect the dynamics of structural change. The relationships of parameters indicate how consolidated status structures are, which has important implications for processes of integration and mobility, the nature of social change, and the depth of social inequalities. The remainder of the paper deals with these three problems.

Differentiation and Integration

Individuals become integrated members of groups through processes of recurrent social interaction and communication. This conceptualization of social integration complements that of social differentiation introduced earlier, integration being defined in terms of intensive social interaction and differentiation in terms of restrictions on social interaction. Social associations establish the networks of interpersonal relations that integrate individuals into cohesive social units. Regular face-to-face contacts in groups socialize new members, furnish continuing social support, create interdependence through social exchange, and thereby make individuals integral parts of groups. These processes of social integration describe conditions in small groups, such as families, friendship cliques, and work groups. But how do individuals and small groups become integrated in entire societies or other collectivities too large for most members to be in direct communication?

The answer often given is that common values are the basis of the social integration of societies. However, common values do not suffice to integrate individuals into a network of social relations. This requires supportive social interaction, which is the reason that integration is assumed to rest on social interaction. Although shared value orientations undoubtedly promote social integration, they do so by encouraging social intercourse among persons when the opportunity arises. Since value orientations are more likely to be shared within groups than by members of different groups, we must still ask what produces the social connections among diverse groups that integrate them and their members into a society. The answer I suggest is that structural differentiation is the condition that brings about macrosocial integration, paradoxical as this seems, inasmuch as differentiation is conceptualized as restricting social intercourse and integration as contingent on it.

IMPLICATIONS OF HETEROGENEITY

Even in small and simple tribes, social integration depends on structural differentiation. The kinship structure is the main basis for differentiation. It divides tribes into clans and families, creating subunits sufficiently small for every member to have daily contact with all others. The intimate and frequent social interaction in families socializes children and transmits the common language and culture to them, and it provides social support to adults as well as children. These social processes make children as well as adults integral parts not only of their families but also of their clans and tribes, because the kinship structure links families in interlocking groups. The incest taboo requires that kin-groups exchange spouses, with the result that marriages give rise to crosscutting ties that strengthen intergroup relations. Hence, the differentiated kinship structure produces the conditions for integrative social associations both within and among kin-groups.

Industrialized societies are much larger and much more heterogeneous than simple tribes, of course. Their sheer size makes it inconceivable that a single kinship system could encompass all members and serve as the basis for an integrated social structure. Their complex heterogeneity, however, furnishes new grounds for social interaction across group boundaries that integrates the diverse groups; but these new conditions alter the character of most human relations and of the social integration rooted in them. The macrostructures of industrial societies are not merely much differentiated in a given dimension; they are differentiated along many distinct lines—religiously, occupationally, ethnically, geographically, politically, and in numerous other ways. Before analyzing such multiform heterogeneity, let us examine the significance of heterogeneity in a single dimension for social integration.

Nominal parameters are reflected in heterogeneity of varying degrees. By definition, a nominal parameter finds expression in disproportionately high rates of sociable intercourse within groups, and recurrent sociable intercourse is the foundation of social integration. Hence, nominal parameters contribute to ingroup integration. The more salient a parameter, the firmer are the group boundaries, and the greater is the tendency to confine sociable interaction to the ingroup. Consequently, salient parameters intensify integrative social interaction within groups, but at the same time they fortify the segregating boundaries between groups. This would impede the macrosocial integration of the diverse groups in society were it not for heterogeneity, which changes the situation.

Whereas heterogeneity creates barriers to social intercourse, much heterogeneity weakens these barriers. This paradoxical conclusion can be derived from two simple assumptions: first, people tend to prefer ingroup to outgroup associates, and second, people tend to prefer associating with outgroup members to not associating with anybody and remaining isolated. The first assumption is true by definition, because the criterion of a group is an excess of ingroup over outgroup social associations.[12] The second is not, but it seems plausible; and it is testable, directly and through its implications for intergroup relations.

The more pronounced the heterogeneity, the greater are the chances that people's casual encounters involve members of different groups. Much heterogeneity, therefore, often forces people to choose between interacting with others who are not members of their ingroups and not engaging in social interaction at all. Although individuals may have intimate associates in their own groups, increasing heterogeneity makes the occasions more frequent when the only alternative to socializing with outsiders is to withdraw from social

---

[12] If it is also assumed that firm group barriers make ingroup choices as likely in small as in large groups, it follows that very small groups, whose few members restrict the choice of ingroup associates, exhibit denser social intercourse, more overlap of friendships, and consequently higher social integration than large groups. (It should be noted that normally a group's small size exerts pressures to make outgroup choices and depresses the rate of ingroup choices below that in large groups.) Here again we arrive from different premises at a conclusion akin to one of Simmel's (1950:89–90), who points out that the small size of sects whose dogma and distinctive practices insulate them from other groups is essential for their strong ties of social solidarity.

intercourse for the time being. Given the second assumption—that people usually prefer outgroup associates to no associates—heterogeneity exerts structural constraints to enter into social interaction with persons who are not members of one's own group and establish intergroup relations. Group boundaries are barriers to sociable relations, but the proliferation of boundaries implicit in great heterogeneity lessens these barriers and encourages intergroup relations.

The physical separation of groups obliterates this effect of heterogeneity. If the various groups are located in different towns and neighborhoods, most encounters involve members of the same group, notwithstanding the heterogeneity of the total population. In this situation, there is little opportunity for intergroup contacts. The consequent restriction of most social intercourse to members of the same group strengthens group barriers and increases social distances among groups. In other words, differences in location that are highly correlated with people's differences in another respect suppress the impact of heterogeneity on intergroup relations. But this is not a distinctive feature of location; high correlations between two or more kinds of differences among people generally suppress the impact of heterogeneity.

MULTIFORM HETEROGENEITY

In industrialized societies, numerous nominal parameters produce multiform heterogeneity, which means that every person belongs to a variety of groups and has multiple roles. Although this multiform heterogeneity has been alluded to before, it has not yet been explicitly taken into account in the analysis. Heterogeneity in a single dimension, though pronounced, does not greatly constrain people to establish intergroup relations in a large society. Even when the population is divided into thousands of groups, most groups contain still thousands of persons, which makes it easy to realize ingroup preferences and confine most sociable interaction to the ingroup. But intersecting lines of differentiation increase heterogeneity exponentially, which reduces the size of perfectly homogeneous subgroups to the vanishing point and thereby reinstates the structural constraints to participate in intergroup relations that society's large size would otherwise nullify.[13]

[13] If parameters were perfectly orthogonal, p parameters each of which divides the population into s subgroups would produce s^p completely homogeneous

Multiform heterogeneity compels people to have associates outside their own groups, because it makes ingroup relations simultaneously intergroup relations in terms of different parameters. We cannot help associating with outsiders, because our ingroup associates in one dimension are, in several others, members of outgroups (Merton, 1972:22–25). For people to realize ingroup preference with respect to the most salient parameters, they must maintain intergroup relations along other parameters. This is by no means a minor constraint. In complex social structures, so many roles are important that people often must set aside ingrained ingroup prejudices for the sake of other roles. The common interests of automobile workers constrain blacks and whites to join in a union and engage in social interaction, and the common interests of blacks constrain unskilled workers and professionals to join in common endeavors and associate with each other.

From another perspective, multiform heterogeneity means that people in different groups also hold group memberships in common. There are few if any people who do not differ in some group affiliation, and there are few who do not share some group affiliation. The shared attributes of persons in different groups are a basis for social interaction when the occasion arises and for developing social relations across group boundaries. This conclusion can be formally derived from the definition of nominal parameters in terms of ingroup associations and the assumption that multiform heterogeneity is so extensive that virtually no persons have all group affiliations in common. If people are predisposed to associate with others who share their group affiliations and if nearly all people differ in some affiliation, though they share others, it follows that the common group affiliations of persons who in any given dimension belong to different groups will promote social associations across group boundaries in this dimension.

Social norms influence these group processes, but their influence is not independent of the structural conditions resulting from heterogeneity. In largely homogeneous communities, sociable contacts tend to be confined to ingroups, and socializing with persons outside one's own group is a deviant practice likely to be disapproved by normative expectations. The pressures exerted by increasing heterogeneity

---

subgroups, which is likely to exceed the number of persons, even in a large society. Parameters are more or less interrelated, of course. Nevertheless, if only two were orthogonal and all other coincided with them, surely an extreme and unrealistic assumption, heterogeneity would increase exponentially.

make social intercourse between members of different groups more frequent and thus a less deviant pattern. The growing prevalence of intergroup relations enlarges the social circles who accept them, which implies that such relations encounter less social disapproval and that normative expectations gradually adjust to them. This oversimplifies the dynamics of developments, however, because deep-seated social norms tend to resist the pressure for change engendered by new conditions. Persisting strong normative disapproval of intergroup contacts often inhibits them despite enhanced heterogeneity. Intensified ethnocentrism when a community becomes ethnically mixed is an example.

But when multiform heterogeneity is pronounced, the predominant ingroup relations along some lines enforced by social norms are necessarily accompanied by intergroup relations along other lines. Besides, different group affiliations are most salient in different contexts—sometimes people's union, sometimes their church, sometimes their neighborhood—and the changing ingroup preferences, depending on the situation, undermine social norms that would preserve certain ingroup preferences. Although social norms can discourage particular intergroup relations, they cannot neutralize the compelling pressure of multiform heterogeneity on the proliferation of intergroup relations generally, nor are the norms themselves immune from this pressure.

The multiple roles and group affiliations in complex social structures weaken the hold of ingroup ties and alter the form of social integration. People have wider circles of less intimate associates. The cocktail party is symbolic. The attenuation of profound social bonds that firmly integrate individuals in their communities is often deplored. But strong ingroup bonds restrain individual freedom and mobility, and they sustain rigidity and bigotry. Diverse intergroup relations, though not intimate, broaden horizons and promote tolerance, and they are the basis of macrosocial integration. Intimate relations, like those in the conjugal family and between good friends, are the main source of social support for individuals. Since intimate relations tend to be confined to small and closed social circles, however, they fragment society into small groups. The integration of these groups in the society depends on people's weak ties, not their strong ones, because weak social ties extend beyond intimate circles (Granovetter, 1973) and establish the intergroup connections on which macrosocial integration rests. The social integration of individuals in contemporary society is no longer based exclusively on

the support of particular ingroups but in good part on multiple
supports from wider networks of less intimate relations.[14] To use an
analogy, a Gothic structure supported by multiple counterbalancing
buttresses has replaced a Norman structure with a uniform solid
foundation.

It must be stressed that this analysis of the structural constraints
that promote intergroup relations assumes that multiform heterogeneity actually exists, which requires that nominal parameters are
not strongly related and various lines of differentiation intersect. If
parameters are highly correlated—for example, if ethnic differences
largely coincide with differences in religion, occupation, and politics—group differences reinforce each other and discourage intergroup relations. Only cross-cutting group affiliations impel people
to choose among their various ingroup preferences and set aside
some, entering into certain intergroup relations, for the sake of
others. Coinciding group affiliations, in contrast, make the various
ingroup preferences cumulative and strengthen tendencies to restrict
sociable intercourse to persons who share most of one's affiliations.
The previously mentioned correlation of location with group differences that counteracts the effect of heterogeneity on intergroup
relations is simply a special case of the general principle that correlated parameters counteract the impact of heterogeneity.

STATUS INEQUALITY

The effects of status inequality on social relations and on the
integration of social strata in society depend on the form the inequality takes. Diversity of status, which means that few people are
roughly equal in status, does not have the same implications for
social interaction and communication as a concentration of status
resources and powers, which means that a small elite is far superior
to the majority. The absence of large and diversified middle strata
is the criterion of elite concentration, not the absolute social distance between the elite and lower strata, whatever the measure. Although the difference between the most educated minority and the

[14] Simmel (1955:163) notes that the individual in modern society "is deprived
of many supports and advantages associated with the tightly-knit, primary
group. [But] the creation of groups and associations in which any number of
people can come together on the basis of their interest in a common purpose,
compensates for that isolation of the personality which develops out of breaking away from the narrow confines of earlier circumstances."

majority with only compulsory education may be the same in two countries, for instance, elite concentration would be higher in the one having fewer persons with intermediate amounts of education, because a larger share of the total educational resources would be concentrated in the elite. The same applies to distributions of wealth, income, power, or other status attributes. The distinction between status diversity and elite concentration is an analytical one, and actual status structures reveal combinations of both in varying degrees.

Status differences inhibit social intercourse. That fact is inherent in the very concept of status, and it has therefore been made a defining criterion of graduated parameters. However, great diversity in status promotes social interaction among persons whose status differs, just as great heterogeneity promotes social interaction between persons in different groups. Much status diversity reduces the social distance between strata and thus the status barriers to sociability. It also creates intervening links between strata, as people bring together acquaintances of higher and lower status than their own. In addition, diversity increases the probability that social encounters will involve persons whose status differs and hence the frequency of occasions for social intercourse that crosses status lines. Moreover, the multiform status diversity that occurs when graduated parameters exhibit weak correlations leads to sociability among persons whose status, though alike in some ways, is not alike in all. For example, people may socialize with others whose status origins, wealth, and income are similar to their own, but whose education and political power are not. Whereas status diversity does not make interpersonal relations between the highest and lowest strata likely, it links them indirectly by fostering personal relations between strata that are not far apart.

Elite concentration of such status attributes as wealth, power, and education is expected to discourage social intercourse between the elite and other strata and encourage it among these other strata, for several reasons. It entails great social distance between the elite and the majority. It implies a small middle class and thus few intervening links that could help bridge the gap between the elite and the rest of the population. It reduces the likelihood of chance encounters between the large majority and the small elite. And it makes the elite interested in preserving their superior position. These very conditions that impede communication between the elite and other strata are likely to facilitate communication across status lines among other strata. The great social distance from the elite and the small size of the middle class diminish the social distance among the lower strata, both in absolute terms and in terms of reference-group comparisons, because whatever status differences exist among them pale by comparison with the difference between them and the elite. The probability of social encounters between persons in the various lower strata is very great, owing to the large proportion of the population they compose. And the vested interest of the elite to maintain superior status has its counterpart in the common interest of the lower strata to improve their status, providing common grounds for social associations.

What are the implications of status diversity and elite concentration for macrosocial integration? Status diversity contributes to macrosocial integration, as heterogeneity does, though not as much, because it furnishes only indirect links between social strata that are widely separated. Some great social distances that inhibit sociable interaction and free communication are a built-in trait of great status diversity, but deep ingroup prejudices that similarly inhibit sociability and communication are not inherent in much heterogeneity. The multiform differentiation resulting from many weakly correlated parameters, in particular, enhances macrosocial integration. Elite concentration, while it furthers integrative relations among lower strata, widens the breach between them and the top stratum. This adverse effect on the integration of the entire society is magnified if different resources and powers are concentrated in the same elite and consolidate its dominant position. The last section of the paper will deal with the problem of consolidation in social structures.

Division of Labor

The next topic is designed to illustrate the analysis of specific forms of differentiation and their relationships. For this purpose, an inquiry into the division of labor is presented, distinguishing its forms, inferring the conditions that govern its forms, and examining its implications for status inequalities. The division of labor refers to the distribution of people among occupational position. It therefore is synonymous with occupational differentiation.

The division of labor in societies is closely connected with their status structure. Differences in occupational positions are associated with differences in status—in education, income, prestige, and power. In the terms adopted, occupation is a nominal parameter that is associated with several graduated parameters. One might readily assume on the basis of these associations that the degree of occupational differentiation—the division of labor—is similarly associated with the degree of status differentiation—the extent of inequality in status. But this assumption is not warranted. The relationship between two forms of differentiation is often confused with the relationship between the two underlying attributes of individuals, as Coleman (1973b:1525) notes. Although the occupation and education of individuals are correlated, in our society and undoubtedly in most, this does not tell us whether the amount of variation among individuals in occupation and in education are correlated. This can only be determined by comparing different societies or historical periods. As a matter of fact, occupational differentiation is variously related to different forms of status inequality, as we shall see. But first the distinct forms of occupational differentiation need to be analyzed.

ROUTINIZATION AND SPECIALIZATION

The division of labor increases when new jobs are added to those being performed or when present jobs are subdivided into a larger number.[15] The one is illustrated by the job of computer operator, which did not exist until recently, and the other by automobile mechanics in large garages who have come to specialize in repairing only certain parts of cars. Subdividing jobs narrows the range of different tasks of all jobs or many of them, but the total repertory of tasks remains presumably the same. For instance, if all clerks once both typed and filed, and now some only type and others only file, the range of tasks for each is narrower than before, but the tasks performed by the entire group have apparently not changed. Actually, however, the sheer subdivision of work often gives rise to new tasks.

The subdivision of jobs may take two forms. On the one hand, it may routinize work, because the narrower range of tasks simplifies

[15] The variation in the number of different occupational positions is a simple indicator of the division of labor. A more refined one, like the Gibbs-Martin index, takes also the distribution of the labor force among the various positions into account.

jobs and reduces the training and skills required to perform them, as when work originally carried out by craftsmen is broken into simple routines on an assembly line. On the other hand, it may make work more specialized, as exemplified by the differences between general practitioners and medical specialists. Here the narrower range of tasks permits greater expertness to be acquired and applied to the work, increasing the training and skills needed to perform it. Note that medical specialists execute tasks that general practitioners cannot undertake. The subdivision of work in the form of specialization, without supposedly adding any new work, in fact leads to the performance of new tasks, adding to the range of tasks accomplished by the collectivity while narrowing the range of tasks of individuals.

The basic difference between routinization and specialization is that the first lowers and the second raises the levels of training and skills required of the labor force. The associations of the division of labor with years of training and degrees of skills thus indicate which one of the two forms it assumes. This difference implies that routinization decreases but specialization increases labor costs, which are reflected directly in the wages and salaries an organization must pay its employees and indirectly in the resources a society must devote to vocational training and education. Since it lessens training time and labor costs, routinizing work is a means for improving input-output efficiency and augmenting the results attainable with given manpower resources. By routinizing some of the work of physicians to enable nurses to perform it, expanded health services can be provided by the available labor force without a rise in costs. Specialization reduces strictly economic efficiency, because it requires long training and costly manpower, but it makes completely new accomplishments possible. Medical specialists can accomplish cures unheard of before the age of specialization, and plumbers can accomplish repairs handymen cannot do. Routinization contributes to the quantity and specialization to the quality of achievements.

By enlarging output at given labor costs, routinization improves labor productivity, whereas specialization depends on other conditions to improve it and thereby to release the time and resources needed to train specialists. Routinization can consequently help supply the manpower resources specialization demands, which implies that routinization furthers the growth of specialization. Accordingly, the increasing division of labor simultaneously makes some jobs more routine and others more specialized, enhancing the differences in skills among the labor force, which may be called a bifurcation of skills. In short, routinization, by raising labor productivity, promotes specialization, and the progressing division of labor is therefore accompanied by a growing bifurcation of skills.

This conclusion must be qualified, however, by emphasizing that routinization, though it can contribute to the development of specialization, is neither a necessary nor a sufficient condition for its development. It is not necessary, because other conditions can improve labor productivity and free manpower for specialized training and work, for example, advances in technology. It is not sufficient, because the mere fact that routine work is performed by people with little training and few skills obviously does not enhance labor productivity. What does is the effective *organization* of complex responsibilities through subdivision into simpler duties that reduce the qualifications needed to perform them. Only within the context of a systematically organized division of labor is routinization likely to raise labor productivity and thus free resources for specialization.

THE FORMAL ORGANIZATION OF WORK

Formally established work organizations—organizations whose members are employed to perform work—play an essential part in the development of the division of labor in society. They are the institutionalized mechanism for organizing work in the pursuit of given objectives. Work organizations bring large numbers of people together, and they require joint endeavors that involve dense social interaction and communication. These conditions—large volume and social density—are the two Durkheim (1947:256–62) specified as the main determinants of the division of labor. Indeed, research has shown that the division of labor in organizations increases as the number of employees does, from which one might infer that it also increases with communication density, on the assumption that many employees entail extensive communication. Conditions in organizations are conducive to the proliferation of the division of labor, especially in the form of extensive routinization.

In contrast to emergent social structures, like those of entire societies, organizations have stipulated objectives, such as a government agency's mission, a factory's product, or a corporation's profit.

These given ends specify the nature of the output, supplying criteria for defining efficiency and creating budget constraints to minimize labor costs per output.[16] Besides, organizations have administrators responsible for the efficient attainment of objectives, who have the authority and the incentives to organize the work force for this purpose. An organization's division of labor is administratively enacted as a means to improve operations, unlike society's division of labor, which is the emergent result of the actions of many people pursuing diverse ends, in socialist as well as capitalist countries, the difference between them being a matter of degree.

Organizations meet the conditions necessary for the systematic routinization of work, since their division of labor is administratively instituted as a means for efficient performance at minimum labor costs. Hence, the above considerations imply primarily that an organization's division of labor takes the form of routinization, and that the routinization of some jobs is accompanied by the specialization of others, manifesting a bifurcation of skills. There are indications that this is the case. A study of American government offices finds that the division of labor is positively related to the proportion of personnel in routine clerical jobs (Blau and Schoenherr, 1971: 93, 218). A study of British organizations reports a parallel correlation and also finds positive correlations of the division of labor with the standardization and formalization of work, two other expressions of routinization (Pugh *et al.*, 1968:83).[17] A study of matched British and American manufacturing firms reveals that the division of labor is positively related to formalization in both (Inkson *et al.*, 1970:361).[18]

By routinizing work, the organizational division of labor helps mobilize resources for specialists. The study of government offices

[16] Such budgetary constraints do not exist only in profit-making enterprises, and they put pressure on administrators to try to maximize efficiency by reducing costs, even when doing so sacrifices quality, as is likely unless objectives are sufficiently precise to permit quantitative calculation of results.

[17] The measure of the division of labor in the American study is the number of occupational positions; that in the British study is the number of *a priori* specified functions performed by at least one full-time employee, which is called "role specialization" (Pugh *et al.*, 1968:72–74, 93–96; for the measures of standardization and formalization, see 74–76, 96–102).

[18] The measures of the two variables—"functional specialization" and "formalization of documentation"—are reported by Inkson and colleagues (1970:352,354) to be similar to, though not identical with, those in the British study just cited.

indicates that the proportion of routine clerical personnel, independent of its relationships with the divisions of labor, is positively related to superior qualifications of the professional personnel (Blau and Schoenherr, 1971:218–19). Such bifurcation of skills is also observable in universities and colleges, inasmuch as the academic division of labor is positively related to superior qualifications of the faculty as well as high proportions of routine clerical personnel (Blau, 1973:71–72, 82–83).[19] The resources needed for highly qualified specialists intensify budget pressures in organizations to routinize work and enable less costly personnel to perform it.[20]

The bifurcation of skills implies that the division of labor intensifies status inequalities. If the manpower resources for specialists come partly from savings realized by routinizing the work of others, specialization and routinization increase together as the division of labor does, extending differences in education and qualifications, and quite possibly in rewards and influence too. Under these conditions, the higher status of the specialists rests on the labor productivity of the low-status workers in routinized jobs. This seems to be the situation in many formal organizations. It may well also be the situation in societies during early stages of industrialization, when much routine work of peasants and laborers is required to support a small minority of specialists. However, it apparently is not the prevailing situation in contemporary industrial societies.

DIVISION OF LABOR AND INEQUALITIES

The division of labor in contemporary societies is predominantly in the form of specialization, as indicated by the positive relationships of occupational differentiation with higher levels of training and skills—of educational and occupational qualifications. Both historical trends and cross-national comparisons reveal these relation-

---

[19] The measure of division of labor is the number of academic departments in a university or college, controlling its size; that of faculty qualifications is the percent of the faculty who have Ph.D.'s or advanced professional degrees (Blau, 1973: 29, 79–80) .

[20] In most organizations, the savings in labor cost achieved through routinization may actually supply the resources for hiring specialists with superior qualifications. In academic institutions, the causal nexus is probably the reverse, and the cost of highly qualified faculty creates pressures to save other labor costs and faculty time by routinizing much administrative work.

ships. Occupational differentiation has steadily increased in the United States since the beginning of this century,[21] the population's education has risen dramatically in that period,[22] and so has the proportion of the labor force in professional and technical occupations.[23] Data on more than sixty countries similarly show that a society's occupational differentiation exhibits substantial positive correlations with the level of education (.73) and with the proportion of the male labor force in professional and related occupations (.55).[24]

If the growth of specialization in today's societies depended on a growth in routinization and hence on a bifurcation of skills, then the advancing division of labor would be positively related to inequality in educational qualifications, whereas it actually is negatively related. A pronounced division of labor reduces elite concentration

---

[21] From .919 in 1900 to .990 in 1970, using the Gibbs-Martin index for detailed occupations. Computed from data in U.S. Bureau of the Census (1960: 75–78 and 1973:1–718–24). If broad occupational groups are used, the increases in occupational differentiation, as measured by the Gibbs-Martin index, are concealed after 1930 (the values are .784 for 1900, .897 for 1930, and .869 for 1970), because some of the formerly small occupational groups have started to expand beyond their proportional share of the labor force, notably "professional, technical, and kindred workers" and "clerical and kindred workers." Detailed occupations reflect the continuing increase in division of labor within these and other major occupational groups.

[22] The median years of school completed has increased from 8.2 at the beginning of the century to 12.6 in 1970. The first figure is estimated and the second computed from U.S. Bureau of the Census (1960:214 and 1973:1–1623–1624). Years of schooling is naturally an imperfect indication of vocational training (see Berg, 1971); yet, broadly speaking, better-educated people tend to have superior occupational qualifications.

[23] The increase in "professional, technical, and kindred workers" has been more than threefold, from 4.3 to 14.5 percent, between 1900 and 1970 (U.S. Bureau of the Census, 1960: 74 and 1973: 1–718).

[24] The measure of occupational differentiation is the Gibbs-Martin index, based on ten occupational categories, computed from data in International Labor Office (1972). (The problems encountered with measuring occupational differentiation in terms of broad categories in the United States—see footnote 21—are unlikely to distort the comparisons substantially, because most countries have only small proportions of their labor force in expanding occupations and because the variation in the differentiation index is so great, ranging from .23 to .83.) The measure of education is the adjusted school enrollment ratio, the proportion of the estimated population 5–19 years of age who attend school (see Taylor and Hudson, 1971: 39–40). The number of cases is sixty-four for the first and sixty-five for the second correlation reported. These results (and others cited later) have been obtained in a preliminary analysis of cross-national data for 1965 by Zeev Gorin and myself. The major source of these data is Taylor and Hudson (1971).

of superior education,[25] and possibly enhances diversity in education, because people cannot engage in a variety of more or less specialized work if most have only a few years of schooling. The increase in the division of labor in the United States during this century has been accompanied by a decline in educational inequality, as observed in two different analyses of census data, one using the Gini coefficient (B. Duncan, 1968: 619) and the other the coefficient of variation (Jencks, 1972: 20–21). Although cross-national data to measure educational inequality are unavailable, a rising level of school attendance, which is the cross-national measure of education, virtually always reflects a decline in educational inequality. Hence, the strong correlation between occupational differentiation and education (.73) makes the inference highly probable that a country's division of labor is inversely related to its inequality in education.[26]

The expansion of specialization is contingent on society's industrial development, however. As long as the efforts of most people are needed to provide food and other means of subsistence, few can engage in specialized pursuits. Technological and economic developments are essential to lift these restraints and free the time of many for specialized work. A society's technological development, as indicated by energy consumption per capita, is substantially correlated with its occupational differentiation (.51), its population's education (.57), and the proportion of its labor force in professional work (.69), and so is a society's economic development, as indicated by gross national product per capita (the three correlations are .50, .62, and .74, respectively). These strong influences of industrial developments raise the suspicion that the correlations of the division of labor with education and with professionalization may be spurious, resulting from the dependence of all three factors on industrialization. But the cross-national data reveal that this is not the case.

---

[25] All empirical measures of inquality used in research refer primarily to elite concentration rather than status diversity, as noted before.

[26] If a pronounced division of labor in today's industrial societies results primarily in more specialization and lessens inequalities in educational qualifications, why does a pronounced division of labor within numerous organizations in highly industrialized societies promote primarily routinization and enhance inequalities in skills? Two admittedly speculative answers may be suggested. First, the budgetary constraints in work organizations may make hiring specialists conditional on savings effected by routinizing other work. Second, unskilled workers can more easily be replaced than those with specialized skills, which weakens their bargaining power and strengthens administrative authority over them; these advantages of routinization for organizations and their administrators may influence the administrative decisions that govern the subdivision of work.

When technological or economic developments are controlled, the division of labor continues to exhibit positive relationships with education and professionalization.[27] The components of specialization—advanced division of labor, superior training, and high skills —all depend on technological and economic conditions, but the division of labor is related to training and skills independent of these conditions, which supports the conclusion that the increasing division of labor in contemporary societies promotes extensive specialization.

In terms of the earlier theoretical analysis, technological advances improve labor productivity and free manpower resources for specialized training and work, thereby making specialization no longer largely conditional on the labor productivity effected through extensive routinization. Yet routinization plays an important part in this development. The more the division of labor has routinized jobs, the easier it becomes to have them done by machines. Routinization creates the conditions that enable organizations to mechanize and automate operations, and the savings in labor costs that can be realized furnish incentives for installing modern technical equipment. As machines are substituted for men and women in routine jobs, growing proportions engage in skilled and specialized work. An example is the empirical finding that automating operations in government offices reduces the proportion of personnel in routine clerical jobs (Blau and Schoenherr, 1971: 60–61, 93–94, 123–24). Widespread routinization seems a stage in the development of the division of labor that intensifies inequalities in training and skills, but further developments of the division of labor resulting from technological progress apparently diminish these inequalities by expanding the specialized and reducing the routine work.

Since an advanced division of labor tends to lessen inequality in education, it should also lessen inequality in income. Whether this is so is a moot question, however. What the American trend

[27] The high correlation (.92) between energy consumption per capita and GNP per capita (for variable definitions, see Taylor and Hudson [1971:59–60, 65]) make it impossible to control both simultaneously. The results of the four regression analyses are: (1) with education as dependent variable, the beta weight for energy is .27 and that for DoL (division of labor) is .59; (2) with education as dependent variable, the beta weight for GNP is .34 and that for DoL is .56; (3) with professionals (% of male labor force in professional and related occupations) as dependent variable, the beta weight of energy is .55 and that of DoL is .27; (4) with professionals as dependent variable, the beta weight of GNP is .63 and that of DoL is .23. All beta weights are more than twice their standard error. The number of cases is sixty-four in the first three analyses and sixty-five in the last.

in income inequality has been is in dispute. The best evidence indicates that income inequality is lower today than early in the century but that nearly the entire decline occurred around World War II, with inequality remaining nearly constant in the two decades before and in the two since (H. P. Miller, 1966: esp. 15–28).[28] Occupational differentiation reveals a different trend line, with a steady slow increase. Should one emphasize that today the division of labor is more pronounced and income inequality less pronounced than two generations ago, which implies a negative relationship, or that the trend lines are not parallel, which implies no connection? The cross-national data do not resolve the issue. Whereas occupational differentiation and income inequality are negatively correlated for the twenty countries for which fairly reliable income data exist (–.40),[29] the small number of cases and the data's questionable reliability undermine confidence in the finding. The conservative conclusion is that the division of labor is little related to the distribution of incomes, though there are limited indications that it is inversely related to income inequality.[30]

In sum, the division of labor in highly industrialized societies tends to take the form of expanding specialization and be accompanied by reduced inequalities in education and qualifications, and possibly also in income and prestige. Does inequality of power simi-

[28] Data from 1970 reveal little change in income inequality since 1960, the last year for which Miller presents data. The Gini coefficient of income inequality —computed from data in Jencks (1972:210) —is .360 for 1970, and that for 1960 that Miller (1966:24) presents is .369. The pioneering work on income inequality is Kuznets' (1953; see also 1966), but his argument that income inequality has declined in recent years seems to be convincingly refuted by Miller (1966: 20–26).

[29] Based on the Gibbs-Martin index of occupational differentiation and the Gini coefficient of income inequality among occupational groups. The income data are taken from Secretariat (1967) and Economic Commission (1971), supplemented by the data on a few additional countries from Kravis (1973: 67). When the more widely available data on income inequality *among industrial sectors* (Taylor and Hudson, 1971:82–83) are used as proxy for *occupational income inequality,* as suggested by Kuznets (1963), they reveal a significant negative correlation (–.46) with occupational differentiation (based on forty-three countries).

[30] The reason that educational inequality has declined substantially while income inequality has declined less (B. Duncan, 1968: 618) may be that people's successful demand for more education, which helped raise the level and reduce the inequality of education, has exceeded the qualifications needed by employers (Berg, 1971). A further reason is perhaps that executives have been unwilling to make the technological adjustments required to capitalize on this educated labor force.

larly decline with growing industrialization and specialization? Although no direct measures of power distributions exist, the role of formal organizations in industrial societies makes this most doubtful. Power in contemporary society is primarily exercised through organizations, the largest of which are giants, in manpower and economic resources, and continue to expand. In manufacturing, for example, firms with more than 1000 employees increased their proportion of all employees from 15 to 33 percent between 1909 and 1967.[31] And the share of all corporate assets in manufacturing held by the 100 largest firms rose from 35 to 48 percent between 1925 and 1967 (U.S. Cabinet Committee, 1969: 45, 92). The concentration of manpower and economic resources in huge organizations implies a corresponding concentration of the powers senior executives derive from their authority over many employees and vast financial assets. While inequality in education has declined in the United States, and inequality in income has at least not increased, the concentration of resources and powers in giant organizations and their top executives has grown.

Consolidated Inequalities

The final topic is the significance that the interrelation or consolidation of parameters has for social change and life in society. These relationships between parameters must be clearly distinguished from the relationships analyzed in the preceding discussion between one form of differentiation and another. Instead of asking how strongly society's division of labor is related to inequalities in education and incomes, for instance, the question now is how strongly the occupational positions of individuals are related to their education and income, their sex and race. Most social research deals with such associations between attributes of individuals. Concern here, however, is not with accounting for variations in one social characteristic of individuals by variations in others, as in conventional survey research, but with the extent of association of these characteristics as a distinctive emergent attribute of social structure. Strong associations reveal that the social structure and inequalities in it

---

[31] Computed from U.S. Bureau of the Census (1917:391 and 1971:2–5). Data for eight intervening years were also computed (using corresponding Census sources for other years), which show that the sharpest increases occurred during World War I and World War II.

have become consolidated, which has important consequences for social change and for social life generally.

THE DYNAMICS OF MOBILITY AND CONFLICT

Multiform differentiation is at the roots of the dynamics of social change. It attenuates ingroup relations, which confine people's perspectives, and intensifies intergroup relations, which foster tolerance and flexibility in adjusting to new social conditions. It stimulates not only processes of social interaction and communication among diverse groups but also processes of social mobility. Firm ingroup bonds impede intergroup mobility. Highly integrated groups do not readily accept outsiders, and strong ingroup loyalties discourage persons from leaving their groups. Lack of opportunity for social mobility fortifies ingroup allegiances. As social mobility, broadly conceived, is essential for change, profound ingroup bonds tend to inhibit structural change.

Social mobility is the process through which social structures adjust to changing conditions by changing themselves, inasmuch as structural change involves, in terms of the conception employed, that the distribution of people among social positions is altered, typically as the result of people's movements between positions. For example, conditions produced by the Industrial Revolution gave rise to more urbanized and industrialized social structures, and these changes were brought about by two kinds of movements of persons, migration from rural to urban places and occupational mobility from farm to industrial work. Recent advances in technology and productivity altered the occupational structure and expanded the professions by opening channels of upward mobility into professional jobs. Emergent value orientations engender structural change also by precipitating moves of people from one group to another. The Reformation changed the religious structure of societies, because it prompted people to leave their religious group and move to another church. For a new ideology to change the political structure, it must induce supporters of the old parties to abandon their political positions and join the new social movement. Implementing demands for the redistribution of wealth requires downward mobility of wealthy persons.[32]

---

[32] Not all changes in the social structure depend on social mobility, though most do. A notable exception is differential fertility, which changes the population

The processes of social mobility that adjust social structures to changing conditions stimulate further mobility by weakening ties within subgroups and strengthening those among different groups. Outmobility at high rates disrupts the network of close social relations that unifies a subgroup and sets it apart. Inmobility of many newcomers—"strangers in our midst"—undermines group solidarity and exclusiveness. Extensive intergroup mobility gives many persons social connections in two groups. The consequent lower barriers among groups encourage intergroup mobility independent of any new conditions creating pressures on people to alter their group affiliation, and the prevalence of mobility makes social structures more flexible and less resistant to change when new conditions do call for structural adjustments. In short, social mobility and structural change reinforce each other. Once deep attachments to narrow social circles have begun to dissolve, mobility and change gather momentum. But this trend may be reversed if the consolidation of various lines of differentiation creates new structural rigidities.

The significance of multiple lines of group affiliation for conflict and change has been analyzed by Coleman (1957: 21–23) and Lipset (1960: 21–32, 88–92). Change in society is often preceded by social conflict, and the pattern of conflict and change depends on the form of differentiation. In a complex social structure with many lines of differentiation, every person is affiliated with a variety of overlapping groups. Conflicts in this situation tend to lead to different alignments on different issues. For instance, union and management, on opposite sides at the bargaining table, may fight together for higher tariffs for their industry. When a controversy arises, many individuals are put under cross-pressure, because they belong to groups or have friends in groups on both sides; and many organized groups experience internal disputes over what side to take, because their membership includes persons whose other group affiliations and associates pull them to opposite sides. These internal conflicts of individuals and internal disagreements in groups discourage extreme positions and drastic measures against the opposition. They thus dissipate the conflict over the issue in society. Besides, the regroupings that divide society along new lines in different controversies prevent antagonisms from becoming unre-

---

distribution without involving moves of people among groups or strata. But the structural adjustments that often occur in response to the changed conditions produced by differential fertility do entail social mobility. For example, the high birth rates of farmers create pressures to move from farms to cities.

lenting hostilities between the same opposing camps. The less severe conflicts permit piecemeal adjustments, and social change is incremental, occurring in response to diverse forces at varying rates in different spheres.

What the authors just summarized fail to stress, however, is that multigroup affiliation is not a sufficient condition for these ameliorative social processes of recurrent adjustments and gradual change. Another condition that is necessary is that the various lines of differentiation—parameters, in my terms—neither coincide nor are closely interrelated. For lasting cleavages and disruptive strife to be averted, people must not only have multiple roles and group affiliations, which is inevitable in complex society, but the various parameters that differentiate their social positions must be independent dimensions that subdivide them in entirely different ways, which is by no means inevitable. Granted that industrial societies are characterized by many lines of differentiation, this fact does not produce interlocking groups and strata that mitigate conflict unless these lines of subdivision are by and large uncorrelated. Only more or less orthogonal parameters generate the multiplicity of intersecting groups that underlie gradual adjustment and change. Consolidated lines of differentiation completely alter the situation, with profound implications for society's integration, social change, and human experience.

STRUCTURAL CONSOLIDATION

A social structure is consolidated if parameters are substantially correlated and social differences among people in one respect are markedly related to their differences in others. Of special significance are interdependent graduated parameters, because they have a direction whereas nominal parameters do not. Vertical status differences are cumulative in a sense in which horizontal group differences are not. The more closely correlated are differences in resources, training, skill, prestige, authority at work, economic power, and political power, the more consolidated is the status structure. When these graduated parameters are also closely related to such nominal parameters as race, sex, and religion, consolidation is still more pervasive.

Consolidated parameters counteract multiform differentiation and consequently impede macrosocial integration, which rests in a large society on the intergroup connections engendered by cross-cutting lines of differentiation. Highly correlated parameters transform a multitude of subgroups that differ in some ways yet have something in common into relatively few larger subgroups that differ in many ways and have little in common. To use a grossly over-simplified illustration, five dichotomous parameters generate thirty-two subgroups, all but two of which share at least one attribute—unless the five parameters coincide, in which case there are only five subgroups whose members differ in all five ways and have nothing in common. The social distinctions resulting from consolidated parameters reinforce one another and widen the social barriers among groups, compelling individuals to turn to their ingroups for social support, which fortifies subgroup solidarities and inhibits the intergroup relations that are essential for macrosocial integration.

Moreover, the consolidation of lines of differentiation makes the social structure more rigid and resistant to change. If groups and strata intersect little, the scarcity of social connections between them reduces flexibility by depriving the social structure of channels of mobility and communication for making adjustments when conditions change and for reaching compromise when interests conflict. In a situation in which people exhibit largely parallel social differences, conflicts over various issues do not give rise to realignments of allies but entail confrontations of the same opponents in controversy after controvery. Entrenched positions encompassing numerous issues and mounting hostilities leave little room for concessions to arrive at mutual adjustments. Rigidity in consolidated structures is an impediment to gradual social change and fosters the revolutionary situation described by Marx in which social change is repressed until it erupts violently.

Last but not least, consolidated lines of differentiation greatly intensify status inequalities by making them cumulative. The consolidation of graduated parameters is the structural counterpart of status consistency, but what looks like perfect balance from the sociopsychological perspective—the consistency of the various statuses of individuals—turns out to be an extreme imbalance from the structural perspective—all status privileges accrue to some people and all status burdens are imposed on others. Although conditions are never that extreme, they are more likely to resemble this polar case than its opposite. If superior income compensates for inferior prestige, for example, inequalities are alleviated. Income and prestige are not inversely related, however, nor are most other aspects of hierarchical status. Social inequalities are greatly magnified when strongly correlated parameters produce status distinctions along lines that reinforce one another and some people enjoy many status advantages while others are oppressed by multiple status handicaps.

Highly differentiated social structures are unavoidable in industrial societies, and though not all forms of differentiation involve inequalities, some status inequalities may also be inescapable. Yet it surely is not impossible to diminish the severe inequalities engendered by pronounced consolidation of status. Here we are admittedly in the realm of value judgments. Structural consolidation not only aggravates inequalities but simultaneously has detrimental consequences for both the integration of diverse groups in society and the dynamics of adjustive change of society. The combination of these three implications of consolidation is the reason that extreme forms of it create a revolutionary situation, when there is much incentive to adopt a radical ideology for groups who have long suffered from multiple inequalities, who are not integrated in the mainstream of society, and who have experienced little adjustment of their deprived conditions. This describes the circumstances of American blacks, which makes it not surprising that some of them, after centuries of oppression, advocate revolutionary change.

How pervasive is structural consolidation throughout American society? The empirical evidence gives an equivocal answer. On the one hand, many parameters are far from perfectly correlated, which shows that cross-cutting boundaries and interlocking groups exist. On the other hand, many social differences among people are substantially correlated, which reveals considerable consolidation. Let us assume we can usually account for about one half of people's differences in one status attribute by their other differences, which is not implausible. Would this indicate much consolidation or little? The answer depends on one's perspective, particularly since we lack similar data from other societies or earlier periods to make comparative judgments. Whether resources and powers are less consolidated and centralized in the United States than in other countries, as we blithely assume, is not at all certain. But even if true, a threat of growing consolidation exists in our society and other industrial ones.

THE THREAT OF CONSOLIDATION

What poses this threat is the dominant position of powerful organizations in contemporary society, such as the Pentagon, the

White House, and huge conglomerates. The trend has been toward increasing concentration of economic and manpower resources and the powers derived from them in giant organizations and their top executives, which implies a growing consolidation of major resources and forms of power, notably authority over employees, power in diverse markets, and political influence. This consolidation of powers is incompatible with democracy, which depends on checks and balances to protect the sovereignty of the people. That some other societies are still more centralized than ours is small consolation if we are, as we seem to be, on a rapid course to join them.

Such consolidation of powers in formal organizations may well recreate the rigid social structures that in earlier eras resulted from undeviating ingroup loyalties, but without the firm social support and deep social roots characteristic of integration in a clan. The extreme inequality entailed by consolidation, moreover, impedes the macrosocial integration of society. Although large organizations are essential for industrialized society and, indeed, for modern democracy, their consolidated powers seriously endanger the integration of the diverse parts in industrial society and the counteracting forces permitting gradual change in democracy.

This is the challenge of the century: to find ways to curb the power of organizations, in the face of their powerful opposition, without destroying in the process the organizations or democracy itself. Unless we can meet this challenge, the growing consolidation effected by organizations is likely to replace democratically instituted recurrent social change with alternate periods of social stagnation and revolutionary upheaval.

The threat is serious, and the time is late. Let us remember that we are within a brief decade of 1984. And let us endeavor to prove Orwell a false prophet.

Bibliography

ABEL, THEODORE
  1930   "The Significance of the Concept of Consciousness of
              Kind," *Social Forces* 9: 1–10.

AGASSI, JOSEPH
  1963   *Towards an Historiography of Science, History and
              Theory.* Beiheft 2. 's-Gravenhage: Mouton & Co.

  1974   "Critical Study. Postscript: On the Futility of Fighting
              Philistines." *Philosophia* 4 (January) : 163–201.

AKULA, JOHN L.
  1973   *"Law and the Development of Citizenship,"* unpublished
              dissertation, Department of Sociology, Harvard University.

ALLARDT, ERIK
  1975   "A Comparative Study of Need-Satisfaction, Alienation
              and Discontent in the Scandinavian Countries." Paper pre-
              pared for the conference on "Recent Political Trends in
              the Scandinavian Countries," Washington, D.C.: American
              Enterprise Institute (February 10–11) .

ALLISON, PAUL D. AND JOHN A. STEWART
  1974   "Productivity Differences Among Scientists: Evidence for
              Accumulative Advantage." *American Sociological Review*
              39 (August) : 596–606.

ARISTOTLE
  1941   *The Basic Works of Aristotle.* New York: Random House.

ARON, RAYMOND
  1955   "Fin de l'age ideologique." Pp. 219–33 in T. W. Adorno
              and Walter Dirks (eds.) , *Sociologica.* Frankfurt: Euro-
              paische Verlaganstalt.

ARROW, KENNETH
1959 *Social Choice and Individual Values*. New York: Wiley, revised edition.

ATKINSON, DICK
1971 *Orthodox Consensus and Radical Alternative*. London: Heinemann Educational Books.

AUDEN, W. H.
1966 "Under Which Lyre: A Reactionary Tract for the Times." Pp. 221–25 in Auden, *Collected Shorter Poems 1927–1957*. London: Faber & Faber.

BANDYOPADHYAY, PRADEEP
1971 "One Sociology or Many: Some Issues in Radical Sociology." *Science and Society* 35 (Spring) : 1–26.

BARBANO, FILIPPO
1959 "L'Opera del Merton nella sociologia contemporanea." Pp. ix–xxvi in Introduction to R. K. Merton, *Teoria e Struttura Sociale*. Bologna: Il Mulino.

1966 "R. K. Merton e le analisi della sociologia." Pp. vii–lviii in Introduction to *Teoria e Struttura Sociale*, 2d ed. Bologna: Il Mulino.

1968 "Social Structures and Social Functions: the Emancipation of Structural Analysis in Sociology." *Inquiry* 11: 40–84.

1971 "La teorie sociologiche tra storicita e scienza." Pp. vii–xxxiv in *Teoria e Struttura Sociale*, 3d ed.

BARBER, BERNARD
1961 "Resistance by Scientists to Scientific Discovery." *Science* 134: 592–602.

BARNARD, CHESTER I.
1938 *The Functions of the Executive*. Cambridge, Mass.: Harvard University Press.

BARTON, ALLEN H.
1973 *The Limits of Consensus Among American Leaders* (a preliminary report of the American Leadership Study) . New York: Bureau of Applied Social Research, Columbia University.

BEACH, FRANK
1950 "The Snark Was a Boojum." *American Psychologist* 5: 115–24.

BECKER, GARY S.
1964 *Human Capital*. New York: National Bureau of Economic Research.

1973   "A Theory of Social Interactions," mimeographed, University of Chicago (October) : 13–14.

BELL, DANIEL
1960   *The End of Ideology.* New York: Free Press.
1973   *The Coming of Post-Industrial Society.* New York: Basic Books.

BELLAH, ROBERT
1964   "Durkheim and History." Pp. 85–103 in W. J. Cahnman and A. Boskoff (eds.), *Sociology and History.* New York: Free Press.

BEN-DAVID, JOSEPH
1973   "The State of Sociological Theory and the Sociological Community." *Comparative Studies in Society and History* 15 (October) :448–72.

BENDIX, REINHARD AND S. M. LIPSET
1953   *Class, Status and Power: A Reader in Social Stratification.* (Eds.) Glencoe: Free Press.

BENSON, LEE
1973   "Group Cohesion and Social and Ideological Conflict." *American Behavioral Scientist* 16 (May–June) : 741–67.

BERG, IVAR
1971   *Education and Jobs.* Boston: Beacon Press.

BERGHE, PIERRE VAN DEN
1963   "Dialectic and Functionalism: Toward a Theoretical Synthesis." *American Sociological Review* 28:695–705.

BERSHADY, HAROLD J.
1973   *Ideology and Social Knowledge.* New York: John Wiley.

BIERSTEDT, ROBERT
1974   "Once More the Idea of Progress." Pp. 63–73 in Ronald Fletcher (ed.), *The Science of Society and the Unity of Mankind.* London: Heinemann.

BIRNBAUM, NORMAN
1971   *Toward a Critical Sociology.* New York: Oxford University Press.

BLAU, PETER M.
1960   "Structural Effects." *American Sociological Review* 25:178–93.
1964   *Exchange and Power in Social Life.* New York: Wiley.
1973   *The Organization of Academic Work.* New York: Wiley.

BLAU, PETER M. AND RICHARD A. SCHOENHERR
1971   *The Structure of Organizations.* New York: Basic Books.

BOUDON, RAYMOND
1968   *A quoi sert la notion de structure?* Paris: Gallimard.
1970   "Notes sur la notion de theorie dans les sciences sociales." *Archives Européennes de Sociologie* 11:201–51.
1971a   *The Uses of Structuralism,* Donald MacRae trans. London: Heinemann.
1971b   *La crise de la sociologie.* Paris-Geneva: Droz.

BOYER, PAUL, AND STEPHEN NISSENBAUM
1973   *Salem Possessed: The Social Origins of Witchcraft.* Cambridge: Harvard University Press.

BRAIDWOOD, ROBERT
1960   "The Agricultural Revolution," *Scientific American* 203 (September) : 130–48.
1968   "Domestication: The Food Producing Revolution," *International Encyclopedia of the Social Sciences* 4:245–50.

BRINTON, CRANE
1933   *English Political Thought in the Nineteenth Century.* London: E. Benn. (Cambridge: Harvard University Press, 1949.)

BUCHANAN, JAMES
1968   *The Demand and Supply of Public Goods.* Chicago: Rand McNally.

BUCHANAN, JAMES, AND GORDON TULLOCK
1962   *The Calculus of Consent.* Ann Arbor: University of Michigan Press.

BUKHARIN, NIKOLAI
1925   *Historical Materialism: A System of Sociology.* New York: International Publishers.

BUNGE, MARIO
1964   *The Critical Approach to Science and Philosophy: Essays in Honor of Karl Popper.* (Ed.) New York: Free Press.
1974   "The Concept of Social Structure." Pp. 81–121 in W. Leinfellner and E. Kohler (eds.) , *Recent Developments in the Methodology of Social Science.* Dordrecht and Boston: D. Reidel.

BUTTERFIELD, HERBERT
1951a   *History and Human Relations.* London and Glasgow: Collins.

1951b   *The Whig Interpretation of History.* New York: Charles Scribner's Sons.

CAMPBELL, DONALD T.

1969   "Ethnocentrism of Disciplines and the Fish-Scale Model of Omniscience." Pp. 328–48 in Muzafer Sherif and Carolyn Sherif (eds.), *Interdisciplinary Relationships in the Social Sciences.* Chicago: Aldine Publishing Co.

1970   "Natural Selection as an Epistemological Model." Pp. 51–85 in R. Naroll and R. Cohen (eds.), *A Handbook of Method in Cultural Anthropology.* Garden City, N.Y.: The Natural History Press.

1974   "Evolutionary Epistemology." Pp. 413–63 in Paul A. Schilpp (ed.), *The Philosophy of Karl Popper.* LaSalle, Illinois: Open Court.

CAMPBELL, NORMAN R.

1920   *Physics: The Elements.* Cambridge: At the University Press.

CHILDE, V. GORDON

1936   *Man Makes Himself.* London: Watts.

1956   *Society and Knowledge.* London: Allen & Unwin.

CHOMSKY, NOAM

1969   "Linguistics and Politics." *New Left Review* No. 57 (September-October) :21–34.

CLARK, GRAHAME

1957   *Archaeology and Society: Reconstructing the Historic Past.* London: Methuen.

1970   *Aspects of Prehistory.* Berkeley: University of California Press.

COHEN, L. JONATHAN

1973   "Is the Progress of Science Evolutionary?" *British Journal of the History of Science* 24:41–61.

COHEN, PERCY

1968   *Modern Social Theory.* New York: Basic Books.

COLE, JONATHAN R., AND STEPHEN COLE

1973   *Social Stratification in Science.* Chicago: University of Chicago Press.

COLEMAN, JAMES S.

1957   *Community Conflict.* Glencoe: Free Press.

1963   "Comment on 'On the Concept of Influence'." *The Public Opinion Quarterly* 27:63–82.

1971 "Collective Decisions." In *Institutions and Social Change: The Sociologies of Talcott Parsons and George C. Homans,* edited by Herman Turk and Richard L. Simpson. Indianapolis: Bobbs-Merrill.

1972 "Systems of Social Exchange." *Journal of Mathematical Sociology* 2: 145–63.

1973a *The Mathematics of Collective Action.* London: Heinemann.

1973b Book Review of *Inequality* by Jencks *et al. American Journal of Sociology* 78:1523–27.

In Press "Social Action Systems." In K. Szaniawski (ed), (title not set).

CONNOR, WALTER
1972 *Deviance in Soviet Society: Crime, Delinquency, and Alcoholism.* New York: Columbia University Press.

COSER, LEWIS A.
1956 *The Functions of Social Conflict.* New York: Free Press.

1967 *Continuities in the Study of Social Conflict.* New York: Free Press.

1974 *Greedy Institutions: Patterns of Undivided Commitment.* New York: Free Press.

DAHRENDORF, RALF
1967 *Pfade aus Utopia.* Munchen: R. Piper & Co.

DAVIDSON, BASIL, WITH F. K. BUAH
1966 *A History of West Africa.* New York: Doubleday Anchor.

DAVIS, KINGSLEY, AND WILBERT E. MOORE
1945 "Some Principles of Stratification." *American Sociological Review* 10 (April):242–49.

DEMERATH III, N. J.
1967 "Synecdoche and Structural-Functionalism." Pp. 501–18 in N. J. Demerath III and R. A Peterson (eds.), *System Change and Conflict.* New York: Free Press.

DEVEREUX, JR., EDWARD C.
1961 "Parsons' Sociological Theory." Pp. 1–63 in Max Black (ed.), *The Social Theories of Talcott Parsons.* Englewood Cliffs, N.J.: Prentice-Hall.

DEVORE, IRVEN
1965 *Primate Behavior: Field Studies of Monkeys and Apes.* (Ed.) New York: Holt, Rinehart and Winston.

DOWNS, ANTHONY
1957 *An Economic Theory of Democracy.* New York: Harper.

Dubos, René
1968   *So Human an Animal.* New York: Charles Scribner's Sons.

Ducrot, Oswald, *et al.*
1968   *Qu'est-ce que le Structuralisme?* Paris: Editions du Seuil.

Duhem, Pierre
1969   *To Save the Phenomena: An Essay on the Idea of Physical Theory from Plato to Galileo.* Chicago: The University of Chicago Press.

Duncan, Beverly
1968   "Trends in Output and Distribution of Schooling." Pp. 601–72 in Eleanor B. Sheldon and Wilbert E. Moore (eds.), *Indicators of Social Change.* New York: Russell Sage Foundation.

Duncan, Otis Dudley
1961   "A Socioeconomic Index for All Occupations." Pp. 109–38 in Albert J. Reiss, Jr. *et al., Occupations and Social Status.* New York: Free Press.

1964   "Social Organizations and the Ecosystem." Pp. 36–82 in R.E.L. Faris (ed.), *Handbook for Modern Sociology.* Chicago: Rand McNally.

Durant, Will
1926   *The Story of Philosophy.* New York: Simon and Shuster.

Durkheim, Emile
1938   *The Rules of Sociological Method.* Chicago: University of Chicago Press.

1947   *The Division of Labor in Society.* New York: Free Press.

1951   *Suicide: A Study in Sociology.* New York: Free Press.

1964   *The Division of Labor in Society.* Translated by George Simpson. Originally published in French in 1893. New York: Free Press.

Economic Commission for Latin America
1971   *Income Distribution in Latin America.* New York: United Nations.

Eisenstadt, S. N.
1964   "Institutionalization and Change." *American Sociological Review* 29 (April): 235–47.

1973a   "Some Reflections on the 'Crisis' in Sociology." *Sociologische gids* 4 (July–August) :255–69.

1973b   *Tradition, Change and Modernity.* New York: Wiley.

1974   "Some Reflections on the Crisis in Sociology." *Sociological Inquiry* 44:147–57.

EISENSTADT, S. N., AND MR. CURELARU
In preparation Sociological Theory, the Sociological Community and the "Crisis" of Sociology.

ELKANA, YEHUDA
1974 "Scientific and Metaphysical Problems: Euler and Kant." Pp. 277–305 in R. S. Cohen and M. W. Wartofsky (eds.), *Methodological and Historical Essays in the Natural and Social Sciences. Boston Studies in the Philosophy of Science* 14. Dordrecht, Holland: D. Reidel Publishing Co.

ENGELS, FRIEDRICH
1957 "Ludwig Feuerbach and the End of Classical German Philosophy" Pp. 212–66 in K. Marx and F. Engels, *On Religion*. Moscow: Foreign Languages Publishing House.

ETZIONI, AMITAI
1968 *The Active Society*. New York: Free Press.

FEUER, LEWIS S.
1942 "Ethical Theories and Historical Materialism." *Science and Society* 6 (Summer) : 242–72.

1955 *Psychoanalysis and Ethics*. Springfield: Charles C. Thomas.

1962 "The Social Theories of Talcott Parsons: A Critical Examination." *The Journal of Philosophy* 59 (March 29):182–93.

FEYERABEND, PAUL
1965 "Problems of Empiricism." Pp. 145–260 in R. Colodny (ed.), *Beyond the Edge of Certainty*. Englewood Cliffs, N.J.: Prentice-Hall.

1970a "Consolations for the Specialist." Pp. 197–230 in Imre Lakatos and Alan Musgrave (eds.), *Criticism and the Growth of Knowledge*. Cambridge: University Press.

1970b "Against Method: Outline of an Anarchistic Theory of Knowledge." Pp. 17–130 in M. Radner and S. Winokur (eds.), *Minnesota Studies in the Philosophy of Science* 4. Minneapolis: University of Minnesota Press.

1975 *Against Method*. London: NLB.

FEYNMAN, RICHARD
1965 *The Character of Physical Law*. London: Cox and Wyman.

FLACKS, RICHARD
1972 "On the New Working Class and Strategies for Social Change." Pp. 85–98 in P. G. Altbach and R. S. Laufer (eds.), *The New Pilgrims*. New York: David McKay.

FREIDSON, ELIOT
1973a "Professions and the Occupational Principle." Pp. 19–38 in

E. Freidson, *The Professions and Their Prospects.* Beverly Hills: Sage Publications.

1973b   "Professionalization and the Organization of Middle-Class Labour in Post-Industrial Society." *The Sociological Review* Monograph No. 20:47–59.

Friedrich, C. J.
1963   *Man and His Government: An Empirical Theory of Politics.* New York: McGraw-Hill.

Friedrichs, Robert W.
1970   *A Sociology of Sociology.* New York: The Free Press.
1972   "Dialectical Sociology: An Exemplar for the 1970s." *Social Forces* 50 (June) : 447–55.

Gallino, Luciano
1972   "Crisi della sociologie, ricerca sociologica, ruolo del sociologo." Pp. 309–26 in Pietro Rossi (ed.) , *Ricerca Sociologica e Ruolo del Sociologico.* Bologna: Societa Editrice il Mulino.

Gibbs, Jack P., and Walter T. Martin
1962   "Urbanization, Technology and the Division of Labor." *American Sociological Review.* 27:667–77.

Giddens, Anthony
1971   *Capitalism and Modern Social Theory.* Cambridge: Cambridge University Press.

Gillispie, Charles Coulston
1968   "Remarks on Social Selection as a Factor in the Progressivism of Science." *American Scientist* 56:439–50.

Goddijn, H. P. M.
1963   *Het Funktionalisme in de Sociologie.* Assen: Van Gorcum.

Godelier, Maurice
1967   "System, Structure and Contradiction in Capital." *The Socialist Register*: 91–119. London.

Goode, William J.
1973   *Explorations in Social Theory,* N.Y.: Oxford University Press.

Gorz, André
1969   *Réforme et Révolution.* Paris: Seuil.

Gouldner, Alvin W.
1957–58   "Cosmopolitans and Locals: Toward an Analysis of Latent Social Roles." *Administrative Science Quarterly* 2: 211–306; 444–80.

1959	"Reciprocity and Autonomy in Functional Theory." Pp. 241–70 in Llewellyn Gross (ed.), *Symposium on Sociological Theory*. Evanston: Row, Peterson.
1970a	*The Coming Crisis of Western Sociology*. New York: Basic Books.
1970b	"Toward a Radical Reconstruction of Sociology." *Social Policy* 1 (May–June) :18–25.
1973a	*For Sociology*. New York: Free Press.
1973b	"Foreword." Pp. ix-xiv in Ian Taylor, Paul Walton and Jock Young, *The New Criminology: For a Social Theory of Deviance*. London: Routledge & Kegan Paul.

GOULDNER, ALVIN W., AND HELEN P. GOULDNER
1963	*Modern Sociology: An Invitation to the Study of Human Interaction*. New York: Harcourt, Brace & World.

GOULDNER, ALVIN W., AND J. T. SPREHE
1965	"Sociologists Look at Themselves." *Trans-Action* 2 (May–June) : 42–44.

GRANOVETTER, M. S.
1973	"The Strength of Weak Ties." *American Journal of Sociology* 78:1360–80.

GREENBERG, DANIEL S.
1967	*The Politics of Pure Science*. New York: New American Library.

GURVITCH, GEORGES
1956	"La crise de l'explication en sociologie." *Cahiers Internationales de Sociologie* 21 (July–Dec.) :3–18.
1962	*Traité de Sociologie*. Paris: Presses Universitaires de France, 2nd revised edition.

HAGGETT, PETER
1967	"Network Models in Geography." Pp. 607–68 in Richard J. Chorley and Peter Haggett (eds.), *Models in Geography*. London: Methuen and Co.

HAGSTROM, WARREN
1965	*The Scientific Community*. New York: Basic Books.

HAMMOND, MASON
1972	*The City in the Ancient World*. Cambridge: Harvard University Press.

HANSON, N. R.
1958	*Patterns of Discovery*. Cambridge: At the University Press.

HARRIS, LOUIS
1973	*The Anguish of Change*. New York: W. W. Norton.

HARRIS, MARVIN
    1968   *The Rise of Anthropological Theory.* New York: Thomas
                Y. Crowell.

HAWLEY, AMOS H.
    1971   *Urban Society: An Ecological Approach.* New York:
                Ronald.

HEILBRONER, ROBERT
    1974   *An Inquiry into the Human Prospect.* New York: Norton.

HENDERSON, L. J.
    1932   "An Approximate Definition of Fact." University of Cali-
                fornia Publications in Philosophy 14:179–99.

HERNES, GUDMUND
    1971   "Interest, Influence, and Cooperation: A Study of the Nor-
                wegian Parliament." Johns Hopkins University. Unpub-
                lished Ph.D. dissertation.

HOBBES, THOMAS
    1651   *The Leviathan: Or the Matter, Form and Power of
                a Commonwealth, Ecclesiastical and Civil.* London:
                Crooke.

HOBSBAWM, E. G.
    1973a   "Karl Marx's Contribution to Historiography." Pp. 265–
                83 in Robin Blackburn (ed.), *Ideology in Social Science.*
                New York: Vintage Books.

    1973b   *Revolutionaries.* London: Weidenfeld and Nicolson.

HOLE, FRANK, AND ROBERT HEIZER
    1965   *An Introduction to Prehistoric Archaeology.* New York:
                Holt, Rinehart and Winston.

HOLTON, GERALD
    1973   *Thematic Origins of Scientific Thought.* Cambridge, Mass.:
                Harvard University Press.

HOMANS, GEORGE C.
    1961   *Social Behavior.* New York: Harcourt.

    1964   "Contemporary Theory in Sociology." Pp. 951–77 in
                Robert E. L. Faris (ed.), *Handbook of Modern Sociology.*
                Chicago: Rand McNally.

    1967   *The Nature of Social Science.* New York: Harcourt Brace
                Jovanovich.

    1971   "Commentary." Pp. 363–79 in Herman Turk and Richard
                L. Simpson (eds.), *Institutions and Social Exchange.* In-
                dianapolis: Bobbs-Merrill.

1974   *Social Behavior: Its Elementary Forms* (Revised Edition). New York: Harcourt Brace Jovanovich.

HOMANS, GEORGE C., AND SCHNEIDER, DAVID M.
1955   *Marriage, Authority, and Final Causes.* Glencoe, Ill.: The Free Press.

HORKHEIMER, MAX
1932   "Bemerkungen über Wissenschaft und Krise." *Zeitschrift für Sozialforschung* 1:1–7.

HOYLE, SIR FRED, AND GEOFFREY HOYLE
1971   *The Molecule Men.* New York: Harper & Row.

HUGHES, EVERETT
1961   "Ethnocentric Sociology." *Social Forces* 40 (October): 1–4.

HUGHES, H. STUART
1951   "The End of Political Ideology." *Measure* 2 (Spring) :146–58.

INGLEHART, RONALD
1971   "The Silent Revolution in Europe: Intergenerational Change in Post-Industrial Societies." *American Political Science Review* 65 (December) :991–1017.

1973   "Industrial, Pre-Industrial and Post-Industrial Political Cleavages in Western Europe and the United States." Paper prepared for the 1973 meeting of the American Political Science Association (September 4–8).

INTERNATIONAL LABOUR OFFICE
1972   *Year Book of Labour Statistics,* 1972. Geneva (Switzerland) : I.L.O.

INKSON, J. H. K. *et al.*
1970   "A Comparison of Organizational Structure and Managerial Roles." *Journal of Management Studies* 7:347–63.

JACOB, FRANÇOIS
1973   *The Logic of Life.* New York: Pantheon Books.

JENCKS, CHRISTOPHER, AND DAVID RIESMAN
1968   *The Academic Revolution.* Garden City: Doubleday.
1972   *Inequality.* New York: Basic Books.

JESSOP, BOB
1972   *Social Order, Reform and Revolution.* London: Macmillan.

JOHNSTONE, J. W. C., E. J. SLAWSKI, AND W. W. BOWMAN
1972–73   "The Professional Values of American Newsmen." *Public Opinion Quarterly* 36 (Winter) :522–40.

Kadushin, Charles
1974   *American Intellectual Elite.* Boston: Little, Brown.

Kaiser, Robert G.
1974   "Soviet Life Oriented Toward Family." *The Washington Post* (June 20) : 1, 10.

Kaláb, Miloš
1969   "The Marxist Conception of the Sociological Method." *Quality & Quantity* 3 (January) :5–23.

Kemeny, John G., Snell, J. Lawrie, and Thompson, Gerald L.
1956   *Introduction to Finite Mathematics.* Englewood Cliffs, N.J.: Prentice-Hall.

Keniston, Kenneth
1960   "Alienation and the Decline of Utopia." *The American Scholar.* (Spring) :1–10.

Keynes, John Maynard
1972   Essays in Biography, Volume X of *The Collected Writings of John Maynard Keynes.* London: The Macmillan Press Ltd.

Kirschheimer, Otto
1957   "The Waning of Opposition in Parliamentary Regimes." *Social Research* 24 (Summer) :127–56.

Klima, Rolf
1971   "Theorienpluralismus in der Soziologie." Pp. 198–219 in A. Diemer (ed.) , *Der Methoden-und Theorienpluralismus in den Wissenschaften.* Meisenheim-am-Glan: Verlag Anton Hain.

1972   "Theoretical Pluralism, Methodological Dissension and the Role of the Sociologist." *Social Science Information* 11: 69–108.

Koertge, Noretta
1971   "Inter-theoretic Criticism and the Growth of Science." Pp. 160–73 in R. Buck and Robert Cohen (eds.) , *Boston Studies in the Philosophy of Science.* Vol. VIII. Dordrecht, Holland: Reidel.

Korzybski, Alfred, Count
1949   *Science and Sanity,* 3d ed. Lakeville, Conn.: The International Non-Aristotelian Library Publishing Company.

Kravis, Irving B.
1973   "A World of Unequal Incomes." *The Annals* 409:61–80.

Kuhn, Thomas
1962   *The Structure of Scientific Revolutions.* Chicago: University of Chicago Press.

1968	"The History of Science." Pp. 74–83 in Volume 14 of *International Encyclopedia of the Social Sciences*. New York: Macmillan and Free Press.
1970a	*The Structure of Scientific Revolutions,* 2d ed. Enlarged by Postscript 1969. Chicago: University of Chicago Press.
1970b	"Reflections on My Critics." Pp. 231–78 in Imre Lakatos and Alan Musgrave (eds.), *Criticism and the Growth of Knowledge.* Cambridge: University Press.
1974	"Second Thoughts on Paradigms." Pp. 458–82 in Frederick Suppe (ed.), *The Structure of Scientific Theories.* Urbana: University of Illinois Press.

KUZNETS, SIMON

1953	*Shares of Upper Income Groups in Income and Savings.* New York: National Bureau of Economic Research.
1963	"Quantitative Aspects of the Economic Growth of Nations: VIII. Distribution of Income by Size." *Economic Development and Cultural Change* 2 (January, Part 2).
1966	*Modern Economic Growth.* New Haven: Yale University Press.

LADD, JR., EVERETT, AND SEYMOUR MARTIN LIPSET

1975	*The Divided Academy: The Politics of Academe.* New York: McGraw-Hill.

LAKATOS, IMRE

1968	"Criticism and the Methodology of Scientific Research Programmes." *Proceedings of the Aristotelian Society* 69: 149–86.
1970	"Falsification and the Methodology of Scientific Research Programmes." Pp. 91–195 in Imre Lakatos and Alan Musgrave (eds.), *Criticism and the Growth of Knowledge.* Cambridge: University Press.
1971	"History of Science and Its Rational Reconstructions." Pp. 91–182 in R. Buck and Robert Cohen (eds.), *Boston Studies in the Philosophy of Science.* Vol. VIII. Dordrecht, Holland: Reidel.
1974	"Popper on Demarcation and Induction." Pp. 241–73 in Paul A. Schilpp (ed.), *The Philosophy of Karl Popper.* LaSalle, Illinois: Open Court.

LAMMERS, CORNELIS J.

1974	"Mono- and poly-paradigmatic developments in natural and social sciences." Pp. 123–47 in Richard Whitley (ed.), *Social Processes of Scientific Development.* London: Routledge and Kegan Paul.

Landecker, Werner S.
1960   "Class Crystallization and Its Urban Pattern." *Social Research* 27 (April) :308–20.

Lane, David
1971   *The End of Inequality? Stratification Under State Socialism.* Baltimore: Penguin.

Lasswell, H., and A. Kaplan
1950   *Power and Society.* New Haven: Yale University Press.

Laughlin, William S.
1968   "Hunting: An Integrating Biobehavior System and Its Evolutionary Importance." Pp. 304–20 in Richard Lee and Irven DeVore (eds.) , *Man The Hunter.* Chicago: Aldine.

Lazarsfeld, Paul F.
1972   *Qualitative Analysis: Historical and Critical Essays,* Chapter 2, "Historical Notes on the Empirical Study of Action: An Intellectual Odyssey." Boston: Allyn and Bacon.

Lazarsfeld, Paul F., and Herbert Menzel
1964   "On the Relation between Individual and Collective Properties." Pp. 422–40 in Amitai Etzioni (ed.) , *Complex Organizations.* New York: Holt.

Leach, E. R.
1970   *Lévi-Strauss.* London: Fontana/Collins.

Lenin, V. I.
1932   *State and Revolution.* New York: International Publishers.

Lennon, Lotta
1971   "Women in the USSR." *Problems of Communism* 20 (July–August) :47–56.

Lenski, Gerhard, and Jean Lenski
1974   *Human Societies.* New York: McGraw-Hill.

Leontief, Wassily
1937   "Implicit Theorizing: A Methodological Criticism of the Neo-Cambridge School." *Quarterly Journal of Economics* 51 (February) : 337–51.

1952   "Some Basic Problems of Structural Analysis." *Review of Economics and Statistics* 34 (February) :1–9.

Lévi-Strauss, Claude
1949   *Les Structures élémentaires de la parenté.* Paris: Presses Universitaires de France.

1952   "Social Structure." Pp. 321–90 in A. L. Kroeber (ed.) , *Anthropology Today.* Chicago: University Press.

LICHTHEIM, GEORGE
1969   "A New Twist in the Dialectic." *New York Review of Books* 12 (January 30):33–38.

LIDZ, VICTOR
1974   "Blood and Language: Analogous Media of Homeostasis." Paper submitted to a Daedalus Conference on the Relations between Biological and Social Theory. Cambridge, Mass.

In Press   "The Analysis of Action at the Most Inclusive Level: An Introduction to Essays on the General Action Systems." In J. Loubser *et al.* (eds.), *Explorations in General Theory in Social Science.* New York: Free Press.

LIDZ, VICTOR, AND CHARLES LIDZ
In Press   "The Psychology of Intelligence of Jean Piaget and Its Place in the Theory of Action." In J. Loubser *et al.* (eds.), *Explorations in General Theory in Social Science.* New York: Free Press.

LIPSET, SEYMOUR MARTIN
1950   *Agrarian Socialism.* Berkeley: University of California Press.
1960   *Political Man.* Garden City: Doubleday.
1967   *Student Politics.* (Ed.) New York: Basic Books.
1970   *Revolution and Counterrevolution.* Garden City: Doubleday-Anchor Books.
1972a   "Academia and Politics in America." Pp. 211–89 in T. J. Nossiter *et al.* (eds.), *Imagination and Precision in the Social Sciences.* London: Faber.
1972b   "Ideology and No End." *Encounter* 39 (December):17–22.
1972c   *Rebellion in the University.* Boston: Little, Brown.

LIPSET, SEYMOUR MARTIN, AND PHILIP ALTBACH
1969   *Students in Revolt.* (Eds.) Boston: Houghton-Mifflin.

LIPSET, SEYMOUR MARTIN, AND RICHARD B. DOBSON
1972   "The Intellectual as Critic and Rebel: With Special Reference to the United States and the Soviet Union." *Daedalus* 10 (Summer): 137–98.

LIPSET, SEYMOUR MARTIN, AND EVERETT C. LADD, JR.
1972   "The Politics of American Sociologists." Pp. 67–104 in Robert K. Merton *et al.* (eds.), *Varieties of Political Expression in Sociology.* Chicago: University of Chicago Press.

LOCKWOOD, DAVID
1964   "Social Integration and System Integration." Pp. 244–57 in

G. K. Zollschan and W. Hirsch (eds.), *Explorations in Social Change*. Boston: Houghton, Mifflin.

LOMAX, ALAN, AND CONRAD ARENSBERG
1968   *Folk Song Style and Culture*. Washington, D.C.: American Association for the Advancement of Science.

LOOMIS, CHARLES P.
1967   "In Praise of Conflict and Its Resolution." *American Sociological Review* 32 (December) :875–90.

LOOMIS, CHARLES P., AND ZONA K.
1961   *Modern Social Theories*. Chapter 5. New York: D. Van Nostrand.

MACDONALD, DWIGHT
1957   *Memoirs of a Revolutionist*. New York: Farrar, Straus and Cudahy.

MACIVER, ROBERT M.
1937   *Society: A Textbook of Sociology*. New York: Rinehart.
1942   *Social Causation*. Boston: Ginn and Co.

MACRAE, DONALD
1968   "Introduction." Pp. vii–viii to Percy Cohen, *Modern Social Theory*. New York: Basic Books.

MALEWSKI, ANDREZEJ
1959   "Der empirische Gehalt der Theorie des historischen Materialismus." *Kölner Zeitschrift für Soziologie und Sozialpsychologie* 11:281–305.
1967   *Verhalten und Interaktion*. Tübingen: J. C. B. Mohr (Paul Siebeck).

MANNHEIM, KARL
1949   *Ideology and Utopia*. New York: Harcourt, Brace and Co.
1950   *Man and Society in an Age of Reconstruction*. New York: Harcourt, Brace and Co.
1956   "The Sociological Problem of Generations." In Karl Mannheim, *Essays on the Sociology of Culture*. New York: Oxford University Press.

MANUEL, FRANK
1965   *Shapes of Philosophical History*. Stanford: Stanford University Press.

MAQUET, JACQUES
1972   *Africanity*. Joan Rayfield, trans. New York: Oxford University Press.

MARCUSE, HERBERT
1964   *One-Dimensional Man*. Boston: Beacon Press.

MARSHALL, T. H.
1950   *Citizenship and Social Class.* Cambridge: Cambridge University Press.

1965   *Class, Citizenship and Social Development.* Garden City: Anchor Books.

MARX, KARL
1936a   "Preface to a Contribution to the Critique of Political Economy." Pp. 354–59 in Karl Marx, *Selected Works.* Vol. I. New York: International Publishers.

1936b   "Wage, Labour and Capital." Pp. 242–81 in Karl Marx, *Selected Works.* Vol. I. New York: International Publishers.

1959   *Capital.* Vol. I. Moscow: Foreign Languages Publishing House.

MASTERMAN, MARGARET
1970   "The Nature of a Paradigm." Pp. 59–90 in Imre Lakatos and Alan Musgrave (eds.), *Criticism and the Growth of Knowledge.* Cambridge: University Press.

MAYR, ERNST
1974   "Behavior Programs and Evolutionary Strategies." *American Scientist* 62:650–59.

MEDVEDEV, ZHORES, AND ROY MEDVEDEV
1971   *A Question of Madness.* New York: Knopf.

MEHRING, F.
1935   *Karl Marx: The Story of His Life.* E. Fitzgerald, trans. New York: Covici Friede.

MELLAART, JAMES
1965   *Earliest Civilizations of the Near East.* London: Thames and Hudson.

MERTON, ROBERT K.
1936   "The Unanticipated Consequences of Purposive Social Action." *American Sociological Review* 1:894–904.

1945   "Sociological Theory." *American Journal of Sociology* 50 (May):462–73.

1948   "On the Position of Sociological Theory." *American Sociological Review* 13 (April): 164–68.

1957   *Social Theory and Social Structure.* New York: Free Press.

1965   *On the Shoulders of Giants.* New York: The Free Press and Harcourt Brace Jovanovich.

1968   *Social Theory and Social Structure.* New York: Free Press. (3d enlarged edition).

1971   "Social Problems and Sociological Theory." Pp. 793–846 in R. K. Merton and R. A. Nisbet (eds.), *Contemporary Social Problems*. New York: Harcourt Brace Jovanovich, 3d ed.

1972   "Insiders and Outsiders." *American Journal of Sociology* 78:9–47.

1973   *The Sociology of Science*. Norman Storer (ed.). Chicago: University of Chicago Press.

MERTON, ROBERT K., AND ELINOR BARBER
1963   "Sociological Ambivalence." Pp. 91–120 in E. A. Tiryakian (ed.), *Sociological Theory, Values, and Sociocultural Change*. New York: The Free Press.

MICHELS, ROBERT
1959   *Political Parties*. Eden and Cedar Paul, trans. New York: Dover.

MILL, JOHN STUART
1909   *Principles of Political Economy*. Edited with an introduction by W. J. Ashley. First published in 1848. London: Longmans, Green and Co.

MILLER, GEORGE A., EUGENE GALANTER, AND KARL A. PRIBRAM
1960   *Plans and the Structure of Behavior*. New York: Holt.

MILLER, HERMAN P.
1966   *Income Distribution in the United States*. (A 1960 Census Monograph.) Washington: U.S.G.P.O.

MILLS, C. WRIGHT
1956   *The Power Elite*. New York: Oxford University Press.

1959   *The Sociological Imagination*. New York: Oxford University Press.

MINCER, JACOB
1974   *Schooling, Experience, and Earnings*. New York: National Bureau of Economic Research.

MINCER, JACOB, AND S. POLACHEK
1974   "Earnings of Women," *Journal of Political Economy*, Part II, March–April.

MITROFF, IAN
1974   "Norms and Counter-Norms in a Selected Group of the Apollo Moon Scientists: A Case Study in the Ambivalence of Scientists." *American Sociological Review* 39 (August): 579–95.

MOORE, JR., BARRINGTON
1958   *Political Power and Social Theory*. Cambridge: Harvard University Press.

1966 *Social Origins of Dictatorship and Democracy.* Boston: Beacon Press.

MOORE, WILBERT E.

1960 "A Reconsideration of Theories of Social Change." *American Sociological Review* 25 (December) :810–18.

1963 *Social Change.* Englewood Cliffs, N.J.: Prentice-Hall.

MORGENSTERN, OSKAR

1972 "Thirteen Critical Points in Contemporary Economic Theory." *Journal of Economic Literature* 10 (December) : 1163–89.

MULKAY, M. J.

1971 *Functionalism, Exchange and Theoretical Strategy.* London: Routledge & Kegan Paul.

MUSGRAVE, ALAN

1968 "On a Demarcation Dispute." Pp. 78–85 in I. Lakatos and E. A. Musgrave (eds.), *Problems in the Philosophy of Science.* Amsterdam: North-Holland Publishing Co.

1971 "Kuhn's Second Thoughts." *British Journal of the Philosophy of Science* 22:287–306.

1973 "Falsification and its Critics." Pp. 393–406 in P. Suppes *et al.* (eds.), *Logic, Methodology and Philosophy of Science* 4. Amsterdam and London: North-Holland Publishing Co.

MYRDAL, GUNNAR

1944 *An American Dilemma.* New York: Harper and Brothers.

NADEL, S. F.

1957 *The Theory of Social Structure.* New York. Free Press.

NAESS, ARNE

1972 *The Pluralist and Possibilist Aspect of the Scientific Enterprise.* Oslo: Universitetsforlager.

NEWELL, ALLEN, AND HERBERT A. SIMON

1972 *Human Problem Solving.* Englewood Cliffs, N.J.: Prentice Hall.

NISBET, ROBERT A.

1966 *The Sociological Tradition.* New York: Basic Books.

1969 *Social Change and History.* New York: Oxford University Press.

1970 "Developmentalism: A Critical Analysis." Pp. 167–294 in John C. McKinney and Edward A. Tiryakian (eds.), *Theoretical Sociology.* New York: Appleton-Century-Crofts.

1972 *Social Change.* (Ed.) New York: Harper & Row.

NOWAK, STEFAN
   1974   "Empirical Knowledge and Social Values in the Cumula-
              tive Development of Sociology." Revision of paper pre-
              pared for the Round Table "Is There a Crisis in Sociology?"
              at the VIIIth World Congress of Sociology, Toronto
              (August).

OBRADOVIC, JOSIP
   1972   "Distribution of Participation in the Process of Decision
              Making on Problems Related to the Economic Activity of
              the Company." Vol. 2, pp. 137–64 in Eugen Pusic (ed.),
              Participation and Self-Management. Zagreb: First Interna-
              tional Sociological Conference on Participation and Self-
              Management.

OLSON, MANCUR
   1965   The Logic of Collective Action. Cambridge: Harvard Uni-
              versity Press.

OPP, KARL-DIETER
   1970   Methodologie der Sozialwissenschaften: Einfuhrung in
              Probleme ihrer Theorienbildung. Hamburg: Rowohlt.

PARETO, VILFREDO
   1935   The Mind and Society. New York: Harcourt Brace, 4 vols.

PARSONS, TALCOTT
   1937   The Structure of Social Action. New York: McGraw-Hill.
              Reprinted by Free Press, New York, 1949.

   1948   "The Position of Sociological Theory." American Socio-
              logical Review 13 (April) :156–64.

   1949   Essays in Sociological Theory. New York: Free Press.

   1951   The Social System. New York: Free Press.

   1954   Essays in Sociological Theory. New York: Free Press.

   1959   "A Rejoinder to Ogles and Levy." American Sociological
              Review 24 (April) :248–50.

   1960   Structure and Process in Modern Societies. New York: Free
              Press.

   1961a   "An Outline of the Social System." In Talcott Parsons,
              Edward Shils, Kaspar D. Naegele, and Jesse R. Pitts (eds.),
              Theories of Society. New York: Free Press.

   1961b   "The Point of View of the Author." Pp. 311–63 in Max
              Black (ed.), The Social Theories of Talcott Parsons.
              Englewood Cliffs, N.J.: Prentice-Hall.

   1963a   "On the Concept of Political Power." Proceedings of the
              American Philosophical Society 107. Reprinted in Parsons,
              1969:352–404.

1963b   "On the Concept of Influence;" "Rejoinder to Bauer and Coleman." *The Public Opinion Quarterly* 27:37–62, 87–92. Reprinted in Parsons, 1969.

1964   "A Functional Theory of Change." Pp. 83–97 in Amitai Etzioni and Eva Etzioni (eds.), *Social Change*. New York: Basic Books.

1966   *Societies: Evolutionary and Comparative Perspectives.* Englewood Cliffs, N.J.: Prentice-Hall.

1967   *Sociological Theory and Modern Society.* New York: Free Press.

1968   "On the Concept of Value-Commitments." *Sociological Inquiry* 38. Reprinted in Parsons, 1969:439–72.

1969   *Politics and Social Structure.* New York: Free Press.

1970a   "Equality and Inequality in Modern Society, or Social Stratification Revisited." *Sociological Inquiry* 40 (Spring): 13–72.

1970b   "Some Problems of General Theory in Sociology." In John C. McKinney and Edward A. Tiryakian (eds.), *Theoretical Sociology: Perspectives and Developments.* New York: Appleton-Century-Crofts.

1971   *The System of Modern Societies.* Englewood Cliffs, N.J.: Prentice Hall.

1973   "Durkheim on Religion Revisited: Another Look at the Elementary Forms of the Religious Life." In Charles Y. Glock and Philip E. Hammond (eds.), *Beyond the Classics? Essays in the Scientific Study of Religion.* New York: Harper and Row.

1974   "The University 'Bundle': A Study of the Balance Between Differentiation and Integration." Epilogue in N. Smelser and G. Almond, *Public Higher Education in California: Growth, Structural Change and Conflict.* Berkeley: University of California Press.

In Press   "Social Stratification" (Social Class). *Enciclopedia Italiana.*

PARSONS, TALCOTT, ROBERT F. BALES, AND EDWARD A. SHILS

1953   *Working Papers in the Theory of Action.* New York: Free Press.

PARSONS, TALCOTT, AND GERALD M. PLATT

1968a   "The American Academic Profession: A Pilot Study." Cambridge, Mass.: multilith.

1968b   "Considerations on the American Academic System." *Minerva* 6, No. 4 (Summer).

PARSONS, TALCOTT, AND GERALD M. PLATT
　1973　　　*The American University.* In collaboration with Neil J.
　　　　　　　Smelser. Cambridge, Mass.: Harvard University Press.

PARSONS, TALCOTT, AND EDWARD A. SHILS
　1951　　　*Toward a General Theory of Action.* Cambridge, Mass.:
　　　　　　　Harvard University Press.

PARSONS, TALCOTT, AND NEIL J. SMELSER
　1956　　　*Economy and Society.* New York: Free Press.

PEEL, J. D. Y.
　1971　　　*Herbert Spencer: The Evolution of a Sociologist.* New
　　　　　　　York: Basic Books.

PFEIFFER, JOHN E.
　1972　　　*The Emergence of Man.* New York: Harper & Row.

PIAGET, JEAN
　1970　　　*Structuralism.* New York: Basic Books.

PIRENNE, HENRI
　1914　　　"The Stages in the History of Capitalism." *American His-
　　　　　　　torical Review* 19, No. 3.

PIZZORNO, ALESSANDO
　1972　　　"Una crisi che non importa superare." Pp. 327–53 in Pietro
　　　　　　　Rossi (ed.), *Ricerca Sociologica e Ruolo del Sociologico.*
　　　　　　　Bologna: Società Editrice il Mulino.

PLANCK, MAX
　1949　　　*Scientific Autobiography and Other Papers.* New York:
　　　　　　　Philosophical Library.

POLANYI, MICHAEL
　1958　　　*Personal Knowledge.* London: Routledge & Kegan Paul.

　1962　　　"Tacit Knowing: Its Bearing on Some Problems of Philoso-
　　　　　　　phy." *Review of Modern Physics* 34:601–15.

POPOVITCH, M.
　1966　　　"What American Sociologists Think About Their Science
　　　　　　　and Its Problems." *American Sociologist* 1 (May): 133–35.

POPPER, KARL R.
　1959　　　*The Logic of Scientific Discovery.* New York: Basic Books.
　1962　　　*Conjectures and Refutations: The Growth of Scientific
　　　　　　　Knowledge.* London: Routledge & Kegan Paul.

　1972　　　*Objective Knowledge: An Evolutionary Approach.* New
　　　　　　　York: Oxford University Press.

　1974　　　"Replies to My Critics." Pp. 961–1197 in Paul A. Schilpp
　　　　　　　(ed.), *The Philosophy of Karl Popper.* LaSalle, Illinois:
　　　　　　　Open Court.

POWERS, WILLIAM T.
1973   *Behavior: The Control of Perception.* Chicago: Aldine.

PRICE, DEREK J. DE SOLLA
1961   *Science Since Babylon.* New Haven: Yale University Press.
1963   *Little Science, Big Science.* New York: Columbia University Press.

PUGH, D. S. *et al.*
1968   "Dimensions of Organization Structure." *Administrative Science Quarterly* 13:65–105.

RADCLIFFE-BROWN, A. R.
1913   "Three Tribes of Western Australia." *Journal of the Royal Anthropological Institute* 43:143–94.

1940   "On Social Structure." *Journal of the Royal Anthropological Institute* 70:1–12.

RADNITZKY, GERARD
1970   *Contemporary Schools of Metascience.* Goteborg: Akademiforlaget.

1971   "Theorienpluralismus-Theorienmonismus." Pp. 135–84 in Alwin Diemer (ed.), *Der Methoden- und Theorienpluralismus in den Wissenschaften.* Meisenheime: Hain.

1973a   "Life Cycles of a Scientific Tradition." *Main Currents in Modern Thought* 29 (Jan.–Feb.) :107–16.

1973b   "Philosophy of Science in a New Key." *Methodology and Science* 6:134–78.

1974   "From Logic of Science to Theory of Research." *Communication & Cognition* 7:61–124.

RAWLS, JOHN
1971   *A Theory of Justice.* Cambridge: Harvard University Press.

RIESMAN, DAVID
1959   "Introduction." Pp. 11–24 in Stimson Bullitt, *To Be a Politician.* New York: Doubleday and Co.

RIKER, WILLIAM, AND PETER ORDESHOOK
1973   *An Introduction to Positive Political Theory.* Englewood Cliffs, New Jersey: Prentice Hall.

ROBEY, DAVID
1973   *Structuralism: An Introduction.* (Ed.) Oxford: Clarendon Press.

ROCHER, GUY
1972   *Talcott Parsons et la Sociologie Americaine.* Paris: Presses Universitaires de France.

Rokkan, Stein
    1958   *Sammenlignende Politisksosilogi*. Bergen: Chr. Michelsens Institutt.

Rossi, Pietro
    1972   *Ricerca Sociologica e Ruolo del Sociologico*. (Ed.) Bologna: Società Editrice il Mulino.

Roth, Guenther
    1963   *The Social Democrats in Imperial Germany*. Totowa, N.J.: Bedminster Press.

Rowntree, John, and Margaret Rowntree
    1968   "Youth as Class." *Our Generation* 6 (May–June) :155–90.

Runciman, W. G.
    1963   *Social Science and Political Theory*. Cambridge: University Press.

    1970   *Sociology in Its Place*. Cambridge: University Press.

Rüschemeyer, Dietrich
    1974   "Reflections on Structural Differentiation." *Zeitschrift fur Soziologie* 3 (June) :279–94.

Sahlins, Marshall
    1960   "Evolution: Specific and General." Pp. 12–44 in Marshall Sahlins and Elman Service (eds.) , *Evolution and Culture*. Ann Arbor: University of Michigan Press.

Samuelson, Paul A.
    1973   "Reply on Marxian Matters." *Journal of Economic Literature* 11 (March) :64–68.

    1974   "Merlin Unclothed, a Final Word." *Journal of Economic Literature* 12:75–77.

Sawyer, Jack
    1967   "Dimensions of Nations: Size, Wealth, and Politics." *American Journal of Sociology* 73 (September) : 145–72.

Scheuch, Erwin
    1974   "Die politischen und sozialen Aurwirkungen der Wirtschaftskrise." Expert Opinion Report prepared for the Chancellor's Office. Bonn (December 30) .

Scheffler, Israel
    1967   *Science and Subjectivity*. Indiana: Bobbs-Merrill.

    1972   "Vision and Revolution: A Postscript on Kuhn." *Philosophy of Science* 39 (September) :366–74.

Schnore, Leo

1958   "Social Morphology and Human Ecology." *American Journal of Sociology* 63 (May) :620–34.

SCHULTZ, THEODORE
1963   *The Economic Value of Education.* New York: Columbia University Press.

SECRETARIAT OF THE ECONOMIC COMMISSION FOR EUROPE
1967   *Incomes in Postwar Europe.* New York: United Nations.

SHAPERE, DUDLEY
1964   "The Structure of Scientific Revolutions." *Philosophical Review* 73:383–94.
1971   "The Paradigm Concept." *Science* 172:706–9.

SHILS, EDWARD
1955   "The End of Ideology." *Encounter* 5 (November) : 52–58.

SHKLAR, JUDITH N.
1957   *After Utopia: The Decline of Political Faith.* Princeton: Princeton University Press.

SIMMEL, GEORG
1950   *The Sociology of Georg Simmel.* Glencoe: Free Press.
1955   *Conflict and The Web of Group-Affiliations.* Glencoe: Free Press.

SJOBERG, GIDEON
1967   "Contradictory Functional Requirements and Social Systems." Pp. 339–45 in N.J. Demerath III and R. A. Peterson (eds.) , *System, Change and Conflict.* New York: Free Press.

SKLAR, MARTIN J.
1969   "On the Proletarian Revolution and The End of Political-Economic Society." *Radical America* 3 (May–June) :23–36.

SMELSER, NEIL
1962   *Theory of Collective Behavior.* London: Routledge & Kegan Paul.

SMITH, ADAM
1904   *An Inquiry into the Nature and Causes of the Wealth of Nations.* Edited by Edwin Cannon. 2 Volumes. London: Methuen and Co.

SOLZHENITSYN, ALEKSANDR I.
1974   *The Gulag Archipelago.* New York: Harper and Row.

SOROKIN, PITIRIM A.
1928   *Contemporary Sociological Theories.* N.Y.: Harper and Bros.

1956 *Fads and Foibles in Modern Sociology and Related Sciences.* Chicago: Henry Regnery.

SPENCER, HERBERT
1925–1929 *The Principles of Sociology.* 3 Volumes. Originally published in 1876–1896. New York: Appleton.

SPREHE, J. T.
1967 *The Climate of Opinion in Sociology: A Study of the Professional Value and Belief Systems of Sociologists.* Ph.D. Dissertation: Department of Sociology, Washington University, St. Louis.

STEINER, HELMUT, AND OWESJ I. SCHKARATAN
1970 "The Analysis of Society as a System and Its Social Structure." Paper presented at the Research Committee of Social Stratification and Social Mobility, 7th World Congress of Sociology, Varna, Bulgaria.

STINCHCOMBE, ARTHUR
1968 *Constructing Social Theories.* New York: Harcourt Brace Jovanovich.
1975 "Merton's Theory of Social Structure." In Lewis A. Coser (ed.), *The Idea of Social Structure.* New York: Harcourt Brace Jovanovich.

STORER, NORMAN
1966 *The Social System of Science.* New York: Holt, Rinehart & Winston.

SUZUKI, H.
1970 *The Urban World.* Tokyo: Seishin Shobo.

SWIDLER, ANN
1973 "The Concept of Rationality in the Work of Max Weber." *Sociological Inquiry* 43 (Spring):35–42.

SZCZEPAŃSKI, JAN
1970 *Polish Society.* New York: Random House.

SZTOMPKA, PIOTR
1974 *System and Function: Toward a Theory of Society.* New York: Academic Press.

TAYLOR, CHARLES L., AND MICHAEL C. HUDSON
1971 *World Handbook of Political and Social Indicators,* II. Ann Arbor: Inter-University Consortium for Political Research.

TEGGART, FREDERIC J.
1939 *Rome and China: A Study of Correlations in Historical Events.* Berkeley: University of California Press.

TINGSTEN, HERBERT
1955   "Stability and Vitality in Swedish Democracy." *The Political Quarterly* 26 (April–June) :140–51.

TOCQUEVILLE, ALEXIS DE
1954   *Democracy in America.* New York: Vintage Books.

TOULMIN, STEPHEN
1972   *Human Understanding.* Volume 1. Princeton: Princeton University Press.

TOURAINE, ALAIN
1971   *The Post-Industrial Society.* New York: Random House.

TRILLING, LIONEL
1965   *Beyond Culture.* New York: Viking.

TROTSKY, LEON
1937   *The Revolution Betrayed.* Garden City: Doubleday, Doran and Co.

TURNER, JONATHAN
1974   *The Structure of Sociological Theory.* Homewood, Ill.: Dorsey Press.

UNITED CHURCH OF CHRIST
1970   News Release on Harris Poll Survey of Culture Critics. March 16.

U. S. BUREAU OF THE CENSUS
1917   *Abstract of the Census of Manufacturers, 1914.* Washington: U.S.G.P.O.

1960   *Historical Statistics of the United States, Colonial Times to 1957.* Washington: U.S.G.P.O.

1971   *Census of Manufacturers, 1967.* Volume 1, Summary and Subject Statistics. Washington: U.S.G.P.O.

1973   *Census of Population: 1970 Detailed Characteristics.* Final Report PC (1) -D1, United States Summary. Washington: U.S.G.P.O.

U. S. CABINET COMMITTEE ON PRICE STABILITY
1969   Studies by the Staff (January). Washington: U.S.G.P.O.

UTZ, PAMELA
1973   "Evolutionism Revisited." *Comparative Studies in Society and History* 15 (March) :227–40.

VAN DEN BERGHE, PIERRE
1963   "Dialectic and Functionalism. Toward a Theoretical Synthesis." *American Sociological Review* 28 (October) :695–705.

VIET, JEAN
   1965   *Les Méthodes Structuralistes dans les Sciences Sociales.*
             Paris: Mouton & Co.

WALLACE, WALTER L.
   1969   *Sociological Theory.* (Ed.) Chicago: Aldine Publishing
             Co.

WASHBURN, SHERWOOD L., AND DAVID A. HAMBURG
   1965   "The Implications of Primate Research." Pp. 607–22 in
             Irven DeVore (ed.), *Primate Behavior: Field Studies of
             Monkeys and Apes.* New York: Holt, Rinehart and Win-
             ston.

WATANUKI, JOJI
   1975   "Report of Governability of Democracy Task Force
             (Japan)." Paper prepared for the Trilateral Commission.
             Tokyo (January 15).

WATKINS, J. W. N.
   1964   "Confirmation, the Paradoxes, and Positivism." Pp. 92–115
             in M. Bunge (ed.), *The Critical Approach to Science and
             Philosophy.* New York: The Free Press.

   1970   "Against 'Normal Science'." Pp. 25–37 in Imre Lakatos
             and Alan Musgrave (eds.), *Criticism and the Growth of
             Knowledge.* Cambridge: University Press.

WATSON, WILLIAM
   1966   *Early Civilization in China.* New York: McGraw-Hill.

WEBER, MAX
   1946a   "Class, Status and Party." Pp. 180–95 in H. H. Gerth and
             C. W. Mills (eds.), *From Max Weber: Essays in Sociology.*
             New York: Oxford University Press.

   1946b   *From Max Weber: Essays in Sociology.* H. H. Gerth and
             C. Wright Mills (eds.). New York: Oxford University Press.

   1947a   "Power, Authority and Imperative Control," Pp. 152–53 in
             T. Parsons (ed.), *The Theory of Social and Economic Or-
             ganization.* Translated by A. M. Henderson and T. Par-
             sons. New York: Free Press.

   1947b   *The Theory of Social and Economic Organization.* T.
             Parsons (ed.). New York: Oxford University Press.

   1968a   *Economy and Society.* New York: Bedminster Press.

   1968b   *On Charisma and Institution Building.* Chicago: Univer-
             sity of Chicago Press.

WESOLOWSKI, WLODZIMIERZ
1969   "Strata and Strata Interest in Socialist Society." Pp. 465–77 in Celia S. Heller (ed.), *Structured Social Inequality*. New York: Macmillan.

WESSLER, IRA E.
1973   The Political Resolutions of American Learned Societies. Ph.D. Dissertation: Department of Sociology, New York University.

WILLIAMS, JR., ROBIN
1966   "Some Further Comments on Chronic Controversies." *American Journal of Sociology* 71 (May):717–21.

ZEITLIN, IRVING M.
1971   *Liberty, Equality and Revolution in Alexis de Tocqueville*. Boston: Little, Brown.

ZUCKERMAN, HARRIET
In Press   *Scientific Elite*. Chicago: University of Chicago Press.

ZUCKERMAN, HARRIET, AND JONATHAN R. COLE
1975   "Women in American Science." *Minerva* 12 (January).

ZUCKERMAN, HARRIET, AND ROBERT K. MERTON
1972   "Age, Aging and Age Structure in Science." Pp. 292–356 in Matilda White Riley *et al.* (eds.), *A Sociology of Age Stratification*. New York: Russell Sage Foundation.

Name Index

Subject Index

Academic institution: *see* University
Action: *see also* Behavior; Rationality
    purposive, 10–11, 77–79, 82–83, 93,
      121–34
    system, 104–10, 116, 120
    theory, 76–134
Ad-hoc hypothesis, 23, 24, 33, 62
Affect, 109–10; *see also* Sentiments
Ahistorical, 6–7, 208
Altruism, 124, 130–31
Antinomianism, 28*n.*–29*n.*, 45, 46*n.*–
    47*n.*, 51–52, 194–97
Antithesis, 7–9, 18–19, 37
Ascription, 111, 114, 185–86, 197, 226–
    27
Association: *see also* Interaction, social
    collegial, 107–08
    fiduciary, 101, 107–08, 126, 129
    types of, 107–08
Atomism, 123–24, 133
Authority, 35, 74, 96, 98, 111, 112, 150,
    153, 189, 226, 241, 247, 250, 253
Axiomatic theory: *see* Theoretical, ax-
    ioms; Theory, deductive

Behavior
    deviant, 35, 37–39, 63, 178, 186–87
    elementary, 4, 7, 64
    enduring, 7, 11, 53–55, 57, 64, 67,
      68
    expected, 12, 35, 122, 178
    purposive, 10–11, 77–79, 93, 121–25
    system, 104, 105, 109
Bindingness, 99–104

Capitalism, 14, 111, 133, 150–52, 160,
    162–68, 170, 191, 193, 196, 202,
    208, 217–19, 241
Castes, 225–27
Change, 2, 6, 7, 8, 13, 14, 16–18, 25,
    35–36, 48–49, 69, 90, 135–53, 155–
    58, 160–67, 173–84, 187–88, 191–
    94, 197–98, 202–07, 209–19, 229,
    248–53
Circulation, 96, 106–07, 128
Class conflict, 13, 118, 163, 165–67, 176,
    189, 218–19
Coercion, 99–100, 102–03, 108, 119,
    145–56, 188–90
Collective decisions, 84–85
Collective interest: *see* Interest, of col-
    lectivity
Collectivities, 12, 14, 97, 100, 107–10,
    218; *see also* Interest, of collec-
    tivity of scientists, 44, 47, 48
Communication: *see* Interaction, so-
    cial; Language; Media
Competence, 103–05, 239–45
Complexity: *see* Differentiation
Configuration, 5, 8–9, 10–11, 18–19,
    74, 81–87, 125, 129–30, 222
Conflict, 8–9, 14, 16, 35–36, 37–39,
    76–77, 87–88, 172–74, 177–78, 183,
    184, 187, 194, 201, 204, 209, 249–51
    between individual and society, 131–
      32
    class, 13, 118, 163, 165–67, 176, 189,
      218–19
    due to tensions, 178, 214–15
    generational, 26–27, 153, 191–95,
      198–201
    means–ends, 12–13, 191–203